D0906178

The Films of
Martin Scorsese, 1963–77

Authorship and Context

Leighton Grist
Lecturer in Film and Media Studies
King Alfred's College
Winchester

First published in Great Britain 2000 by
MACMILLAN PRESS LTD
Houndmills, Basingstoke, Hampshire RG21 6XS and London
Companies and representatives throughout the world

A catalogue record for this book is available from the British Library.

ISBN 0–333–75412–3

 First published in the United States of America 2000 by
ST. MARTIN'S PRESS, INC.,
Scholarly and Reference Division,
175 Fifth Avenue, New York, N.Y. 10010

ISBN 0–312–22991–7

Library of Congress Cataloging-in-Publication Data
Grist, Leighton.
The films of Martin Scorsese, 1963–77 : authorship and context / Leighton Grist.
p.   cm.
Filmography: p.
Includes bibliographical references and index.
ISBN 0–312–22991–7 (cloth)
1. Scorsese, Martin—Criticism and interpretation.   I. Title.

PN1998.3.S39 G75   2000
791.43'0233'092—dc21

99–047321

This book is printed on paper suitable for recycling and made from fully managed and sustained forest sources.

10   9   8   7   6   5   4   3   2   1
09   08   07   06   05   04   03   02   01   00

Printed and bound in Great Britain by
Antony Rowe Ltd, Chippenham, Wiltshire

Aum dakshane Ganeshaya namah

Contents

List of Plates

See page ix for sources of the plates.

Acknowledgements

This study started as a PhD thesis at the University of Warwick. I would like to thank the Department of Film and Television Studies for their help and support, but especially my supervisor Victor Perkins, as well as Ed Gallafent and Richard Dyer. I would also like to thank Richard Dyer, again, and Tom Ryall for being the most gentlemanly of examiners.

Thanks in addition to my parents for the life-saving (and still working) Amstrad; to friend and colleague Michael Walker for his calmness and sound advice; to Anil for the tape of *Bloody Mama*; and, last but certainly not least, to my wife Rita for inspiration, patience, understanding and good humour far beyond the call of duty.

Stills are courtesy of the Ronald Grant Archive and the following: Joseph Brenner Associates (*Who's That Knocking at My Door?*), American International Pictures (*Boxcar Bertha*), Warner Bros (*Mean Streets*, *Alice Doesn't Live Here Anymore*), Columbia Pictures (*Taxi Driver*) and United Artists (*New York, New York*).

1
Introduction: Martin Scorsese, Authorship, Context

In analysing the work of a film director the issue of authorship is often inescapable. It becomes pressing when discussing the early work of Martin Scorsese. Firstly, the films have been posited not only as the expression of a personal worldview, but as constituting displaced autobiography, a post-Romantic means of understanding the self through the aesthetic objectification of experience: 'If my films aren't quite autobiographies, there are certain feelings in the characters which I identify with ... if I were disinterested in the characters or couldn't relate to them, I couldn't make a film about them' (Taylor 1981: 294). Secondly, Scorsese has admitted auteurism as an influence on his career: 'They told us at film school that we had to like only Bergman ... . Sarris and the "politique des auteurs" was like some fresh air' (Pye and Myles 1979: 191). As late as 1993, Scorsese was describing direction as 'using the lens like a pen'; an account that recalls Alexandre Astruc's influential pre-auteurist concept of the *caméra-stylo*.[1]

However, as an approach to cinema, auteurism has been a contested practice. In the seventies and eighties, while it became a commonplace of middlebrow and popular criticism, auteurism was – in academic terms – virtually a dead language, having been superseded in film studies by a combination of post-structuralist and historical methodologies. Seeming to provide a more rigorous account of the construction of meaning, such were seen institutionally to have enacted, following Roland Barthes, the death of the author.[2]

But concern with authorship was less killed off than discursively marginalized. Author-centred film studies courses continued to be taught, and auteurist articles continued to appear in 'progressive' journals like *Film Comment* and *CineAction*. In the past decade, not only have James Naremore (1990), Timothy Corrigan (1991) and Dudley

1

Andrew (1993) respectively proclaimed auteurism's tenacity, refiguration and revival, but work on authorship has begun to re-appear in *Screen*, historically a prime conduit of post-structuralist thought; albeit this has largely occurred under the vindicating aegis of gay and feminist criticism.[3] Latterly, however, the possibility and very fact of film authorship have been problematized and even denied from within the contrasting realms of analytic philosophy and newspaper journalism.[4] It would therefore seem to be as appropriate a time as any to return to the debate over authorship. For while the primary focus of this study is the discussion of Scorsese's early films, it also seeks to enact an intervention in that debate, to reconstitute authorial analysis on a more theoretically sound basis, one that accepts and integrates many of the challenges that would appear to question its validity.

Auteurism is fundamentally a critical practice that seeks to obtain meaning from a group of films through the examination of stylistic and thematic features that can be related to a single creative figure, usually the director.[5] As John Caughie notes, within its 'distinguishable currents' – *Cahiers du cinéma/la politique des auteurs* in France, *Movie* in the UK, Andrew Sarris in the USA – auteurism, while differently inflected, 'shares certain basic assumptions' (1981c: 9).[6] Most notably, that a film is more probably of value if it is controlled by its director, and that for a director to be considered an *auteur* – or author – his or her work has to evince a stylistic and, above all, thematic consistency. Before auteurism, author-directors had been heralded within, for example, European or Japanese art cinema, but only occasionally, in exceptional instances of control of 'genius', within Hollywood: witness Charlie Chaplin, John Ford or Orson Welles. Auteurism stressed the incidence of authorship across the generality of Hollywood directors.

This emphasis on Hollywood was in part an incitement of established film criticism that tended to dismiss Hollywood as a commercial and industrialized 'assembly line' inimical to personal, 'artistic' expression. However, by focusing upon Hollywood, auteurism foregrounds the central problem of assigning individual authorship within a collaborative, technically determined, highly regulated and largely generic medium. Early auteurist analyses are often guilty of an essentialist Romantic celebration of autonomous, all-embracing creativity. This also had connotations for the evaluation of films. The aim of Romantic-orientated criticism tends to be the discovery of the author in a work. Hence the 'second premise' of Sarris's conception of 'the *auteur* theory', that proclaims 'the distinguishable personality of the director as a criterion of value' (1962: 7).

While Romantic essentialism is common within early auteurism, it is not a monolithic trait. In the article, 'La politique des auteurs', André Bazin sought to correct the 'excesses' of auteurism from within the pages of *Cahiers du cinéma* itself. He attacks the tendency to use personality as a measure of value – '*Auteur*, yes, but what *of?*' (1957: 155) – and declares the necessity of considering the influence of context when analysing a filmmaker's work. He thus confronts the difficulty of adducing authorship within a collaborative, institutionalized form. Writing about Hollywood, he notes the significance of the 'vigour and richness' of the 'cinematic genres' (*ibid.*: 153) and suggests that personnel other than the director can contribute to a film's quality. Further: 'The American cinema is a classical art, but why not then admire in it what is most admirable, i.e. not only the talent of this or that filmmaker, but the genius of the system, the richness of its ever-vigorous tradition' (*ibid.*: 154). Bazin similarly raises the significance of environment and culture on a filmmaker's work: 'the individual transcends society, but society is also and above all *within* him. So there can be no definitive criticism of genius or talent which does not first take into consideration the social determinism, the historical combination of circumstances, and the technical background which to a large extent determine it' (*ibid.*: 142).

Bazin's institutional and ideological contextualization of the *auteur* foreshadows certain foundational criticisms of auteurism that attended developments in structuralist and post-structuralist theory. Moreover, in positing the filmmaker's ideological determination he confronts another Romantic assumption that informs much auteurist writing: that of the unified, freely creative and even self-determined individual. Since Freudian psychoanalysis revealed the self to be the fissured site of conflicting, often unconscious impulses, the notion of the unified, autonomous personality has become difficult to sustain. This difficulty has been heightened by subsequent developments in psychoanalytic and Marxist theory, within which bodies of thought the individual's psycho-sexual conditioning has increasingly been seen to be imbricated with its ideological constitution, the marks of its – again, often contradictory – material, historical situation.[7]

The introduction of structuralist ideas into Anglophone film criticism has been ascribed to a group of British critics dubbed the *auteur*- or cinestructuralists. Influenced by the structuralist analyses of folktales and myth by the likes of Vladimir Propp and, especially, Claude Lévi-Strauss, *auteur*-structuralism sought to divorce auteurism from Romantic idealism. Geoffrey Nowell-Smith defined *auteur*-structuralism's project thus:

'to uncover behind the superficial contrasts of subject and treatment a structural hard core of basic and often recondite motifs. The pattern formed by these motifs, which may be stylistic or thematic, is what gives an author's work its particular structure, both defining it internally and distinguishing one body of work from another' (1967: 10). As these motifs could be, to quote Peter Wollen, 'conscious or unconscious' (1972: 113), the *auteur*-structuralists felt that they had circumvented the problem of Romantic authorial intentionality.

Auteur-structuralism foundered upon its insufficient critical and theoretical design. Critically, despite the claim that motifs could be 'stylistic or thematic', *auteur*-structuralism rather emphasizes thematic structures to the extent that they overwhelm the crucial consideration of *how* the structures are realized, weighted and presented to the spectator through, say, *mise-en-scène*. Theoretically, *auteur*-structuralism's appropriation of Lévi-Strauss was unsupportably instrumentalist. Lévi-Strauss's writing on myth stresses the trans-individual, cultural creation of meaning; a concept far removed from *auteur*-structuralism's relation of meaning to a single individual.[8] In a tacit acknowledgement of the theoretical deficiency of *auteur*-structuralism, Wollen, in his 'Conclusion' to the revised edition of *Signs and Meaning in the Cinema*, states that the authorial structures previously designated 'conscious or unconscious' were now 'unconscious, unintended' (1972: 167), with the *auteur* relegated to the role of 'unconscious catalyst': 'Fuller or Hawks or Hitchcock, the directors, are quite separate from "Fuller" or "Hawks" or "Hitchcock", the structures named after them, and should not be methodologically confused' (*ibid.*: 168). However, while accepting that authorial analyses are, like the results of any exegetic process, critical constructs, to deny the director any conscious intention is as unsustainable as affording the *auteur* total creativity.

Another of *auteur*-structuralism's problems lay with structuralism as an analytic practice. In its revelation of explanatory, underlying relationships structuralism inclines toward essentialist prescription. *Auteur*-structuralism effectively replaced one ahistorical ideal (the Romantic artist) with another (the immutable structure). Moreover, in an ironic reflection of auteurist Romantic excess, for *auteur*-structuralism anything filmically exterior to the authorial structure tends to be disregarded, being dismissed in Wollen's initial formulation of authorship as '"noise"' 'inaccessible to criticism' (1972: 104, 105).

Wollen's 1972 'Conclusion' yet suggests another way forward: '*auteur* analysis ... does no more than provide one way of decoding a film, by specifying what its mechanics are at one level ... . Beyond that, it is an illusion to think of any work as complete in itself ... . Different codes may run across the frontiers of texts at liberty, meet and conflict within them' (*ibid.*: 168–70). This approaches a post-structuralist position, from which texts – no less than the individual or the social formation – embody 'a structured play of forces, relations and discourses' (Caughie 1981b: 1) each of which can be related to specific historical conjunctures. Rather than a film being regarded as the site of a single, discrete meaning, it is posited as a text constituted by an (ideologically determined) 'heterogeneity of structures, codes, languages' (Heath 1973: 89). These cross the text in various configurations of meaning, none of which embodies an all-embracing statement.

Already denied autonomous subjectivity, the author as punctual, much less sole, source of meaning would thus appear to be radically displaced, even rendered redundant. Redemption is nevertheless offered from within post-structuralism via the 1970 'collective text' by the Editors of *Cahiers du cinéma*, 'John Ford's *Young Mr Lincoln*'. Reflecting both theoretical developments and the revised critical position of *Cahiers* following *les événements* of May 1968, the piece constructs *Young Mr Lincoln* (Ford, 1939) as 'a play of tensions, silences and repressions' (Caughie 1981c: 14) between its constituent elements, not least of those between its ideological and institutional determination and the operation of what is called Ford's authorial inscription – a term for the film's authorial connotations that has been variously re-worked in post-structuralist criticism as the authorial code, sub-code or even Metzian 'sub-system' (Nowell-Smith 1976: 30). Extending this, we can posit a model of 'situated' film authorship wherein, while the fact of stylistic and thematic links between the films of many directors is admitted, any film text remains a complex structured by multiple determinants. Authorship, yes, but also genre, budget, narrative structure, studio policy, historical situation and so on. Moreover, authorship itself is likely to be multiple rather than single, attributable not just to the director but to the input of other involved personnel. Any of the text's elements or inputs can be separated or analysed in isolation or in combination with any of the others. But while each is determined by and brings the text into a (frequently displaced and highly mediated) relation with its broader cultural context, it also mutually interacts with and disrupts the text's other elements and inputs to produce an historically specific collocation of structures, representations and determinants.

As this model of film authorship aligns auteurism with post-structuralism, so its emphasis on material determination both confronts the ahistoricity of much auteurist writing and intersects with the interests of the historical criticism that has emerged as part reaction to, part continuation of post-structuralism.[9] The model likewise rescues the author from both Romantic idealization and Barthesian obsolescence. The author instead survives as one of a number of active elements that cohere in the creation of meaning. Hence for *Cahiers'* reading of *Young Mr Lincoln* the agency of Ford's inscription would seem to be central in problematizing the text's putatively reactionary intent: 'The film's ideological project ... finds itself led astray by the worst means it could have been given to realise itself (Ford's style, the inflexible logic of his fiction)' (1970: 43).

But is the notion of inscription, or that of code or sub-code, adequate to account for this authorial agency? Robin Wood notes a 'certain ambiguity' about what inscription 'actually means': 'it can easily become synonymous with "direction", or even "visual style" ... and that is not enough' (1989: 19). In turn, critical analyses of the author as code or sub-code tend – whatever their theoretical underpinning – reductively to overprivilege the semiotic, frequently rendering the author as just 'an effect of the text' (Heath 1975: 37). Compounding this, the terms 'code' and 'sub-code' semantically evoke a fixity and predictability that – perhaps revealingly – occludes an understanding of authorship, and representation in general, as a *process*. A more apposite concept-cum-designation is that of an authorial *discourse* that is *inscribed* by the text.[10] To a degree, this plays off Michel Foucault's assertion that the author is 'a function of discourse', a designation that serves 'to characterize the existence, circulation, and operation of certain discourses within a society' (1969: 124). However, Foucault is less concerned with how the 'author-function' (*ibid.*: 125) in relation to discourse affects the construal of textual meaning than how it acts within the broader discursive regime and its regulation of power. Following the work of linguist Emile Benveniste, the notion of discourse – that Benveniste describes as 'every enunciation assuming a speaker and a hearer, and in the speaker the intention of influencing the hearer in some way' (1966: 242) – can be seen further to highlight the sense of the way in which authorship inflects a text's address and, correspondingly, the placing of the spectator in relation to that text. Caughie elucidates: 'discourse involves notions of the text as a production and a productivity ... with someone speaking and someone spoken to, and with the positioning of the one by the other. For authorship, to talk of the film as discourse opens it up to questions of the way in which it positions its subjects (enunciating and spectating), and to questions of rhetoric' (1981d: 294).

Reframing authorship as a discourse accordingly encompasses not only repeated authorial concerns, but *how* these concerns are represented and weighted. While this marries the thematic and the stylistic, analysis of authorship as discourse – centring upon its textual inscription – likewise obviates dispute over what is 'intended' or 'unconscious'. With the authorial discourse engaging in a constant interplay with a text's other determinants, the concept also easily accommodates a director's involvement in pre- or post-production. This is important when discussing the films of modern American directors like Scorsese, who tend to have a greater 'hands-on' input throughout a film's making than many directors during the classical period.

Neither does the concept of authorial discourse invalidate the pertinence of the author as a biographical individual. As the authorial discourse presents certain concerns and emphases that are invariably ideological, so they can be related to an individual that is the product of particular material forces. This allows us to consider the significance of the often foregrounded biographical reference of Scorsese's work without reducing it to a 'Romantic' outpouring of self. It can instead be read as an expression of and reflection upon a specific socialization; not least as a central concern of Scorsese's authorial discourse is his characters' ideological and psycho-sexual determination.

This brings us to the sub-title of this study: *Authorship and Context*. The following chapters will be focused upon variously detailed analyses of Scorsese's fictional films, ranging from his student shorts to the big-budget *New York, New York* (1977). The analyses will centre on how the texts' constituent elements interact to create meaning, thereby occasioning consideration of the stylistic and thematic consistencies that shape Scorsese's authorial discourse. These meanings and consistencies will of necessity be read in relation to discussion of the films' industrial, institutional and filmic determination. The films analysed were made within a heterogeneity of production practices – student filmmaking, exploitation cinema, independent production, major studio finance and distribution – each of which differently inflects and (dis-)places Scorsese's authorial discourse. Hence the study's chapter per film or production context structure.

No less than meanings and consistencies, the films' contextual determinants are ideologically informed. Consequently, the subsequent readings cannot be restricted to their authorial or cinematic placement, but will encompass the films' wider historical context; one marked by the acute social and political upheaval of sixties and seventies USA.

The time similarly sees upheaval within Hollywood – numerous crises and changes resultant upon the end of the studio system and the beginnings of Hollywood's renewed, conglomerated dominance. Within this situation, the study specifically traces the genesis, institutional appropriation and consequent rejection of New Hollywood Cinema: that phase of art cinema-influenced, variously oppositional filmmaking, that Scorsese's work typifies, and that, as it embodies both an expression of and response to factors impelling Hollywood's sixties decline, is now widely considered to comprise Hollywood's final 'golden age', 'the last time Hollywood produced a body of risky, high-quality work – as opposed to the errant masterpiece' (Biskind 1998: 17).

Social, political and institutional upheaval have been seen to interact as Hollywood, having ceded its position as the central proponent of the dominant ideology to television, sought, through New Hollywood Cinema, to address an emergent younger, vaguely Left-liberal and cine-literate audience. In turn, the period of New Hollywood Cinema, with its art cinema reference, sped the recognition by Hollywood of the director as *auteur*, with the majors increasingly perceiving author-directors to be key elements in the financing and selling of films. It is with respect to this that Corrigan claims auteurism's refiguration. Writing from a postmodernist position, Corrigan stresses the *auteur* 'as a *commercial* strategy for organizing audience reception', arguing: 'Since the early 1970s, the commercial conditioning of this figure has successfully evacuated it of most of its expressive power and textual coherence' (1991: 103, 135).

At the risk of being (not too uncomfortably) lumped with 'neoro-mantic Marxist critics of postmodernism who cling longingly to the high-modernist conception of filmmaker as expressive artist' (*ibid.*: 106–7), for myself this goes far too far. This evokes other issues. Namely, why Scorsese? And why his early films? Taking the latter first, the films discussed – with the exception of *Taxi Driver* (1976) – have in general lacked the substantive critical treatment enjoyed by some of Scorsese's later projects. Further, Scorsese's experience of different production situations offers a paradigm for that of many other filmmakers associated with New Hollywood Cinema.

Beyond this, the choice of Scorsese's films invariably raises the question of evaluation. Although it is a nonsense to confuse value with the fact of authorship, V.F. Perkins accurately observes: 'The term "author" when used of a film director is almost inevitably a term of acclaim: it is an honorific title – like "artist" – at least as much as it is description' (1990: 59). While Scorsese's early filmmaking shares certain elements with that of other New Hollywood Cinema directors, it is both distinctive and distinguished. To account for this to an extent requires recourse to an older critical language, one that deals with 'such values as eloquence, subtlety, vividness and intensity' (*ibid.*). Certainly, what are claimed to be the most accomplished of Scorsese's films here discussed – *Mean Streets* (1973), *Taxi Driver* and *New York, New York* – imply the criterion of cinematic excellence that Perkins outlines in *Film as Film*: 'The great film approaches an intensity of cohesion such that its elements do not operate solely to maintain or further the reality of the fictional world, nor solely to decorative, affective or rhetorical effect' (1972: 131). The three films demonstrate how, at its best, Scorsese's work affords a heightened fusion of style, narrative and subject matter through which the films' concerns are represented and worked through with a rare, almost confrontational, emotional and intellectual intensity. While these qualities are apparent to a lesser or less extensive degree in the other films analysed, all bear witness to the significance of context to their making and meanings. Thus, to return to Foucault, this study seeks to investigate not only 'the expressive value and fundamental transformations' of Scorsese's authorial discourse, but 'its mode of existence', the 'modifications and variations' of its 'circulation, valorization, attribution, and appropriation', and how, further, it is 'articulated on the basis of social relationships' (1969: 137).

Authorship and context.

2
New York, NYU, and the European Influence: *What's a Nice Girl Like You Doing in a Place Like This?; It's Not Just You, Murray!; The Big Shave*

I

As an avowedly 'personal' director, Scorsese has had his films repeatedly discussed in relation to his biography. Too often this has been the chief or sole reference point, resulting in readings that place the films as unproblematically direct reflections of Scorsese's life and/or construct a simplistic, hagiographic opposition between Scorsese as *auteur* and the commercial imperatives of Hollywood. However, not only does the biographical reference of Scorsese's films vary, but his personal history – while important – is just one of a complex of determinants on his work. Further, this personal history requires to be considered as a particularized articulation of a larger historical context.

Scorsese was born in Flushing, Long Island, on 17 November 1942. The second son of Charles and Catherine Scorsese, second-generation Italian-Americans who worked in the garment trade, he lived until he was 'seven or eight years-old' (Scorsese 1981: 132) in Corona in Queens, New York. Because 'of financial problems and illness' (*ibid.*), the family relocated to the same block on Elizabeth Street, Manhattan, on which both of Scorsese's parents had been born and brought up. Scorsese thus entered the Little Italy of the Lower East Side, an environment that has markedly informed his *oeuvre*: 'Elizabeth Street was mainly Sicilian, as were my grandparents, and here the people had their own regulations and laws' (Thompson and Christie 1996: 3).

Chronically asthmatic, the young Scorsese was frequently taken to the cinema by his parents or by his elder brother, Frank. Scorsese hence began the intensive film-viewing that has continued and influenced his work throughout his career, and that was complemented by the increasing scheduling of films on television, in which his 'movie-buff' father made an early investment (Scorsese 1981: 132). In childhood Scorsese drew 'fictional' titles and posters and 'cartoon' movies, 'a kind of storyboarding' (*ibid.*: 133). When 'twelve or thirteen' he 'abandoned the storyboards' (*ibid.*) and attempted to make some 8 mm films with friends from the neighbourhood.[1]

Apart from cinema, Scorsese's other 'refuge' was the Catholic Church. When 'eight or nine' (Thompson and Christie 1996: 12) Scorsese decided to become a priest: a decision that has become almost a cliché of writing on the director. In 1956 Scorsese entered a prepatory seminary but was expelled because of poor grades and bad behaviour. He subsequently entered a Catholic high school and, still harbouring ambitions for the priesthood, sought to enter the Jesuit Fordham University, only to be rejected because of inadequate grades.

It was almost by default, therefore, that in 1960 Scorsese entered New York University (NYU). Two sociological points are here noteworthy. First, Scorsese was the first member of his blue-collar family to enter university. Second, it is testimony to the insularity of Little Italy life that, before entering NYU, Scorsese had only visited Greenwich Village, the site of the university, once – this despite its being within walking distance of Elizabeth Street.[2] Initially, Scorsese intended to major in English, but on taking a course entitled 'The History of Motion Pictures, Radio and Television' 'found' his vocation and switched from literature to film.

With the University of Southern California (USC) and the University of California at Los Angeles (UCLA), NYU offered one of the first film schools in the USA. The three schools remain the most prestigious. However, while film school graduates are now common among American filmmakers, in proceeding to make features Scorsese became part of the first generation of American film school educated directors – a group that also includes Michael Wadleigh (NYU), George Lucas, John Milius (USC) and Francis Ford Coppola (UCLA). Unlike the situation, say, in Europe, where film schools have had a longstanding relation to national cinemas, previously directors in the main had entered the American film industry from other media (for example, theatre – George Cukor; radio – Orson Welles; television – Sidney Lumet) or from other countries (Michael Curtiz, Fritz Lang, Alfred Hitchcock, *et al.*) or had risen to direct through the industry (Henry Hathaway, Robert Parrish, Don Siegel ...).

While these routes to direction are still extant, the entry of film school graduates into the American industry was, and remains, in part facilitated by the break-up of the studio system, and thus of a structure through which filmmaking talent could be nurtured. The first film school product to direct a feature for a major studio is thought to have been UCLA graduate Brian G. Hutton, whose film *The Wild Seed* was released by Universal in 1965. Before this, few entered film school 'with serious hopes of becoming directors, producers, or writers of any substance in theatrical film' (Pye and Myles 1979: 55).

Film school characteristically involves both practical study of production and academic study of film theory, history and criticism. This has been perceived to have had consequences for the kind of films directed by film-school graduates. With respect to production, 'university training ... [demands] that students learn virtually every phase of the filmmaking process' (Schatz 1983: 204). Correspondingly, the work of film school directors has been variously praised for its intensive technical competence and condemned for a crippling technical, and technological, over-determination. In turn, as film school graduates have 'learned about the history of film and the techniques of its construction outside of the production system', so it has been claimed that this enables a 'more analytic approach than that of their predecessors' (Kolker 1988: 160). This is not to assert that older or other filmmakers are or were ignorant of film history or conventions. It is rather a matter of degree, with film school graduates being seen frequently to construct their films through self-conscious and often explicit reference to filmic precursors.

Certainly, a foregrounded combination of technical prowess, formal awareness and cinematic self-consciousness is diversely apparent in many of the films of the first generation of film school directors. Moreover, these films, in their contrasting critical and commercial prominence, have tended to establish a model of post-film school practice. It is nevertheless perhaps a model as much determined by the historical context of the first generation's study as by the study itself. Namely, the films show the influence of 'the burst of cinematic enthusiasm and creative energy in Europe in the late fifties' wherein filmmakers influentially 're-examined traditions and conventions' (*ibid.*: 8). Scorsese specifies: 'I was a film student from 1960 to 1965, during the height of the French New Wave, the international success of the Italian art cinema and the discovery of the new Eastern European cinema' (Thompson and Christie 1996: 14).

Of these European influences, the most significant is that of the French New Wave, or *nouvelle vague*. Although the movement lacks the broad formal uniformity of, say, Soviet montage cinema or Italian Neo-Realism, some defining elements can be cited. Most notably, there is a fusion of naturalism and stylization, as elements with 'documentary' connotations (long takes, improvisatory acting, location shooting) are combined with a foregrounded use of film style and syntax. This includes a non-realist articulation of filmic space and time (jump-cuts, crossing the line, slow-motion, freeze-frames), the anachronistic resuscitation of 'silent film' devices (irises, masking), 'unmotivated', often virtuoso camerawork and/or overtly commentative music. In short, the *nouvelle vague*, as it strives to represent contemporary actuality, engages self-consciously with cinema as a specific material practice.

Further self-consciousness is apparent in a predilection for cinematic allusion. This is especially a trait of films made by the most critically discussed sub-group of the *nouvelle vague*, that comprising former critics for *Cahiers du cinéma*; primarily Claude Chabrol, Jean-Luc Godard, Jacques Rivette, Eric Rohmer and François Truffaut. The films of this group have in turn tended to dominate notions of what constitutes *nouvelle vague* cinema. Indeed, the above summary of *nouvelle vague* elements more firmly 'fits' the films of the *Cahiers* directors than, for example, those of the Left Bank group.[3]

In tracing the influence of the *nouvelle vague*, we can posit some suggestive parallels between the first generation of American film school directors and, in particular, the *Cahiers* group. First, there is the latter's comparative youth. Chabrol and Truffaut directed their first features (*Le Beau Serge*, 1958, and *Les Quatre Cents Coups*, 1959) when 27, Godard his (*A bout de souffle*, 1960) when 28.[4] Youth, however, is a common factor of the *nouvelle vague*: during its time (approximately 1958–64) over 170 directors made their first features, 67 alone in 1959–60.[5] Accordingly, the films' formal engagement is often far from 'academic', but frequently marked by a 'youthful', even playful, exuberance and audacity. The films likewise represent predominantly young characters in topical situations. Hence the films' naturalistic, 'documentary' imperative: 'The *nouvelle vague* directors wanted ... to show their own generation's ways of living and thinking: to tackle issues not previously raised in the French cinema' (Siclier 1961: 117).

Second, as the *Cahiers* group's self-conscious filmmaking followed an extensive (if informal) study of and critical reflection upon cinema, so it affords a possibly empowering precedent for that associated with film school graduates. A commonplace regarding the *Cahiers* directors is their wide cinematic knowledge, founded upon an obsessive film-viewing. Well-served by fifties Paris, with its many cinemas, cine-clubs and the Cinémathèque Française, this also evokes a more specific parallel with the experience of the young Scorsese. In turn, if the *Cahiers* group's cinephilia became legitimized in their published criticism for *Cahiers du cinéma*, then their films sought to embody the critical position that underlaid their writing: *la politique des auteurs*. Ben Brewster's description of a *politique* is instructive: 'In a *politique* the critical tasks of the present are defined by constructing a history of the art which selects favourite artists or artistic tendencies of the past, and thereby formulates a programme for the artistic creation of the future' (1971: 52).

While Scorsese's auteurist investment has been marked, the practice espoused and acted upon by the *Cahiers* critics-cum-directors also finds certain reflection in the model of filmmaking encouraged at NYU; in particular by Professor Haig Manoogian. Manoogian stressed that films should be personal – Scorsese recalls him repeating 'over and over again: "Film what you know"' (1997a: 3).[6]

II

The first example of Scorsese's filmmaking is accepted to be his 1963 short, *What's a Nice Girl Like You Doing in a Place Like This?*.[7] Shot in 16 mm, the film, nine minutes long, was both directed and written by Scorsese, who claims that it is based on an (unidentified) story by English writer Algernon Blackwood, and concerns a writer known as Harry (Zeph Michaelis) who buys and becomes obsessed by a photograph of a man standing in a boat.

In 1964 Scorsese directed *It's Not Just You, Murray!*. Again shot in 16 mm, the film runs 15 minutes and represents the comic history of an Italian-American mobster, Murray (Ira Rubin), and his relationship with, and exploitation by, his friend, Joe (Sam De Fazio). The film's script was co-written by Scorsese and another student, Mardik Martin, instigating an important collaboration.

While both films broadcast an engaging energy and a precocious cinematic intelligence, they do so somewhat despite their conditions of production. During Scorsese's studentship, the NYU film school was significantly under-resourced. Of cameras, Scorsese remarks: 'We had very little equipment at that time, only a 16 mm Arriflex and a Cine-Special' (Thompson and Christie 1996: 14). Throughout both *What's a Nice Girl Like You Doing in a Place Like This?* and *It's Not Just You, Murray!* there is a very apparent sense of technical and logistical circumscription. Hence the minimal dressing and repeated use of a restricted number of locations, scenes with darkened, setting-obscuring lighting and montages of stills. The ample presence of voice-over implies limited possibilities for recording synchronized sound.[8]

The use of voice-over also operates as an extended allusion to the opening of *Jules et Jim* (Truffaut, 1961). This is but one of a number of specific allusions to (already allusive) *nouvelle vague* films. Truffaut is the key influence: apart from *Jules et Jim*, *What's a Nice Girl Like You Doing in a Place Like This?* especially evokes *Tirez sur le pianiste* (Truffaut, 1960). Scorsese's film replicates the latter's anachronistic use of masking, while a triple jump-cut, with each cut heralding a closer shot of Harry's finger as it moves toward a typewriter, replicates a trope used in *Tirez sur le pianiste* as Charlie (Charles Aznavour) moves his finger toward a door-bell). It is a device that is repeated, often significantly, in Scorsese's later films. *It's Not Just You, Murray!* continues the Truffaut allusions: the freeze-frames that end both the film's narrative proper and its coda recall that which ends *Les Quatre Cents Coups*. More than specific allusions, however, the energetic, elliptical irreverence of Scorsese's student shorts implies a liberating appropriation of what may be termed a *nouvelle vague* sensibility: 'we broke all the rules. That doesn't mean that we did films without learning the rules ... but I was able to draw on many new films and create a vocabulary for myself' (Kelly 1992: 38).

The use of voice-over, and the concomitant sound–image relations, are in addition a major source of the films' humour. In *It's Not Just You, Murray!* a montage sequence outlines the areas 'affected by' Murray and Joe's activities. But when Murray says 'motel chains', we see a shot of a line of prostitutes, 'politics', a shot of a corpse with a knife in its back, and 'undertaking services', a shot of a man being gunned down. In *What's a Nice Girl Like You Doing in a Place Like This?*, sound–image disjunction is combined with a ridiculous literalness. This once more implies *Tirez sur le pianiste*: when the hood, Momo (Claude Mansard), says, 'May my mother drop dead if I tell a lie', we see just that. When Harry says that he has been 'just hanging around the house', we see him hanging from a bar. Likewise, when Harry relates how he broke his obsession with the photograph by falling in love at a party, upon which he is finally able to eat, write and sleep, a series of jump-cuts reveal him doing all three while the party continues around him.

Such absurdity is matched by that of the film's storyline: having been cured of his initial obsession, Harry ends the film trapped in a painting of the sea. Scorsese has claimed that another influence on the film was the cartoon *The Critic* (Ernest Pintoff, 1963), that was written and narrated by Mel Brooks.[9] He extends the Brooks influence to *It's Not Just You, Murray!*, 'that's why the name Murray was used – because Brooks used it' (Kelly 1980: 14). However, in discussing the film, Scorsese privileges other influences: '*Murray* recalls the Warner Brothers films of the late thirties, early forties, films like *The Roaring Twenties* [Raoul Walsh, 1939] ... the gangster filmmaking tradition' (*ibid.*).

Although *The Roaring Twenties* finds specific allusion in the sequence of Murray and Joe's bootlegging, *It's Not Just You, Murray!* tends more broadly to parody the generically familiar 'rise of a gangster' scenario. Complementing this is the 'Love Is a Gazelle' sequence, that – with allusive consistency – burlesques the Busby Berkeley production numbers of the thirties Warners musicals. These generic references expand elements in *What's a Nice Girl Like You Doing in a Place Like This?*. Harry's friend (Fred Sica), with his suit, cigar and dark glasses, implies a screen mobster, while, as Harry watches television, we are given a musical number, 'Swivelhips Sal'.

The films' generic self-consciousness returns us to the *nouvelle vague*, for whom genre comprised another set of conventions open to rearticulation. Hence, *A bout de souffle* and *Tirez sur le pianiste* differently rework *film noir*, while *Une Femme est une femme* (Godard, 1961) deconstructs the musical. For James Monaco the *nouvelle vague* 'centered on the twin concepts of the *politique des auteurs* and film genres .... The auteur "standard of reference" was the vertical axis against which a film was plotted; the horizontal axis was the genre' (1976: 7–8).

In *It's Not Just You, Murray!* Scorsese sought to combine generic parody with 'real stories from the neighborhood I grew up in' (Kelly 1980: 14). Not only was the film 'completely shot in the neighborhood', but, 'of all my films *Murray* is the one that really shows the old neighborhood, the way it looked in the early sixties, right before it began to die out' (*ibid.*: 14, 16). On one hand, this continues the *nouvelle vague*'s 'documentary' impulse: even in its comic illogic, the location-based *What's a Nice Girl Like You Doing in a Place Like This?* conveys a sense of immediate actuality. On the other, it implies the influence of the contemporaneous, New York-centred direct cinema movement associated with the likes of Richard Leacock, D.A. Pennebaker and the Maysles Brothers. Both the *nouvelle vague* and direct cinema were technologically and economically facilitated by the same developments (hand-held cameras, lightweight sound equipment, fast film emulsions and so on) that enabled flexible location shooting with minimal crews. For direct cinema, this also allows the intimate, spontaneous, 'fly-on-the-wall' approach characteristic of the mode. Where the movements primarily diverge is in their narrative address. Simplifying, *nouvelle vague* filmmaking tends, to paraphrase Godard, to emphasize the reality of the representation as much as the reality represented.[10] That is, the films, in their self-consciousness, and with varying degrees of reflexivity, highlight the implication of film form, style and syntax in the creation of meaning. If this in addition implies film's 'subjective' manipulability, then documentary largely foregrounds its 'objective' recording function. Direct cinema predominantly seeks to authenticate the actuality of what is represented. Paradoxically, it is an authentication ratified by signifiers of mediation – unsteady camerawork, grainy visual textures, uneven sound – that are offered as confirmation of the films' capture of contingent actuality.

It is a paradox both exploited and laid bare by the opening of *It's Not Just You, Murray!*. The film begins with a medium shot of a balding, middle-aged man sitting at a desk in a well-appointed office. He leans toward the camera, smiles, winks and says: 'Hi'. Cut to a close-up of a tie. We hear the man's voice: 'See this tie?'. He hand directs the camera up to his face, and he says: 'Twenty dollars'. Cut to a shot of the man's feet: 'See these shoes?'. His hand again directs the camera upward: 'Fifty dollars'. Cut to a medium shot of the man buttoning his suit jacket: 'See this suit?'. Cut to a facial close-up: 'Two hundred dollars'. Cut to a street and a medium shot of a white convertible: 'See this car?'. The hand-held camera moves right to where the man stands: 'Five thousand dollars'. So far the sequence broadly implies direct cinema. For while the man acknowledges, and plays up to, the camera, the shots are, with documentary 'objectivity', (literally) determined by the subject represented. However, on the man offering the camera – and, by implication, the spectator – a 'ride' in his car, the illusion of 'objectivity' is exploded. The man suddenly hesitates and, claiming that he has 'forgot something', walks toward the camera demanding that shooting stop. We faintly hear a voice behind the camera, and the shot cuts to the man once more at his desk: 'I forgot to introduce myself. I'm Murray.' While amusing, this restart goes beyond direct cinema's tacit admission of mediation reflexively to suggest that documentary, no less than any other filmic mode, is a constructed, conventionalized form that, as here, facilitates the 'subjective' manipulation of meaning.

This effective deconstruction is compounded as the film continues as a spoof documentary of Murray's criminal career. Indeed, despite Scorsese's claims, any sense of a documentation of Little Italy life in the film is, at best, tangential. Nevertheless, the beginning of *It's Not Just You, Murray!* highlights a tension between the documentary and the reflexive, the 'objective' and the 'subjective' that, implicit in *What's a Nice Girl Like You Doing in a Place Like This?*, and grounded in the *nouvelle vague*, becomes a defining element of Scorsese's authorial discourse.[11]

III

It's Not Just You, Murray! likewise presents a recognizable Scorsese thematic. Murray is positioned between antithetical forces embodied in the persons of Joe and his mother (Catherine Scorsese). While Joe, louche and well-dressed, suggests an embrace of WASP values, Murray's mother is almost over-insistently Italian-American. The character is not only dressed in a plain, Italianate black dress and shawl, but – in a running joke – repeatedly represented carrying plates of spaghetti to Murray; even to prison, where she feeds it through the wire that separates her from her son. Murray lands in prison after a police raid on his and Joe's bootlegging operation. Typically, Joe flees the situation, leaving Murray to take the rap. By contrast, Murray's mother's spaghetti, while ridiculously obsessive, implies a giving concern. Further, whereas Joe, through his partnership with Murray, is associated with criminality and materialism, Murray's mother's representation hints at a rooted, 'Old World' morality.

It is the latter that is ideologically privileged by the text. Although Murray scorns his mother's basic psychology, 'eat first', Joe's more 'sophisticated' advice is shown to be destructive. Joe impresses on Murray the need to 'always control yourself' – 'when people bother you, hit you, abuse you, curse you ... when they really, really bother you ... don't do nothing'. During this, we see Murray being knocked unconscious, beaten up and gestured at, before a series of shots show Murray, dressed in a dinner suit, but tied up, and smoking a cigarette through a gag with exaggerated 'cool', standing in a bowl into which cement is poured.

While functioning comically, the film's sound–image disparity thus serves further to reveal the 'truth', that is 'guaranteed' textually by the visual. When Murray claims that 'in the course of business' there was 'a misunderstanding', we see Murray arrested in the police raid. Similarly, the sound–image split during Murray's account of his and Joe's success can be considered an exposé of its sordid and violent underpinning.

Moreover, despite Murray's seeming, proud materialism, his stress on his success – 'I'm very rich. I'm very influential. I'm very well liked' – might be read as an overcompensatory attempt to convince himself of his 'sweet life'. Likewise, not only do Murray's euphemistic accounts of his criminality suggest a desire to mask its actuality, but there are intimations that he is repressing an awareness of his exploitation. Just before the bootlegging scene, we hear Murray say, regarding Joe, 'he did set me up', then pause pregnantly before adding, 'in business'. But if such imply a latent apprehension, Murray's words also consistently reveal an embarrassingly limited perception. He can thus declare – without irony – that without Joe 'I wouldn't be what I am'.

Joe's using of Murray culminates in his affair with Murray's wife (Andrea Martin). This again indicts Murray's obtuseness. When Murray watches 'Love Is a Gazelle' from the wings with engrossed, childish delight, Joe and Murray's wife look meaningfully at each other behind Murray's back. Murray's unawareness is later linked with his materialism. As Murray counts a wad of banknotes with more childlike joy, Joe kisses Murray's wife's hand, again behind Murray's back. Before this, Joe lights a cigarette from a votive candle. An act that invites criticism, it is also, in Scorsese's early short films, a rare instance of the Catholic imagery that informs many of his features.

A more problematic 'Catholic' influence is implicit in the film's female representation. Scorsese has admitted that his upbringing instilled a misogynistic view of women: 'I grew up in a certain kind of culture: Sicilian, Roman Catholic; women were separate entities; and the madonna–whore dichotomy encouraged fear of them, distrust, and, because they didn't seem like real human beings, difficulty in relating to them' (Rosen 1975: 43). In *It's Not Just You, Murray!* the madonna–whore dichotomy is literally reproduced. On one hand, there is Murray's mother, devoted to her son. On the other, there is Murray's wife, revealed to be an adulteress. That this is primarily achieved visually not only confirms it as a 'truth' of the text, but yet again critiques Murray's limited perception: he initially terms his wife 'an angel'. It is further significant that neither Murray's mother nor his wife is given a name – they are defined through their relationship to Murray.

The film climaxes when Murray, on saying that Joe is like a 'second father' to his children, is struck by a sudden revelation and calls Joe into his office. When Joe enters screen right, so Murray's mother, with plate of spaghetti, enters, with diegetic illogic, screen left. This places Murray between the embodiments of the film's structuring oppositions, suggesting that choice remains. Murray, however, reverts to habit and, in voice-over, rationalizes his lot: 'times change, things change .... So Joe says I ain't gonna win no father's day award .... We are very happy. ... We got everything that we want.' Disabused of illusions or excusing obtuseness, Murray here presents an especially pathetic figure. This is once more underscored by sound–image disjunction. As Murray's voice-over speaks acquiescence, we see him – as Joe 'explains' everything – looking unhappy. The freeze-frame that ends the scene captures his anguished expression in close-up. The shot is frozen as Murray's voice-over describes a 'new car', this time costing 'ten thousand dollars': a sound–image correlation that crowns the film's critique of materialism by suggesting its insufficiency. It also recalls Murray's earlier proud display of his 'five thousand dollar' car. This returns us to the opening sequence, as does the scene's occurring in Murray's office and another overtly reflexive moment: as Joe begins his explanation, an off-screen voice demands 'cut the sound'. As the film's climax thus reflects its beginning, a sense of cyclicity is evoked; that Murray – and his situation – will continue, and in what the film implies is a negative spiral.

Cyclicity is underscored graphically by the film's coda, in which many of the film's characters dance around Murray's convertible in a circle. This alludes to the ending of *Otto e mezzo* (Frederico Fellini, 1963) – Murray even wears a brimmed hat like that of the film's protagonist, Guido (Marcello Mastroianni). At first, Murray directs events from the car, only for Joe to appear, divest Murray of his megaphone and send him to join the dance, to become 'an extra in his own life' (Kelly 1980: 158). A summation of the 'truth' of Murray and Joe's relationship, the scene – and the film – concludes with a shot of a flash-powder photograph being taken of Murray and Joe, that again freezes.

IV

That Murray and Joe are shown directing the coda's action, and that Murray can be described as an 'extra', raises another reflexive connotation offered by the short's allusiveness. For, as the film implies that Murray has been dominated by Joe, so it suggests that Murray has been dominated, metaphorically, by cinema. This it achieves by implicitly linking the chronology of his relationship with Joe with the development of cinema from its earliest days to the (then) contemporary European art cinema. Near the film's beginning, Murray shows the camera a photograph of Joe aged 'about six or five'. Narratively marking the longevity of Murray and Joe's friendship, the photograph begins to move in a jerky, elliptical manner reminiscent of early cinema, the first moving pictures.[12] The correlation between the progression of Murray and Joe's relationship and that of (in particular American) film continues via the raid on Joe's and Murray's still, that suggests a silent movie chase, and the film's allusions to the gangster film and the musical. When Murray is questioned by an inquiry, the scene's recollection of the House Committee on Un-American

Activities (HUAC) hearings, along with the scene's grainy visual texture and scratchy sound, suggests a newsreel from the forties or fifties. This brings *It's Not Just You, Murray!* to its diegetic present, the point from which the central character recounts his life, appropriately shot in an approximation of direct cinema, before the film's coda brings the film's potted history of cinema further up to date with its Fellini allusion. Finally, as the anachronistic flash-powder camera of the last shot embodies early visual technology, so it recalls Murray's photograph of Joe, again implying cyclicity.

Murray's direction of the dance, and his evocation of Guido, who – in *Otto e mezzo* – is both a film director and figure of Fellini, implies a parallel between Murray and Scorsese. This accords with the film's other biographical intimations. If Murray is represented as dominated metaphorically by cinema, Scorsese's like 'domination' is implied by the enthused engagement with the medium evinced by *It's Not Just You, Murray!* itself. When making the film Scorsese, too, was in a cross-cultural situation – when attending NYU, he still lived in Little Italy. There is also the casting of his mother.

A comparable combination of the reflexive and the biographical is apparent in *What's a Nice Girl Like You Doing in a Place Like This?*. As in *It's Not Just You, Murray!*, the text's sound–image relations privilege the visual as the guarantor of 'truth'. In *What's a Nice Girl Like You Doing in a Place Like This?* this emphasis on image over word is complemented narratively: Harry cannot work as a writer because he becomes obsessed first with a photograph and then painting. The objects of Harry's obsession are suggestively cinematic. The photograph is akin to a film still, and the 'painting' in which Harry becomes trapped is finally represented by a shot of the sea.

Early on, Harry's voice-over states that his real name is Algernon. Given that the film is claimed to derive from a story by Algernon Blackwood, this links Harry with its 'author' and, by extension, with Scorsese. This is complemented via the metonymic relation of photograph and painting, the biographical pertinence of which hinges on an awareness that the man in the photograph is Scorsese. In becoming part of the painting, Harry thus occupies a space analogous to that occupied by Scorsese in the photograph: he becomes Scorsese's substitute.

Yet as both films figuratively imply their central characters' cinematic domination, this carries some negative connotations. In *It's Not Just You, Murray!* it is implicated not only in Murray's exploitation by Joe and what the text represents as an ideologically questionable materialism, but in a denial of Italian-American roots. In *What's a Nice Girl Like You Doing in a Place Like This?*, Harry's end as he is absorbed by the painting (by cinema?) is, in Harry's words, 'fraught with peril'. While the films display a delight in cinema, they also suggest a suspicion of its possibly amoral, possibly deracinating, possibly dehumanizing seductiveness.

Harry's fate again raises the issue of textual misogyny. It is Harry's wife (Mimi Stark) who paints the image in which Harry becomes trapped. She is also another female character who remains unnamed. Moreover, the conclusions of both films privilege the central characters' relationships with their male friends before those with their wives. In *What's a Nice Girl Like You Doing in a Place Like This?* it is Harry's friend who discovers Harry's predicament and to whom Harry's final words are addressed. In *It's Not Just You, Murray!*, Murray's acceptance of his cockolding begins 'Joe and me has always been great friends …'.

V

The Big Shave was made after Scorsese had left NYU and, lasting six minutes, presents his first use of colour. The film was enabled by the Palais des Beaux Arts, Brussels, that, on Scorsese's submission of his script, furnished a grant of ten rolls of colour 16 mm film. Textually, *The Big Shave* extends the absurdist tendencies of Scorsese's student short films into a darkly comic exercise in the excessive and the surreal: when shown at the Fourth International Festival of Experimental Cinema at Knokke-le-Zoute, Belgium, in December 1967 it won Le Prix de L'Âge d'Or.

In *The Big Shave*, a young, blonde-haired man (Peter Bernuth) enters a gleamingly white bathroom and, to the accompaniment of Bunny Berigan's version of 'I Can't Get Started', shaves until he is covered in blood. For Kim Newman, 'The humour and horror of the piece resides in the cool, methodical manner in which the shaver obliterates his own features' (1992: 56). Extending this, the film's effect revolves upon a series of systematic contrasts: between the quotidian and the surreal, between the bathroom's spotless white and the man's dark-red blood, between the man's actions and the song's lyric – 'the problem for the young man in the film is not that "he can't get started" but that he simply cannot stop' (Bliss 1985: 110). The film has in addition an unsettling plausibility – what is represented is eccentric and unlikely, but, for the most part, possible.

Scorsese conceived *The Big Shave* as a comment on American involvement in Vietnam: 'the Tet offensive was on in Vietnam .... In this daily morning ritual, an American is cutting his own throat without realizing it' (Taylor 1981: 307). To push the message home, Scorsese considered ending the film with stock footage of Vietnam, but contented himself with the title 'Viet '67' on the end credit.

Subsequently, Scorsese has regarded *The Big Shave* more an expression of personal difficulties: 'Consciously it was an angry outcry against the war. But in reality something else was going on inside me, I think, which really had nothing to do with the war' (Kelly 1980: 19). Specifically, he has related the film to the break-up of his first marriage and to his failure to find distribution for his first feature, a film that was to become *Who's That Knocking at My Door?*.[13]

3
Entering the Marketplace, Developing a Style: *Who's That Knocking at My Door?*

I

In *The Big Shave* the young man shaves himself bloody while standing before and being reflected in a mirrored cabinet. Accepting the situation's naturalistic pertinence, the mirror, when combined with the man's actions, implies an alienation from self. The connotation is underscored intertextually by the moment in *It's Not Just You, Murray!* when Murray smashes his mirrored reflection. This occurs as we hear Joe conclude his injunction to 'do nothing' by asserting that one day Murray is 'going to see somebody' who is all his assailants 'rolled into one' whom Murray can give 'all he deserves'. Further, not only does Harry's paralysing obsession with the photograph in *What's a Nice Girl Like You Doing in a Place Like This?* suggest an analogous self-alienation, but the figured relation between Harry and the pictured Scorsese renders the photograph a metaphoric mirror.

The opening shot of *Who's That Knocking at My Door?* represents a mirror in which we see reflected a maternal figure (Catherine Scorsese) working at a kitchen table. In the ensuing scene, one of two that precede the film's credits, brief shots show the woman preparing, cooking and serving a dish to five children. The scene hence continues the association in *It's Not Just You, Murray!* of the maternal – and Scorsese's mother – with the provision of food. It also relates the woman with the Madonna. In the opening shot, the mirrored image of the woman is flanked, screen right, by a china statuette of the Madonna and child, close-ups of which intersperse the shots of the woman's actions. Compounding this are a pair of shots, filmed from behind the statuette, that not only imply that the Madonna is supervising the meal's preparation and serving, but find reflection in a shot, filmed from the foot of the table, that lends the woman a similar over-seeing dominance.

The scene cues the film's prime concern: the madonna–whore dicho-tomy. The narrative of *Who's That Knocking at My Door?* centres upon a young Italian-American, J.R. (Harvey Keitel), caught between contrasting cultures, represented through discrete spheres of his experience. On one hand, there is the time that J.R. spends with his friends from 'the neighborhood', Joey (Lennard Kuras) and Sally Gaga (Michael Scala), a seemingly endless round of drinking, driving, whoring or just hanging about. On the other, there is his relationship with a young Caucasian woman, known only as the girl (Zina Bethune). J.R. refuses to have sex with the girl because, thinking her a virgin, it would violate his invest-ment in the madonna–whore dichotomy that, for the benefit of the girl, he defines as the difference between a 'girl' and a 'broad' – 'a broad isn't exactly a virgin … you play around with them … you don't marry a broad'. When the girl tells J.R. that she was raped on a date, he responds viciously, and the relationship splits. J.R. seeks solace in his friends' activities, only to turn up one morning at the girl's apartment. However, the characters' potential reunion degenerates into a bitter confirmation of their cultural dissonance, leaving J.R. nowhere to go but Little Italy.

As *Who's That Knocking at My Door?* thus locates the madonna–whore dichotomy within a defined milieu, so the opening shot of the mirror can be read as framing a culturally determined image. Like intimations are offered by the representation of mirrors in Scorsese's short films. Read biographically, the metaphoric mirror of the photo-graph in *What's a Nice Girl Like You Doing in a Place Like This?* suggests cultural appropriation; Murray's smashing of his reflection can be related to, and underlines, his implied unease regarding his criminal, materialistic existence; while the presence of the mirror in *The Big Shave* suggests situational estrangement whether considered with respect to the USA's self-destructive involvement in Vietnam or to Scorsese's personal and professional difficulties.

Across Scorsese's *oeuvre*, mirrors recurrently comprise a motif that focuses a thematic preoccupation with what the films represent as the predominantly alienating processes and effects of acculturation. With this explored with often foregrounded Freudian reference, the mirror motif in turn evokes and can be further considered in relation to Jacques Lacan's account of psycho-sexual development, that is grounded by his concept of the mirror stage.

In Lacan's re-reading of Freud, the mirror stage instigates the development of the ego. Between six and 18 months, the infant remains physically uncoordinated. However, on perceiving its image in, say, a mirror, the infant mistakes its unified whole for a superior self, that it identifies with and internalizes as an ideal ego. Not that the function of the mirror should be taken literally, it is rather a 'convenient symbol' (Muller and Richardson 1982: 28) – the internalized image can be that of the mother or any 'other'. The infant's identification is nevertheless a misrecognition that contrasts 'with the turbulent movements that the subject feels are animating him' (Lacan 1949: 2). The mirror stage hence 'situates the agency of the ego, before its social determination, in a fictional direction' (*ibid.*), a disjunction between self and image that inaugurates 'the assumption of the armour of an alienating identity, which will mark with its rigid structure the subject's entire mental development' (*ibid.*: 5).[1]

The mirror stage occurs during the pre-Oedipal phase that Lacan designates the Imaginary: a mainly pre-linguistic period of psychic development governed by images and dyadic mother–child relations. For Lacan, the Oedipus Complex marks the transition from the Imaginary to the Symbolic, 'the realm of all discourse and cultural exchange' (Stam, Burgoyne and Flitterman-Lewis 1992: 133). The acquisition of linguistic capability bespeaks the subject's insertion into a social context that – in contrast to the Imaginary, but with Oedipal consistency – is dominated by the patriarchal Law, what Lacan terms the Name of the Father. As the subject has to learn the language and customs of the culture, it is effectively '*spoken* by the culture itself' (*ibid.*: 132).

That this has Saussurean echoes is unsurprising: Lacan reformulates Freud explicitly through the prism of structural linguistics. This finds reflection in *Who's That Knocking at My Door?* in J.R.'s division of 'girls' and 'broads': a distinction that suggests the unequal linguistic – and hence cultural – status of men and women under patriarchy.[2] The patriarchal reference of the implied determination of the woman in the opening scene is flagged by the sight of a painting of a moustached patriarch on the wall above and behind her as she rolls some dough and serves the children. This parallels the Madonna's 'overseeing' of the woman, a link that accords both with the Catholic Church's historical status as a major patriarchal institution and the text's insistent implication of it in the maintenance of the madonna–whore dichotomy. The determining influence of the Church is figured when the woman divides the 'bread-like pastry' that she bakes between the children: a communion-like sharing of food that 'symbolizes the passing on of religion and knowledge to the next generation' (Bliss 1985: 31, 32). This complements the Lacanian connotations of the mirror motif. Although none of the children is between six and 18 months old, they nevertheless sit accepting before and receive from a maternal figure of which the Lacanian mirror is frequently the 'convenient symbol'; both figure and symbol having been visually united in the initial shot.

Retrospectively, the scene's collapsing of the mirror motif, the psycho-sexual, Catholicism and cultural determination has a summary resonance for Scorsese's authorial discourse. Textually, the Lacanian connotations of the mirror motif and, in particular, its diegetic relation to the madonna–whore dichotomy are affirmed by a pair of related scenes.

The first is a flashback that represents Gaga's thoughts, and cuts from a shot of Gaga and a woman (Wendy Russell) necking in Joey's bar, the 8th Ward Pleasure Club, to a mirror shot of the woman brushing her hair and discovering that she has lost $40 from her purse. If in the opening scene the mirror motif is related to a figure of the Madonna, here the situation, and the woman's slatternly appearance, relates it to a 'whore'.

The second scene happens in J.R.'s family apartment. J.R. follows the girl into what appears to be his mother's bedroom and the couple lie on the bed. There ensues a passage of sexual foreplay. Twice J.R. pulls away. The first time he is coaxed back by the girl's kiss, the second time the break is decisive. Although J.R. cannot articulate a response to the girl's concern, the film 'explains' his actions: as the girl asks 'What is it?' we are given a shot of the characters reflected in a dressing-table mirror flanked screen right by another statuette of the Madonna and child. A configuration that recalls the film's opening shot, it is first shown when J.R. and the girl kiss and move toward the bed, as though signalling that their intimacy will be constrained by the madonna–whore dichotomy. Ironically, J.R. initially presses his abbreviated attentions upon the girl as she tries to brush her hair. This links the girl with the woman in Gaga's flashback, foreshadowing J.R.'s recasting of the girl as a 'broad' when she tells him of her rape.

II

The scene's recollection of the opening shot allows the woman at the film's beginning to be read as J.R.'s mother. The Madonna statuette from the opening scene also reappears in a later kitchen scene. The latter scene and that of J.R. and the girl in the bedroom were shot in the kitchen of Scorsese's family's apartment and his parents' bedroom. While this may in part be attributable to the film's limited production finance, it combines with Scorsese again casting his mother equally to suggest a biographical intent.[3] This intersects with the film's 'documentary' imperative. For Scorsese, *Who's That Knocking at My Door?* 'was an attempt to portray just the way I was living', to 'record the daily life of the neighborhood' (Kelly 1980: 16). Unlike the claims for *It's Not Just You, Murray!*, this is borne out by the film's evocation of quotidian actuality. In this, *Who's That Knocking at My Door?* once more plays off direct cinema: the film was shot on location, in everyday settings, in natural light and often with a hand-held camera.

Who's That Knocking at My Door? is nevertheless a fictional narrative. The film's use of direct cinema stylistics relates more precisely to a strand of New York independent filmmaking that, between the mid-fifties and early sixties, used 'documentary' techniques for fictional purposes – witness, for example, the work of Morris Engel, Lionel Rogosin and Shirley Clarke.[4] However, the key influence for Scorsese was John Cassavetes and his first film *Shadows* (1959): 'It was after seeing that, I realized *we* could make films' (1981: 134).

Shadows suggests a clear stylistic and formal precedent for *Who's That Knocking at My Door?*. Shot in unglamorous New York locations, in 16 mm, frequently with a hand-held camera, *Shadows* presents a narrative that is markedly loose and episodic (the film's closing title reads 'The film you have just seen was an improvisation'). *Shadows* might also be read as an enabling influence in terms of production. As for the *nouvelle vague* or the direct cinema documentarists, the advent of portable equipment made filmmaking economically possible for the likes of Cassavetes.[5] Moreover, the production history of *Shadows* exemplifies the doggedness and ingenuity that necessarily underpin much American independent cinema. The total cost of *Shadows* was a meagre $40 000, for which, during 1957–59 Cassavetes partly reshot and edited two versions of the film. Costs were kept down by, for instance, using equipment that was variously 'begged, borrowed, and rented', having an unpaid cast that largely comprised 'unemployed actors from Cassavetes' own drama workshop' (Carney 1985: 37) and Cassavetes himself serving as an uncredited cinematographer and editor. More idiosyncratically, the first $2000 of the film's budget was received in donations after Cassavetes mentioned the project on Jean Shepherd's *Night People* radio show during an interview that was intended to promote *Edge of the City* (Martin Ritt, 1957), in which Cassavetes starred.[6]

Shadows and *Who's That Knocking at My Door?* in addition show narrative likenesses. Broadly, *Shadows*, that centres on a pair of black brothers and their sister, two of whom can pass for white, is, like *Who's*

That Knocking at My Door?, concerned with ethnicity and cross-cultural tensions. Within this, the representation of J.R.'s Little Italy lifestyle finds specific antecedents in the represented experiences of the character Ben (Ben Carruthers). An unemployed, would-be jazz trumpeter in his early twenties, Ben leads an idle, unsettled existence that mainly consists of his hanging around with two friends, Tom (Tom Allen) and Dennis (Dennis Sallas), as they drift from street to bar to pick-up to fight. The obvious parallel with the time that J.R. spends with Joey and Gaga is enhanced by closer comparison. Both sets of characters are similarly represented. Tom and Joey act as self-proclaimed group leaders, Ben and J.R. are troubled by their listless lives, while Dennis and Gaga tend to be patronized by their companions. There are also similarities of incident and detail. The scene in *Shadows* in which Tom 'phones a woman and asks her to bring two friends for Ben and Dennis is reflected by that in *Who's That Knocking at My Door?* in which Gaga is despatched to find some women to entertain guys at a party. Likewise, when Ben bemoans his own and his friends' incessant, meaningless picking-up of girls, Tom corrects Ben's designation of the female with the term that resonates throughout Scorsese's film: 'Broads'.

Further comparable are the way in which the films open and close. *Shadows* begins with Ben crossing a busy day-time street to meet Tom and Dennis on the opposite sidewalk. It ends with Ben again crossing a busy city street, only this time he is walking away from Tom and Dennis and it is night. For all Ben's preceding protestations of change, the scenes imply an unbroken, ongoing cycle of experience.

Following its pre-credit scenes and credits, *Who's That Knocking at My Door?* presents the sight, through a window, of a butcher hacking a piece of meat. The camera zooms out and tracks right along a street to pick up J.R. and Joey as they turn a corner, then tracks left with and zooms in on the characters as they walk down the sunlit street and enter the 8th Ward Pleasure Club. The film closes with the sight of J.R. and Joey saying good night on a similar but night-time street. The camera zooms out as J.R. enters a building screen left and Joey, screen right, walks into the darkness. As in *Shadows*, the shots imply an ongoing cycle of experience – in the latter we hear the characters agreeing to talk 'tomorrow'.

The relation of *Who's That Knocking at My Door?* to *Shadows* is, however, both matched and problematized by Scorsese's continuing debt to the *nouvelle vague*. Throughout *Who's That Knocking at My Door?* 'documentary' representation is stylistically interrupted and italicized by jump-cuts, freeze-frames, the use of slow-motion and – as the post-credit shot demonstrates – often overt technical dexterity. The use of unannounced flashbacks implies a bid to replicate the complex interpenetration of present and past conveyed in *Hiroshima mon amour* (Alain Resnais, 1959).

The *nouvelle vague* devices foregroundedly inscribe Scorsese's discursive agency, not least as they frequently serve to interpret or to comment upon the represented action. It is a 'subjective' address that clashes with Cassavetes's inclination to eschew authorial expression before the 'objective' representation of experience: 'To tell the truth as you see it … is not necessarily the truth. To tell the truth as someone else sees it is, to me, much more important and enlightening' (Gelmis 1970: 78). Accordingly, Cassavetes's films tend to privilege the close representation of the moment-to-moment interplay of character and situation before any explicitly 'imposed' structuring of shot, scene and sequence.[7]

Such 'subjective' self-effacement before an 'objective' pro-filmic reality would seem to return us, once again, to direct cinema. Of note, with regard to this, is Jean-Louis Comolli's recasting of direct cinema as much less as defined documentary mode than a particular *'practice* of cinema' (1969: 243). Embracing the inevitability of mediation, and refusing the conventional distinction between fiction and documentary, Comolli defines direct cinema in terms of reciprocation of the act of filming and that which is filmed, through which the film 'is simultaneously produced by and produces the events and situations' (*ibid.*: 233). To wit, 'the filmed event does not pre-exist the film and the filming, but is produced by it' (*ibid.*: 243). Persuasive in relation to the paradoxical 'objectivity' of direct cinema documentaries, Comolli's conceptualization no less helps to ground Cassavetes's filmmaking epistemologically – indeed, for Comolli *Shadows* embodies one of 'the first experiments in direct fictional cinema' (*ibid.*: 240).[8]

III

Who's That Knocking at My Door? began as a graduate project at NYU, being 'the first student film shot in black and white 35 mm on the East Coast' (Thompson and Christie 1996: 25).[9] Initially titled *Bring on the Dancing Girls*, the film was also intended by Scorsese to be the second part of a trilogy about fundamentally the same character. The first instalment, *Jerusalem, Jerusalem*, has never been made, the third, originally called *Season of the Witch*, became *Mean Streets*.[10] Financed by $6000 raised by Scorsese's father from a student loan, filming of *Bring on the Dancing Girls* began in early 1965 and continued for six months, mainly at weekends.

As in the film's final version, *Bring on the Dancing Girls* cut between scenes of J.R. and his friends and his relationship with a young woman. But when shown at NYU later in 1965, the film was 'a disaster', 'it was 65 minutes long and just confounded everyone' (Thompson and Christie 1996: 25).[11] In 1967 Haig Manoogian, his wife Betzi and lawyer and NYU mature student Joseph Weill raised $37 000 for the film to be partly reshot. The scenes between J.R. and the young woman were reworked and shot in 16 mm with Keitel and Bethune. The new footage was blown up into 35 mm and intercut with the original scenes of J.R. and his buddies. Re-editing took four months, and involved Scorsese, Manoogian, Weill and, in a collaboration which looks forward to Scorsese's later features, Thelma Schoonmaker. Re-titled *I Call First*, the film was premiered at the Chicago Film Festival in November 1967, but failed to find distribution.

Scorsese repaired to Europe. When in Paris, Scorsese was informed by Manoogian that Joseph Brenner Associates, 'a soft-core porn distributor', would distribute *I Call First* if Scorsese added a nude scene: 'Everything was opening up in America at that time: Brenner was going legitimate' (Thompson and Christie 1996: 26). Unable to return to the USA, and unable to film in Paris because of *les événements* of May 1968, Scorsese had Keitel flown to Amsterdam where he shot a scene with Keitel and four women.[12] Given its present title, the film's extant version, including nude scene, was shown at the 1969 Chicago Film Festival before opening commercially in New York.

The need to include a nude scene plainly highlights the constraints that impinged upon the film's production, and Scorsese cut the scene almost contemptuously into the middle of a conversation between J.R. and the girl. However, the nude scene's forced insertion merely compounds the text's reflection of the project's prolonged, difficult gestation: *Who's That Knocking at My Door?* presents a patchwork of jerky transitions, unintegrated stylistic contrasts and varying standards of cinematography and picture quality. Some incidents imply a lack of finance or opportunity for reshooting. When Joey slaps Gaga about early in the film a sound boom enters shot, while when, near its end, J.R. kisses a crucifix and a blob of blood runs from his mouth, the moment is farcically unconvincing.[13]

Yet if *Who's That Knocking at My Door?* bears the scars of its production, it equally suffers from a lack of *beneficial* constraint that marks it, pejoratively, as a student-cum-independent film. Too often Scorsese's direction displays a self-indulgence and lack of control that diversely implies over-eagerness and/or immaturity. For instance, the incessant jump-cuts to images of enclosure (doors slamming, car windows closing, locks clicking shut), while thematically coherent, become over-used to the point of redundancy. It is a redundancy shared by the film's freeze-frames (of J.R. rising from a stool, of J.R. drunk, of J.R. and Joey in the street) that transmit little except the use of a (then) *outré* filmic transition.

Overstatement also mars the film dramatically. In the scenes between J.R. and the girl the dialogue veers toward the forced and contrived, and seems too obviously a means of carrying narrative and character information. Analogous problems attend the seeming improvisation used in the scenes of J.R. and his friends. Granting that this informs the scenes' 'documentary' connotation, it inclines toward a repetitiveness that diffuses rather than enhances the impact of moment and performance. Consider the scene that shows a drunken J.R., Joey and Gaga after J.R. breaks with the girl. Centred on a long, static front-on take, the characters' inebriated antics, as they laugh inanely, throw napkins and annoy each other, are allowed to drift until the scene teeters on the brink of actualizing rather than representing irritating behaviour.

The use of improvisation suggests another link with *Shadows*, even as its effect contrasts with the latter's deceptive dramatic economy. However, *Shadows*, despite its closing title, 'was rehearsed for weeks in advance of the filming in a series of dramatic workshop exercises led, and frequently partially scripted, by Cassavetes himself' (Carney 1985: 57). Further, while essaying an 'ethnographic' representation of marginal New York life, *Shadows* implies a documentary of actors acting, of – following Comolli – the ongoing creation of character within closely observed simulations of everyday situations. It is a reading offered by most of Cassavetes's films that, from this perspective, suggest 'discrete, self-enclosed actors' experiments happening at irregular intervals' (Combs 1992: 24). This emphasis on the actorly, while hardly Brechtian, nevertheless foregrounds, and reflects back upon, the process of (self-)rep-resentation, that becomes as much the films' concern and fascination as that what is purportedly represented.[14]

This finds echoes in *Who's That Knocking at My Door?*. Marion Weiss notes how, in the scenes of J.R. and his friends, as well as those of the male characters in *Mean Streets*, an authentic sense of long-term fellowship – and, one can add, ethnicity – is conveyed by the characters' speech patterns. These largely consist of 'brief sentences, simply syntactical and semantic constructions, rhetorical questions, audible gestures ("hey", "yeah"), storytelling devices, and rapid-fire delivery' (Weiss 1987: 5). However, for Robert Phillip Kolker, such interchanges manifest 'rhythm and energy and concentration greater than could be expected were it merely made up and "overheard" on the spot' (1988: 176). The dialogue consequently evokes the 'craft and planning', the improvisation through which it has been constructed, with its 'artificiality creating the effect of the overheard and the immediate' (*ibid.*).

Scorsese's features tend to be centred on actors versed in the Method.[15] This once again reflects the work of Cassavetes, a Method actor himself.[16] Simplifying, the Method seeks to achieve a greater naturalism than other acting modes via the actor 'feeling his/her way into a role from the inside, temporarily identifying with a character' (Dyer 1979: 161). But while the privileging of 'emotional meaning over all other aspects of character (such as social behaviour and "intellectual physiognomy")' frequently lends performances an emotive actuality, the expression of this 'emotional meaning' also gravitates – lacking exterior reference – toward 'the accumulation of redundant performance signs' (*ibid.*) that foreground acting as acting. Certainly, the performances in Scorsese's films of, most famously, Keitel and Robert De Niro, while purveying a dramatically convincing 'off-handedness' and 'immediacy' (Kolker 1988: 165), are hardly self-effacing *as* performances.

If the Method's emphasis on actor–character identification facilitates improvisation, it has similarly served to generate performances marked by greater emotional intensity than those in other acting styles. Moreover, although 'in principle the Method could be used to express any psychological state', in practice it has largely been used 'to express disturbance, repression, anguish, etc.' (Dyer 1979: 161). This is mirrored by *Who's That Knocking at My Door?*, in which the male characters predominantly display a tense insistence or frustrated unease that repeatedly explodes into outbursts of aggression or violence. Complementing and complemented by this is Scorsese's articulation of a battery of other stylistic elements: witness the film's elliptical editing or its recurrent, often 'unmotivated' camera movement. We can thus discern the emergence of a recognizable stylistic discourse, a characteristic, 'authorial' re-inflection of anterior styles and influences.

IV

Who's That Knocking at My Door? introduces Scorsese's now familiar employment of rock and pop music. This was historically innovative. With *Bring on the Dancing Girls* shown at NYU in 1965, its exhibition pre-dates by two years the release of the film usually cited as the first

American feature to be scored using rock/pop music, *The Graduate* (Mike Nichols, 1967).[17]

What distinguishes Scorsese's use of rock and pop from that of many other filmmakers is a centrality and intelligence of narrative integration that is far removed from the music's over-familiar deployment as what Scorsese scorns as 'an unimaginative device for establishing a time period' (1995: 1) or as primarily a means of selling a film. In *Who's That Knocking at My Door?* the chosen music – positioned prominently in the mix, or even comprising the sole element on the soundtrack – augments the assertive edginess created by the film's other stylistic components, with the use of mainly vocal as opposed to instrumental music frequently contributing to an aural overload correlative to the intensity provoked visually and dramatically.

The energetic, brittle rhythms of the somewhat callow late fifties–early sixties songs that dominate the music track nicely complement the uncertain, immature behaviour of the film's male protagonists. Correspondingly, the selection of The Doors' 'The End', released in 1967, to accompany the nude scene compounds, through the music's more sophisticated knowingness, the scene's disjunctiveness. Even so, the use of the song's explicitly Oedipal section works to comment upon J.R.'s situation. If, for J.R., the girl before she tells of the rape is a madonna-figure, she is also, implicitly, a mother-substitute. Given this, the choice of the maternal bedroom for the abbreviated sex scene obtains further point.

Within the rhythmic fitness of the film's other music, specific sound–image relations evince a diverse complexity. In unpacking this, a convenient starting point is Michel Chion's work on film sound.[18] Elaborating upon the dualistic division of music that underscores and that which counterpoints, Chion proposes a tripartite schema: empathetic music, that expresses 'its participation in the feeling of the scene, by taking on the scene's rhythm, tone, and phrasing'; anempathetic music, that exhibits 'conspicuous indifference to the situation, by progressing in a steady, undaunted, and ineluctable manner' (Chion 1994: 8); and didactic contrapuntal music, that is used 'in a distanciated manner in order to elicit a precise, usually ironic, idea' (Stam, Burgoyne and Flitterman-Lewis 1992: 63). This schema is both demonstrated and complicated by *Who's That Knocking at My Door?*. For example, the choice of Ray Barretto's hypnotic 'El Watusi' to accompany the slow lateral tracks, slow-motion and dissolves of the party scene in which Gaga is 'jokingly' threatened by a guest (Robert Uricola) who wields a loaded gun empathetically enhances the transmission of a sense of sated torpor. Similarly, the rasping energy of Jr Walker and the All Stars' 'Shotgun' as J.R. differentiates between 'girls' and 'broads' can be read as anempathetic, while, lyrically, The Searchers' jejune paean to hopeless devotion, 'Ain't That Just Like Me', heard during the drunk scene, implies an ironic, didactically contrapuntal relation to J.R.'s situation. However, the phallic connotations of the minimal lyrics of 'Shotgun' also ironically reflect upon J.R.'s misogyny, while the loose energy of the beat of 'Ain't That Just Like Me' corresponds with that displayed by the drunken J.R., Joey and Gaga. Once more, the use of vocal music is here significant.

Despite its discursive overstatement, *Who's That Knocking at My Door?* also presents an authorially distinctive development of the film's constitutive interplay of naturalism and stylization. For, as the latter's evocation of an extra-diegetic subjectivity becomes collapsed with and even subsumed by the implication of a reflected diegetic subjectivity, it shades from the expressive to the expressionist: representations that externalize the interiority of characters and situations. Hence the slow-motion party scene, or the complex long take that, as it tracks around, toward and back from J.R. and the girl, reflects and transmits the tentative flux of their first meeting or, in contrasting register, the jarringly jump-cut, overlapping montage that nightmarishly prolongs the representation of the girl's rape.[19]

The cramped and workaday sites that dominate the film's *mise-en-scène* likewise serve as an objective correlative for the characters' repressive determination, functioning dramatically to imply a causal factor in the frustrated, combative behaviour that bespeaks their alienation. Consider the scene in which J.R., Joey and Gaga drive uptown in Joey's car at night. The characters are shot in a single take through the frame-within-frame of the car's windscreen, affording a spatial circumscription that intensifies J.R. and Joey's repetitive argument about whether to go uptown or not. This is characteristically complemented by the scene's use of music. Gaga interjects requests to have the car radio turned up. The music's raised volume contributes to an increasing tension that, reaching a point at which all three characters are yelling, is only released when Joey orders J.R. out of his car.

Psychoanalytically, the implied relation between determination, alienation and aggression once more evokes Lacan, who posits 'aggressivity' as 'a correlative tension of the narcissistic structure in the coming-into-being ... of the subject' (1948: 22). In *Who's That Knocking at My Door?* a link between this 'aggressivity' and the textually particular connotations of the mirror motif is implied through the sexualized reference of the characters' outbursts. In the car scene, not only are the guys going uptown to see a 'broad', but J.R. and Joey's argument centres upon the impugning of the other's masculinity. Thus J.R.'s mocking allusion to the car as Joey's toy, implying penial compensation, or his barb that he would like to see Joey 'get a girl without paying five dollars'. Joey calls J.R. a 'jerk-off' and asserts that J.R.'s reluctance to go uptown is because of his relationship with the girl.

In the scenes at the Pleasure Club the sexual is mapped on to the shabby décor and fittings. On the walls behind and to the left of the bar are fixed nude female pin-ups. Another pops up, with phallic impudence, when Gaga, during his flashback, lifts the bar flap to which it is stuck. Earlier, Gaga is shown assuaging/augmenting his frustrations by reading an issue of *Playboy* – a magazine that J.R. also knows the price of.

V

The second of the film's pre-credit scenes represents a fight between J.R., Joey, Gaga and two other guys and a pair of Puerto Ricans.[20] On one hand, this introduces the cross-cultural element developed by J.R.'s relationship with the girl. On the other, the scene's sequential, if elliptical, connection to the opening, compressed figuration of cultural determination suggests a summary exposition of the pattern of alienation and aggression that informs the narrative. Further, as the opening scene evokes a specifically sexual repression, that which follows implies the displaced return of sexual energy: the opening scene cuts to a close-up of a phallic wooden bar held upright behind Joey's back. The Catholic Church is again involved: the most prominent Puerto Rican crosses himself and kisses his crucifix before the fight begins.[21]

Phallic displacement is subsequently foregrounded when Gaga is threatened by the pistol at the party – earlier in the scene the gun is dropped, in a superimposed close-up, into J.R.'s lap. A similar association of frustrated sexuality and mock-threatening aggression is afforded by the later party sequence in which J.R., unable to wait his turn with the 'broads' whom Gaga has procured, leads a storming of the bedrooms. Notably, the first party immediately follows, in narrative order, J.R.'s sexual denial in the bedroom, while the second is presented after he and the girl break up.

The aggression and, in the later sequence, misogyny that barely underlies both instances of mock violence is revealed when Joey, on discovering that one of the 'broads' has scratched his neck, responds with unwarranted nastiness. This, moreover, not only reflects Joey's similarly over-reactive assault on Gaga at the Pleasure Club, but combines with the character's irascible assertiveness accumulatively to imply an overcompensatory denial of feared masculine lack.

Such intimations implicitly critique the repressions and deformations that accrue from the male characters' cultural conditioning. In turn, their patriarchal (over-)determination, and attendant placing of women as either idealized or reviled 'others', is lent an ironic obverse by the film's suggestion of a tacit homoeroticism. J.R. tends to be more at ease with his male friends than with the girl, with whom he is frequently awkward. More specific homoerotic connotations are supplied by the film's two parties. The representation of the first of these ends with the gun-toting guest shooting a bottle. Michael Bliss declares this 'an obvious substitute' for the 'ejaculation (the shot) that J.R. fails to achieve with his girlfriend' (1985: 39). 'Ejaculation' occurs, moreover, within an all-male context replicated by the second party, into which the two 'broads' are inserted. The proposed shared, if sequential, sex, with its semantic intimations of 'having sex together', implies a displacement of inadmissible homosexual desire. Further, the storming of the bedrooms not only disrupt heterosexual communion, but, as J.R. and Joey laughingly embrace, and the women angrily leave, rapturously reasserts the group's male exclusivity.

J.R.'s relationship with his male friends endures while that with the girl does not. J.R.'s misogyny makes the film's critique of the madonna–whore dichotomy explicit. When the girl recounts her memory of the rape, J.R. reacts with an ugly nastiness that, in its sexual violence and disregard for the girl's feelings, aligns him with the rapist. J.R.'s malevolence is centred on an attack on the girl's probity: 'How do I know you didn't go through the same story with him?'. If this in addition implies a virtually pathological investment in virginity, J.R.'s changed perception of the girl is underlined by his attitude paralleling that of Gaga toward the 'broad' at the Pleasure Club. In a well-worn misogynistic move, both interpret events so as to place the women as culpable for their own violation. When the 'broad' finds that she has lost her money, a flashback within the flashback reveals Gaga stealing the money from her purse as they neck: a shot that, in its Freudian suggestiveness, links the woman's economic and sexual exploitation.[22] Gaga, however, blames the theft on the woman's failure to put her pocket-book 'safely' behind the bar. J.R. blames the rape on the girl allowing her date to take her 'out on some goddamn road'. The girl's account of the rape implicates Little

Italy's sexual mores. She notes that the rapist's car radio was loud; a recollection that flags the scene in which Joey, J.R. and Gaga drive uptown.

J.R.'s inability to overcome his misogynistic acculturation is confirmed by his last scene with the girl. His turning up at her apartment at 6.30 in the morning implies a desire for reconciliation. Indeed, after precipitately trying to kiss the girl and hurting her, J.R. apologizes for his behaviour regarding the rape. However, his physical clumsiness is merely a prelude to his more hurtful emotional obtuseness. He says smugly: 'I forgive you ... and I'm going to marry you anyway.' The girl unsurprisingly demurs, at which J.R. exasperatedly moves from calling the girl a 'broad' to asking jeeringly: 'Who do you think you are, the Virgin Mary or something?'. J.R.'s ready anger can be seen to lay bare the hostility that underpins his 'forgiveness'. Lesley Stern observes, 'the only way J.R. can assimilate the idea that "his" woman has been sexually possessed (in fact raped) by another man is to convert the sense of jealousy and sexual anxiety into "forgiveness" ... for him to forgive is to punish, and to save is to take revenge' (1995: 45). J.R. concludes his tirade by twice calling the girl a 'whore'.

There ensues a forceful montage sequence. The first cuts between shots of J.R. entering and inside a confessional and shots of the character moving toward and kissing the girl in his mother's bedroom; a conjunction that implies that J.R. is seeking absolution for the relationship. There follows a multiplicity of images that include shots of the rape, from the nude scene, of religious statues, of J.R. kissing the crucifix, of his mother and of the girl. Anchored as J.R.'s perception by shots of the character standing in the church, the images both summarize the pressures impinging upon J.R. and, in their increasingly rapid, harsh combination, his unresolved confusion. His confession has seemingly not brought any relief.

Among the statues shown there are, unsurprisingly, representations of the Virgin. One shown recurrently comprises part of a *pietà*, itself one of a number of repeatedly shown statues of Christ crucified. This suggests a (possibly sacrilegious) link with the similarly 'crucified' J.R. There is also an emphasis on stigmata. Not only are the statues' painted wounds clearly apparent, but we are given close-ups of the *pietà* Christ's hand, side and foot. In terms of Freudian dream symbolism, this betokens castration, a reading similarly offered by two close-ups of other statues. One shows a gash on a thigh that, in its vaginal shape, figures the bleeding wound. The other shows a plate bearing a pair of disembodied eyes.[23]

VI

On walking into the confessional J.R. enters a space whose (religiously determined) restriction is affirmed by the dark, close shots of its interior. By contrast, the shots of J.R. and the girl atop the roof of a Little Italy tenement transmit a sense of physical and metaphoric freedom. J.R. and the girl first meet and talk while waiting for and travelling on the Staten Island ferry. That is, in relatively open spaces outside their respective environments. From the first, however, their encounter suggests the cultural differences that will undo their relationship. Respectively dark and blonde-haired, J.R. and the girl's contrasting Italian-American and WASP provenance is underlined by indicators of their unlike ethnic, class and educational status. J.R., speaking with colloquial looseness, evinces a somewhat blinkered outlook. Surprised that a photograph of John Wayne should be in a French magazine, he refers to dubbed 'Italian movies', and compares the Italian magazine *Oggi* to *Life*. The girl evinces a more educated, sophisticated sensibility. Enunciating precisely, she seems to read *Paris Match* easily, despite her disclaimer that she knows 'just a few' French words. She also notes: 'I'm not used to admitting I like westerns.'

The characters' talk about *The Searchers* (John Ford, 1956), around which their meeting revolves, centres upon incidents that foreground racial and cultural difference. J.R. describes the scene in which Ethan Edwards (Wayne) comes face to face with his Comanche adversary and *alter ego*, Chief Scar (Henry Brandon). The girl remembers the film through Martin Pawley (Jeffrey Hunter)'s inadvertent acquiring of a Native American wife, Look (Beulah Archuletta); a relationship that – in its cross-cultural incompatibility and unfortunate end (Look is killed by cavalry, by white men, after fleeing Martin and Ethan) – tangentially foreshadows that which occurs between J.R. and the girl.

Cross-cultural connotations culminate in the scene at the girl's apartment. In contrast to the cramped and dingy Little Italy interiors, the girl's room is spacious and bright, and instead of religious icons or nude pin-ups, prints of paintings adorn the walls. J.R. walks around the room while the girl makes coffee. He notes that the girl does not have a television: the scene comes after the second party, during which the guys watch a Charlie Chan film on television while waiting their turn with the 'broads'. The girl suggests that J.R. put on a record. Getting no joy when he asks whether the girl has any records by Guiseppe De Stefano, an Italian opera singer, J.R. inspects a row of discs and we see albums by Stan Getz and Astrud Gilberto, Frank Sinatra and Dinah Washington as they fall to the ground. On clumsily replacing the records J.R. asks, inconsequentially: 'How about Percy Sledge?'. As J.R.'s liking for Italian opera and sixties soul continues to suggest his ethnic and blue-collar roots, so the girl's jazz records, lack of a television and art prints sustain the sense of her bourgeois taste and upbringing. J.R.'s manhandling of the records is amusing, but equally implies that they are somehow alien; a connotation repeated when he fumbles with a copy of F. Scott Fitzgerald's *Tender Is the Night*.

Whereas J.R. and the girl first meet in the 'neutral' environs of the Staten Island ferry, their relationship becomes strained and breaks in locations redolent of their acculturation. Both J.R.'s denial of the girl in the bedroom and his rejection of her account of the rape in his family's kitchen are tacitly referred to the environments in which the scenes occur. The same holds for the girl's refusal of J.R. in her apartment.

The girl's last words to J.R. – her repeated request that he 'Go home' – once more suggest *The Searchers*. They recall another scene mentioned during the characters' first meeting, that in which Ethan's niece Debbie (Natalie Wood), who, having been captured by Scar, has been the object of Ethan and Martin's five-year search, requests, on being found, that Ethan and Martin return home and leave her with her 'people'. Ethan, however, seeks Debbie not to save her but to kill her for her miscegenation with Scar that, in Ethan's eyes, renders her 'impure'. If this suggests a parallel with J.R.'s response to the girl's rape, his investment in westerns, and more especially the masculinity embodied in the star images of Wayne and Lee Marvin, whose role as the thuggish Liberty Valance in *The Man Who Shot Liberty Valance* (Ford, 1962) he delightedly recounts, imply another factor in – and comment on – his determination.[24]

VII

Not only does J.R.'s cross-cultural situation reflect that of Murray, but his inability to reconcile or choose between attendant, divergent impulses and values is likewise implied to inform his apparent alienation. During the early scenes at the Pleasure Club, J.R. is shown sitting apart from Joey and Gaga and isolated, with rapt expression, in close-up. The intercut shots first of the girl and then of her and J.R.'s meeting suggest the cause of this apartness. Following the drunk scene, Joey helps an inebriated J.R. into his tenement's hallway. Inside, J.R. slides to a sitting position on the floor. The circumscription of the hallway is intensified both by J.R. being shot from a high angle and by his bringing his knees, in an index of repression, up to his chin. J.R. moves his right hand across his body, upon which there is a match cut to the same hand reaching out to touch the girl's hair on the roof. The girl turns, and she and J.R. kiss. As the cut bridges present and past, time and space, so it similarly implies J.R.'s desire for spatial, mental and sexual release. Indeed, the girl – who is represented as 'pure', although not a virgin – can be seen to embody a rebuttal of the madonna–whore dichotomy.

As with Murray, J.R.'s cross-cultural position carries biographical intimations. The character's relationship with the girl has been referred to Scorsese's marriage to fellow NYU graduate Laraine Brennan, 'a liaison that was disintegrating the whole time the director reworked his film' (Keyser 1992: 25). The girl's greater worldliness likewise evokes the broader outlook that Scorsese discovered at NYU: 'I became aware of other people in the world and other life-styles, other views, political or otherwise' (DeCurtis 1993: 206).

In turn, J.R.'s passion for westerns extends the cinematic obsession figured in Scorsese's short films, in particular as it partakes of a certain monomania: 'Everybody should like westerns. Solve everybody's problems if they liked westerns.' Moreover, if cinematic obsession in both *What's a Nice Girl Like You Doing in a Place Like This?* and *It's Not Just You, Murray!* is implicated in their protagonists' alienation, so J.R.'s cinematically founded relationship with the girl informs his cross-cultural dilemma.

Nevertheless, in representing this, *Who's That Knocking at My Door?* would seem to invert the ideological perspective of *It's Not Just You, Murray!*. While in the latter, mainstream WASP society is associated with exploitative materialism and that of Italian-Americans with a rooted morality, in *Who's That Knocking at My Door?* the girl's educated sophistication compares favourably with J.R.'s alienating repression. Symptomatic is the film's representation of mother-figures. Murray's mother embodies a selfless devotion, J.R.'s mother is implicated in her son's repressive determination; albeit in the former's constant, spaghetti-laden attendance there is hinted the cultural and psycho-sexual repression that is foregrounded in Scorsese's first feature.

Ideological inversion would appear to extend to the texts' sexual politics. Both Murray's wife and the girl are blonde and Caucasian, and both are represented as moving – for the protagonists – from purity to corruption. But whereas in *It's Not Just You, Murray!* the representation of Murray's wife ratifies the madonna–whore dichotomy, in *Who's That Knocking at My Door?* J.R.'s treatment of the girl invites its condemnation.

However, if *Who's That Knocking at My Door?* explicitly critiques J.R.'s culturally conditioned misogyny, it is a critique that is implicitly compromised. Although the girl's admitted self-doubt upon the rape is understandable and affecting – 'I felt dirty. I felt I wasn't as good as anyone else. I felt ashamed' – that she has lost her virginity against her will as opposed to consensually in, say, a previous relationship, tacitly upholds J.R.'s stance on female sexuality; as does her assertion that should she and J.R. have sex 'it'd be the first time'.

In addition, not only does the girl, like the female characters in *What's a Nice Girl Like You Doing in a Place Like This?* and *It's Not Just You, Murray!*, remain unnamed, but the outflanking of heterosexual relationship by male friendship is, in *Who's That Knocking at My Door?*, compounded dramatically. Compared to J.R., or even Joey or Gaga, the girl remains a sketchy figure. Further, whereas the scenes between J.R. and the girl incline toward the dramatically stilted, those of J.R. and his friends – while representing limited actions and attitudes – tend, in their energy and apparent unpremeditation, to project a sense of lived, if at times tedious, actuality.

As *Who's That Knocking at My Door?* implicitly upholds what it explicitly critiques, so it suggests a residual investment in Little Italy mores. Read intertextually, it is as though the film holds the obverse ideological perspective of *It's Not Just You, Murray!* in an unresolved tension. Read biographically, it is as though Scorsese is, like J.R., ultimately unable to break from his cultural conditioning. It is maybe unsurprising, therefore, that Scorsese should return to Little Italy, his past and many of the concerns of *Who's That Knocking at My Door?* in *Mean Streets*.

4
Exploitation Cinema and the Youth Market: *Boxcar Bertha*

I

Although *Who's That Knocking at My Door?* received some good reviews at the Golden Siren at the 1970 Sorrento Film Festival, it was not a commercial success. Given the film's limited distribution and its textual infelicities, this is maybe unsurprising. The film's failure has in addition been attributed to it being historically 'out of step'. As much discussed, the sixties saw the dominant American ideology shaken by manifold social and political challenge: civil rights mobilization, assassinations, radical black dissent, the rise of the counter-culture, the New Left, and feminism, anti-Vietnam War protest and so on. Nowhere was pressure more registered than in a liberation of sexual mores; with respect to which, Mary Pat Kelly has posited that *Who's That Knocking at My Door?*, 'a movie that rested on a girl's virginity', was perceived to be 'old-fashioned and puzzling' (1992: 48). The film can nevertheless be read as no less impressed by the decade's ideological shifts than more overt reflectors of cultural change. In terms of representation, *Who's That Knocking at My Door?* veers from the comparative sexual explicitness of, say, the bedroom and rape scenes to the openness of the nude scene. Moreover, the film questions J.R.'s *refusal* to have sex with the girl and, through this, the reactionary social and religious order that determines his refusal.

In 1968, after completing *Who's That Knocking at My Door?*, and making a short for the United States Information Agency that was thought 'so odd that they destroyed it unseen' (Scorsese 1981: 134), Scorsese was hired to direct a low-budget ($150 000) feature, *The Honeymoon Killers*. Scorsese completed pre-production but was unsurprisingly fired after a week's shooting because he 'felt that a director who really knows what he's doing does it in one take' (*ibid.*: 135).[1]

In 1969 Scorsese accepted a teaching post at NYU, where he took classes in film technique and production and in film criticism. For the latter, Scorsese, in a move that reflects auteurist-inflected shifts in film culture, replaced examples of European art cinema with Hollywood films.[2] In 1970 he programmed the Lincoln Center's 'Movies in the Park' screenings in Central Park; an attempt by New York City 'to diffuse the anger in the streets', to preclude 'the riots that had gone on in other cities during past long, hot summers' (Kelly 1992: 58).

An obverse and more direct engagement with the counter-culture and radical protest is reflected in two other projects on which Scorsese worked at this time. In August 1969 Scorsese travelled to upstate New York with Michael Wadleigh and Thelma Schoonmaker to film the three-day Woodstock rock festival. On the ensuing, 184-minute documentary, *Woodstock* (1970), Wadleigh was credited as director, Schoonmaker and Scorsese each as editor and assistant director. During the student strike of May 1970 Scorsese and a number of NYU students joined with a group of independent filmmakers to form the New York Cinetracts Collective.[3] The result was a 75-minute documentary, *Street Scenes 1970* (1970), that centres upon footage of anti-war demonstrations in New York and Washington, DC. Although Scorsese directed only one scene, he was responsible for the film's editing. This was not least because, with $16 000 worth of NYU equipment and film stock having been lost, used or destroyed, college authorities told Scorsese that he could keep his job only if he delivered a film from the raw footage. Even so, Scorsese's investment in 'outside' projects soon led to his dismissal.

In January 1971 Warner Bros flew Scorsese out to Hollywood to re-edit and redeem *Medicine Ball Caravan* (François Reichenbach, 1971), a documentary of a 1970 tour by rock and other artistes. What Scorsese thought was going to be a two-week job took nine months.[4] *Medicine Ball Caravan* was also not a success.

However, during his first week in Hollywood Scorsese had been contacted by producer and director Roger Corman. Having seen *Who's That Knocking at My Door?*, albeit under yet another title, *J.R.*,[5] Corman offered Scorsese the chance to direct a follow-up to *Bloody Mama* (Corman, 1970) – *Boxcar Bertha*. Corman promised a script in six months, that – following Corman's marriage – became nine. By the time Corman called, Scorsese was being supported by John Cassavetes, 'who had become a friend' (Scorsese 1981: 135).

II

In making a film produced by Corman and distributed by American International Pictures (AIP), Scorsese collided with the category of American independent filmmaking known as exploitation cinema. While Aaron Lipstadt aptly notes that *'any* film must have an "exploitable" element' (1981: 10), exploitation remains, in Pam Cook's words, 'a derogatory term, implying a process of "ripping off"' (1985: 367). Within exploitation cinema, 'ripping off' has a multiple reference. It suggests 'an economic imperative – very low budgets, tight production schedules, low-paid, inexperienced, non-union personnel, minimal production values, "sensational" selling campaigns and widespread saturation bookings aimed at specific markets ... all in the interests of making a fast buck' (*ibid.*). This economic 'exploitation' is complemented textually. Frequently lacking that which gives 'big-budget films their coherence (stars, psychological realism, narrative development, expensive production values)' (*ibid.*), exploitation films instead privilege their exploitable elements: an ever-evolving combination of the lurid and the *risqué*, of action, sex, and/or comedy. 'Ripping off' extends to the provenance of the films' narratives. On one hand, there is the exploitation of events or social trends that have captured the public's imagination – or rather that of a targetable audience. On the other, there is the cashing in on mainstream successes via cheaper derivations. Exploitation filmmakers also try to profit from their own successes: exploitation film production typically comprises series of cycles 'which disappear as soon as their audience appeal is exhausted' (*ibid.*: 368).

Exploitation cinema dates from the fifties and resulted from the institutional and social changes that were decimating the majors. The reverberations of the 1948 consent decrees outlawing vertical integration afforded potentially profitable openings for independent producers and distributors. For some it was an opportunity seized by identifying a growing market then ignored by the majors: teenagers and young adults empowered by disposable income and car-ownership – hence the symbiotic relationship of exploitation cinema and drive-ins. It was, moreover, a market 'created' by the very suburbanization that has been cited as a prime factor in the decline of the mainstream Hollywood audience.[6]

Of the companies that sought to exploit the youth market, AIP was the most successful and most influential. The company was founded in 1954 by James H. Nicholson and Samuel Z. Arkoff as American Releasing Corporation (ARC), changing its name in 1956 when it began to make as well as distribute films. The first film to be distributed by ARC, *The Fast and the Furious* (Edwards Sampson and John Ireland, 1954), was produced by Corman, instigating a collaboration that has contributed massively to what we understand to be exploitation cinema. Neither AIP nor Corman shied from catering for 'younger, brighter audiences who might like the sensational, the gruesome, and the suggestive' (Pye and Myles 1979: 35). With regard to production, speed and economy have become bywords for Corman's filmmaking. Most of the films that Corman made in the fifties 'were shot in ten days or less on a budget below $100,000' (Naha 1982: 15). Corman filmed *A Bucket of Blood* (1959) for AIP in five days and *The Little Shop of Horrors* (1960) for his own distribution company, Filmgroup, in two days and a half and at a cost of only $35 000. Tales of other Corman economies abound, and extend from actors having to double-up on roles, through shooting films in tandem on location, to thinking up *The Terror* (Corman, 1963) in order to capitalize on standing sets and two days remaining on Boris Karloff's contract for *The Raven* (Corman, 1963).[7]

For all this, across Corman's films critics have discerned a resonance and discursive consistency that has led to his being proclaimed an *auteur*.[8] Granted, this in part served initially to scandalize orthodox criticism. Nevertheless, a recurrent, admitted preoccupation of films directed by Corman is a concern with 'outsiders, misfits, or antiheroes' (Corman with Jerome 1990: 24). Whether taking the form of, say, overreaching individuals (for example, The Boy/Robert Vaughn in *Teenage Caveman*, 1958, or James Xavier/Ray Milland in *X – The Man with the X-Ray Eyes*, 1963) or groups marginal to mainstream society (like the Hell's Angels in *The Wild Angels*, 1966, or the young survivors in *Gas-s-s-s*, 1970), these outsider figures are repeatedly represented as challenging or being in transgression of the dominant order. This transgression frequently has a gendered aspect, with assertive female characters refusing their subordinate patriarchal positioning (for example, Marie/Peggie Castle in *The Oklahoma Woman*, 1955, Flo/Susan Cabot in *Machine Gun Kelly*, 1958, or the often vengeful female partners of the Edgar Allan Poe adaptations).[9]

Complementing these structures is an often foregrounded psychoanalytic reference. In the Poe films, Poe-inflected preoccupations with incest, necrophilia and the death instinct are played out within decaying mansions that stand as metaphors of the protagonists' tortured psyches. Xavier's scientific-cum-religious overreaching, his desire 'to see what no man has ever seen', can likewise be read as an Oedipal transgression, a refusal of symbolic castration, while Paul (Peter Fonda)'s LSD experience in *The Trip* (1967) is represented as a simulation of the psychoanalytic encounter. In *Bloody Mama* the criminality of the film's outlaw group embraces robbery, murder and extortion. This, however, is textually subordinated before the group's psycho-sexual transgressiveness, its denial of the patriarchal Law. Not only is the group ruled by *Ma* Barker (Shelley Winters), but it is a site for the engagement in that which the Law represses and declares taboo: mother–son incest, sado-masochism, homosexuality.

Similar concerns are apparent in films that Corman has produced.[10] As much is demonstrated by some early cycles invested in by New World Pictures, the successful production and distribution company co-founded by Corman in 1970: witness the putative feminism of the company's nurse and women-in-prison films or the counter-culture sympathies of its biker films.[11] Consistency is maybe unsurprising given the control that Corman as producer asserts over pre- and post-production. Not only does Corman have the final say on a film's budget, shooting schedule, cast, crew and locations, but he takes a 'hands-on' interest in script development: 'I will generally have a first or second draft screenplay written before I bring the director in to ensure that the basic structure of the script is what I'm looking for.'[12] He likewise oversees the film's advertising and distribution and its final cut.

However, in ascribing Corman's authorial discourse we must tread carefully, for within exploitation cinema the creative is at every step imbricated with the commercial. For example, Corman's films' proclivity for busy shot composition, comparatively rapid cutting and camera movement implies an economic as much as a stylistic imperative, an approach that seeks to obviate limited production values. Similarly, New World's production of the nurse cycle was more a market than an ideological decision: 'The first two pictures we had were a motorcycle picture and a nurse picture ... . Both films were successful, but the nurse film was more successful than the motorcycle film. It was a very simple decision at that point to make another nurse film' (Morris 1975: 22–3).

Perhaps ultimately a defining element of Corman's work as director and producer is a dichotomy between the profitable and the progressive, the pragmatic and the idealistic. Such certainly informs his legendary employment of new talent. For over 30 years Corman, as producer, has granted early opportunities to many major figures in American filmmaking. Most notably, he has given breaks to directors ranging from Francis Ford Coppola, Monte Hellman and Peter Bogdanovich to Scorsese and, subsequently, the likes of Jonathan Demme and Ron Howard.[13] On one hand, this suggests philanthropy on Corman's part: 'I know that it is still extraordinarily difficult to get the first assignment as a director' (1974: 23). Further, for all his involvement in pre- and post-production,

Corman prefers 'to retire to a suitably executive distance during the actual shooting so that the young director relies on his own authority and judgement on the set' (*ibid.*: 24). On the other hand, the situation lends Corman clear benefits. Apart from young directors being potentially in tune with the youth audience, they provide Corman with a pool of cheap, eager non-union labour that, given its chance, will possibly work harder than more experienced, but less desperate, filmmakers who would cost more money. If this affords yet another meaning to the term exploitation cinema, in this case 'the "exploitation" is mutual' (Cook 1985: 368).

Accordingly, Scorsese has stated that he 'would have *paid Roger*' to direct *Boxcar Bertha* (Corman with Jerome 1990: 185). However, as exploitation cinema foregrounds cinema's economic resolution, so its obsessive market orientation highlights some of the difficulties in attributing individual authorship within commercial film.

III

Boxcar Bertha begins with a biplane crash that kills Bertha (Barbara Hershey)'s crop-dusting father. Travelling through the Depression South, Bertha takes up first with union radical Bill Shelley (David Carradine) and then with Yankee card-sharper Rake Brown (Barry Primus). Both men are imprisoned, and Bertha frees them from a chain-gang, along with her father's black mechanic, Von Morton (Bernie Casey). With Bertha and Bill resuming their relationship, the quartet engage in a criminal campaign against the Reader Railroad. This comes to grief with a failed attempt to kidnap the railroad's owner, H. Buckram Sartoris (John Carradine). Rake is killed, Bill and Von are again imprisoned and Bertha drifts into prostitution. Time passes, and Bertha once more finds Bill, only for their reunion to be interrupted by the railroad's paid thugs. These crucify Bill by nailing him to a boxcar, but are shot dead by Von, who is nevertheless unable to prevent the train taking Bill's body away from a distraught Bertha.

Boxcar Bertha derives from Bertha Thompson's 1937 autobiography, *Sister of the Road*. A first script was written by Joyce H. and John William Corrington. This was rewritten – freely but uncredited – by Scorsese. Neither was Scorsese credited with the film's editing that, unusually for Corman, the director also undertook.[14] The film was shot on a tight schedule and budget of 24 days and $650 000. During this, Scorsese was characteristically granted comparative autonomy. Moreover, Corman defended Scorsese; on viewing rushes, Arkoff and others at AIP called for his dismissal.

In part, Arkoff and AIP were troubled by Scorsese's use of *nouvelle vague* devices.[15] However, in *Boxcar Bertha* these are subordinated before the text's realist address. Largely leached of the expressionist pertinence that such devices obtain in *Who's That Knocking at My Door?*, they are mainly used to enhance local dramatic impact. Hence the jump-cuts that follow the pre-credit scene's 'plane crash, the freeze-frame that ends the first sex scene between Bertha and Bill or the 'virtuoso' backward zoom and jump-cuts as Bill storms down an enclosed, sun-flared corridor. In the main, the film stylistically conforms to Corman's preferred low-budget approach. Note, for instance, the post-jailbreak scene in a disused factory, and its combination of composition in depth, frequent camera movement, varied set-ups and sharp cutting.

Indeed, Scorsese's liberty to rework the script, direct it and edit the resultant footage was circumscribed throughout by a necessary adherence to exploitation cinema's reciprocal aesthetic and commercial demands. In rewriting the script he was impressed upon by Corman: 'to make sure there's a touch of nudity or a promise of a touch of nudity every fifteen pages. And violence – there had to be a certain amount' (Kelly 1992: 67–8). Similarly pragmatic were Corman's instructions regarding post-production: 'you're mixing the entire film in three days: nine reels, three days. The first reel has to be good because people coming to the drive-in have to hear what's going on. Forget the rest of the film until you get to the last reel, because they just want to know how it turned out' (Thompson and Christie 1996: 34).

Compounding such inhibitions, *Boxcar Bertha* demonstrates a number of specific prescriptions cited by director Jonathan Kaplan in relation to another 1972 Corman production, *Night Call Nurses*: 'Exploitation of male sexual fantasy, a comedic subplot [Rake's incompetence, cowardice and unease in the South], action and violence ... a slightly-to-the-left-of-centre subplot [the film's pro-union, anti-capitalist/anti-racist perspective] ... then frontal nudity from the waist up [Bertha], total nudity from behind [Bertha and Bill], no pubic hair, and get the title in the film somewhere [Sartoris mentions it during the scene in which he questions his chief hit-men, the McIvers/David R. Osterhout and Victor Argo]' (Hillier and Lipstadt 1986: 44).

Originally, the script ended with Bertha ensconced in a black quarter of New Orleans.[16] The extant ending – in its shaky motivation, forced coincidence and jarring transitions – offers a synecdoche of the effects of the film's downgrading of narrative reason before its exploitative elements. The irruption of the railroad's thugs into Bertha's tender reconciliation with an apparently wizened Bill lacks any seeming logic, but no more than Bill's sudden rejuvenation in the ensuing struggle, Von's retributive appearance or the train's inexplicable pulling out with Bill's body. The sequence thus jumps typically through a series of weakly constructed but impactful moments; a structure that further reflects upon the film's specific use of *nouvelle vague* tropes.

A reason why the original ending was dropped was that the shooting of *Boxcar Bertha* was restricted – in a representative Corman economy – to a corner of Arkansas served by a steam railway. This limited location becomes foregrounded as the characters repeatedly cross paths in a manner that, as it strains credibility, exacerbates the film's narrative illogic. For example, upon fleeing the card game during which Bertha shoots a railroad lawyer, Mendez, not only do Bertha and Rake 'coincidentally' take refuge in a shack situated next to a field in which Bill and some strikers are camping just at the moment when, as predicted in the previous scene, the latter are attacked by railroad heavies, but on boarding a boxcar a little later they 'just happen' to choose the one in which Bill and some of the same strikers are travelling.

IV

Although *Boxcar Bertha* is nominally a sequel to *Bloody Mama*, both films are better seen as 'exploitations' of the success of *Bonnie and Clyde* (Arthur Penn, 1967). Common elements range from broad similarities like their rural Depression settings and concern with the flagrant and violent criminality of a small band of outlaws to more specific details that in *Bloody Mama* and *Boxcar Bertha* operate as markers of exploitative intent. For example, all three films contain extended, country-road car chases and feature bluegrass music on their soundtracks, while *Boxcar Bertha* also reworks the scene in *Bonnie and Clyde* in which Buck (Gene Hackman) reads aloud to the rest of the Barrow Gang a newspaper report of their exploits.

Beyond this, *Bloody Mama* and *Boxcar Bertha* can be placed within a cycle of films that, instigated by *Bonnie and Clyde*, crosses mainstream and exploitation cinema. Considered by Robert Phillip Kolker a development of 'the minor country thieves variation of the gangster film' (1974: 237), the cycle also contains *Dillinger* (John Milius, 1973), *Badlands* (Terrence Malick, 1973), *The Sugarland Express* (Steven Spielberg, 1973) and *Thieves Like Us* (Robert Altman, 1974). Historically, the cycle finds precedent in the outlaw-couple films that recur between the thirties and the fifties, a category that includes *You Only Live Once* (Fritz Lang, 1937), *They Live by Night* (Nicholas Ray, 1948), of which *Thieves Like Us* is a remake, *Shockproof* (Douglas Sirk, 1949), *Gun Crazy* (Joseph H. Lewis, 1950) and *Where Danger Lives* (John Farrow, 1950).[17] Crime narratives set, at least in part, in the country instead of the city, the outlaw-couple films also repeatedly represent their protagonists on the road and on the run. Following this, the country thieves cycle specifically comprises a sub-generic hybridization of the gangster film and the road movie, with the rise–fall trajectory of the gangster film protagonist mapped on to the picaresque, episodic narrative progression of the road movie.[18]

As exploitation cinema foregrounds, the economic rationale of cycles is that of 'a short-term attempt to rework a proven success' (Krutnik 1991: 12). However, as 'a historical, sub-generic grouping', cycles can also be read as conduits for the articulation of contemporary concerns, having 'an affirmatory function in that they provide a consolidatory framework and a channel of comprehensibility whereby the new can be both bonded to, and embodied via, the familiar (to the extent of seeming "commonsensical")' (*ibid.*: 12, 13). The country thieves cycle, as it short-circuits and inverts the ideological dynamics of the classical gangster film, implies an intimate relation to the period's cultural conflicts. Rather than the activities of the criminal protagonists increasingly making them unsympathetic and justifying their obliteration by the dominant order, the criminal protagonists of the country thieves cycle remain, in general, if variably, sympathetic before what is frequently represented as the increasingly unjustifiable oppressiveness and brutality of the dominant order. With the cycle hence inverting conventional expectations, and – accordingly – their underpinning ideological postulates, the films can be termed revisionist.

Implicated in this revisionism is a generational conflict, with the films' predominantly young(-ish) and often rootless and unsocialized protagonists placed in opposition to older authority figures and established attitudes. Yet if the films thus address the demographic group most involved in social and cultural challenge during the sixties and seventies, the cycle's mainstream examples, but most patently *Bonnie and Clyde*, can also be read as part of the majors' belated bid to move into the youth market so profitably served by exploitation cinema. By 1970, 'three-quarters of all "frequent moviegoers" (which accounted for about ninety percent of all admissions) were between the ages of twelve and twenty-nine' (Schatz 1983: 190).[19]

The oppositional perspective of the country thieves cycle grounds *Boxcar Bertha*'s 'left-of-centre-subplot'. Comprising a union man, a single, sexual woman, a Jew and a black, the film's outlaw group embodies a confederacy of the marginalized and dispossessed in thirties (and seventies?) USA. The group is also implied to be democratic: before committing their first train robbery they 'vote' to do so by raising their firearms in turn. This contributes to the protagonists' representation as, crucially, much more appealing figures than characters affiliated with the patriarchal capitalist order. In this, the generational aspect of the country thieves cycle comes into play: the central foursome are largely younger and physically more prepossessing than those whom they contest. The latter, moreover, are variously vindictive, vicious and reactionary. Hence the aggressive insensitivity of the landowner who makes Bertha's father fatally fly his damaged biplane, or the cold brutality of the McIvers, who, with their similar hats and frequent blankness, not to mention the larger McIver's Ollie-like moustache, evoke a lumpen Laurel and Hardy. The facially scarred sheriff has Bill beaten because he is 'a nigger lover', Sartoris complains about 'gangs of Communists, whores ... and niggers', while the gross, bald Mendez shifts from complaining about 'Reds' and gloating that Bill is 'gonna get his tomorrow' to eyeing Bertha lasciviously.

Within the film's oppressive patriarchal realm, power is definitively phallic. When early on Bill addresses a group of strikers, his voice is superimposed over a two-shot of baton-wielding policemen. Upon this the batons are brought nearer, in a forceful sound–image correlation, by three jump-cuts to close-ups: 'Railroad took it away from us [cut] we got to get it back.[cut] Organize.[cut] Unionize.' Later, as Deputy Harvey Hall (Harry Northup) misogynistically recounts a sexual encounter, we are shown a close shot of pump-action shotguns leant against a desk. By contrast, Bertha manages to free her companions after Harvey 'castrates' himself by setting his shotgun aside.

Similar emphases proliferate in *Boxcar Bertha*, that, as it thus marries the oppositional and the psycho-sexual, sits comfortably with other films that Corman has produced and/or directed. However, given such emphases' systematic precision, and the relative autonomy granted Scorsese in terms of direction and post-production, they also suggest Scorsese's discursive agency. Like patternings inflect the articulation of incident throughout, at times cutting across and implicitly commenting upon the narrative's forced illogic and attendant – and significant – ideological contradictions.

V

When Bertha joins the group of strikers addressed by Bill, he ups his rhetoric and incites the strikers to attack the McIvers and the police. Plainly Bill does this not in the name of the class struggle but to impress Bertha and to create a diversion that enables him and Bertha to flee. If this use of the political for personal ends rather compromises Bill's probity, he proceeds, upon offering Bertha 'dessert' at a communal kitchen, to walk her to a boxcar where he forces her to have sex.

Formally, Bill's shift from the political and oppositional to the personal and oppressive implicates the narrative's 'exploitation' emphasis, its predication upon the periodic representation of violence and sex. This also here carries critical implication. Ideologically, Bill, in engaging in unequal and gendered exploitation, embodies what the text seemingly condemns. Dramatically, the scene would appear to dissimulate this both by 'amusingly' playing Bill's knowing self-assurance off Bertha's hesitant innocence and by representing Bertha – whose fearful uncertainty connotes virginity – as rapidly, and joyously, accepting Bill's imposition. While the aim is to keep Bill sympathetic, read against the grain Bill's attitude is insidiously patronizing and Bertha's enjoyment suggests a validation of misogynistic maxims regarding 'women who say no' – in particular as the incident can be considered rape.

Such textually specific contradictions compound those that more broadly inform the sexual politics of exploitation cinema, or at least of that associated with Corman. Bertha's representation relates to the mooted 'feminist' emphasis on strong female figures that, whatever their commercial imperative, are apparent across Corman's films. Writing of the 'positive-heroine' figures in Corman's contemporaneous New World productions, Cook notes: 'The woman takes on male characteristics, uses male language, male weapons' (1976: 126). The mildly cursing Bertha is represented as physically active, resourceful and willing to handle firearms. Accepting that Bertha shoots Mendez accidentally, this willingness recurs during the scenes of the protagonists' criminality, being a coextensive legal and psycho-sexual transgression that is foregrounded when she releases Bill, Von and Rake. Bertha teasingly tells Harvey Hall to close his eyes and open his mouth, upon which she cocks – in a symbolic sexual reversal – a loaded pistol in his mouth.

However, Bertha's action only ensures her relationship with, and dependence on, Bill, towards whom she displays a fierce loyalty throughout. This reflects her earlier movement from autonomy to dependence when, having enabled Rake to survive in the South by teaching him unprompted how to speak 'Southern', she is next seen as his intimate companion. The representation of Bertha's gendered subordination even within the film's 'democratic' criminal group is complemented by her repeated sexual objectification and fragmentation.[20] Note, for example, the eroticizing close shots of her naked body in the film's two sex scenes, or the titillating way that the straps of her dress keep slipping from her shoulders during the raid on Sartoris's party. Overwhelming the two 'compensatory' sights of Bill's bare backside, Bertha's functioning as an 'erotic object' (Mulvey 1975: 11) fulfils the film's commercial need to exploit 'male sexual fantasy', encouraging in the spectator the same lascivious regard that is both condemned when embodied diegetically by Mendez and, furthering contradiction, represented as unproblematic when Bill gazes at Bertha scratching her naked thigh during the pre-credit scene – a sight that the spectator also shares.[21]

Similar contradictions infect Bertha's phallic appropriation. Operating narratively and thematically as a mark of transgression, her rendering as phallic can nevertheless be read as enabling a fetishistic disavowal of sexual difference, of the threat of castration that woman embodies. To cite Sigmund Freud, 'the fetish ... remains a token of triumph over the threat of castration and a protection against it' (1927: 363). With Bertha thus represented, symbolically, as 'male', and, further, as achieving her ends through the use of male means and methods, that are – by default – suggested to have an exclusive efficacy, not only is the text made unmenacing for the male spectator, and hence 'safe' for patriarchy, but the putative sexual progressiveness and/or transgressiveness of *Boxcar Bertha* is seriously weakened. The same potentially applies to Corman's films in general.[22]

No less problematic is Bertha's literal movement in the course of the film from virgin to whore. Once more this is attended by narrative contradiction. After the protagonists' first train robbery, Bertha's assertion that a newspaper claim that she is 'a common whore and woman of the streets' is 'a lie' is spoken with dismay, as though the very suggestion is shaming. Later, after Rake's death and Bill and Von's arrest, a man asks Bertha, as she walks alone, 'you sportin' Baby?'. Bertha retorts immediately, if with weary despondency: 'Do I look like I'm sportin'?'. Bertha is accosted by Mrs Mailer (Marianne Dole), whose offer of a place to 'clean up, get some rest' is revealed to be a euphemism for prostitution. Yet while a pair of zip-pans when Bertha enters the brothel transmits her shock, her almost instant acceptance of her lot rather jars against her preceding sad demurrals. Further, although the words of another of the whores, Tillie (Ann Morell), links prostitution with capitalist expropriation – 'We'd never have a day off if they had their way. … They'd just keep on working us to death' – and although we are given some close-ups of a wistful Bertha, Mrs Mailer's house is also represented as a site of comedy (the antics in the parlour), class contestation (Bertha's teasing 'seduction' of the anthropologist) and even tenderness (toward Bertha by some of her clients). Indeed, Bertha's wistfulness is implied to be less related to her situation than to her missing Bill.

Moreover, Bertha is implicitly placed as a whore long before she meets Mrs Mailer. Having had sex with Bill in the boxcar, Bertha wakes the next morning to find that he has left her some money in her shoe.[23] The implication that Bill has 'prostituted' Bertha is underscored by his having left Bertha to sleep alone after the act. Even so, as in the previous scene the negative connotations of Bill's actions are dramatically dissimulated: Bertha, on finding the money, laughs happily, and sexual exploitation becomes a humanistic gesture.

After her deflowerment, Bertha has guiltless, sexual extra-marital relationships (implicitly) with Rake and (explicitly) with Bill. On one hand, this suggests the film's historical context and the protagonists' counter-cultural associations. On the other, it implicates Scorsese's authorial discourse; specifically, its problematic investment in the madonna–whore dichotomy that ultimately informs both *It's Not Just You, Murray!* and *Who's That Knocking at My Door?*. Considered thus, it would appear that Bertha must, to evoke the latter, become a 'broad' rather than a 'girl' before the film will 'allow' her to act sexually. We might also ponder the connotations of Scorsese's diegetic role as one of Bertha's sympathetic clients who, in contrast to Bill, offers her $15 just to stay the night. Is this an attempt to disavow his earlier rendering of her, as director, as a whore?[24]

VI

In 'drawing' Bill from the political to the sexual, Bertha's 'progressiveness' is further problematized by her contention of Bill's socialist conscience. When Bill walks Bertha from communal kitchen to boxcar, she responds to his sympathetic but downbeat account of the strikers' plight by perkily declaring, 'I want something I ain't never had', that – with selfish opportunism – she says that she aims to get by 'grabbing something good when it comes by'. That Bill in effect does this in his sexual use of Bertha is ideologically consonant with the rest of the incident. Bill's ideological commitment is similarly deflected during the second sex scene. Bill and Bertha's love-making is interrupted by Bill's unease that he 'ain't done an honest day's work in months'. Discussion proceeds to Bill telling Bertha that she can leave if she wishes. Bertha exclaims, 'I ain't leaving', and they fall again to sexual activity, Bill's qualms apparently overcome.

In turn, as Bertha frees Bill and the others from the chain-gang with the use of a stolen car, that is placed across the tracks to halt the train they rob, she is instrumental in Bill's criminal involvement. This creates a painful dilemma for Bill, who is caught between his political ideals and his position as a union man and his new standing as a criminal; a tension that is signalled by his recurrent disquiet about his changed status. The last of the protagonists to 'vote' to rob the train, he repeatedly complains that he is not meant for his new 'kind of life'.

Bill's alienating predicament is highlighted by the scene in a disused church that immediately follows Bill's repudiation by the union official (Joe Reynolds) to whom he donates his $3000 cut of the train robbery. The scene is marked by a controlled staging. The space shown is divided by an altar-rail. Before the rail sit Rake, Bertha and Von. Comfortable in their criminality, all three had tried to prevent Bill's union donation. Behind the rail stands Bill, backed by a mural of Christ. As with J.R. during the climactic montage in *Who's That Knocking at My Door?*, a parallel between Bill and Christ is suggested. Bill walks around the altar-rail to join his companions. This has evaluative implications: Bill both moves away from the mural and sits instead of stands, 'lowers' himself to his companions' level. Bill despondently notes that the union does not want him, and that the railroad 'goes on starving kids, bustin' heads, making money'. Bertha retorts – with typical apoliticalness – that Bill 'don't need no union' to 'get back' at the railroad. This is supported both by Rake, who repeats that Bill 'don't need no union' to 'go for more' payrolls, and by Von. As Rake speaks, he sets a flame to a glass of spirits that, on him asking, 'What else we gonna do?', Bill, as though in reply, blows out.

In *Boxcar Bertha* fire is implicitly linked with the malignancy of the dominant order, most obviously when the strikers' camp is set aflame. During this, moreover, Rake prevents Bertha from joining Bill, but only after he is shown lighting a (phallic) cigar; a moment reprised when one of the heavies lights a cigar after crucifying Bill. Given such, Rake's setting light to the spirits reflects upon the venality of the group's mooted criminality – a venality that Bill's 'reply' would appear to deny. This is confirmed when the scene cuts to Bill, Bertha and Rake forcing the railroad's payroll-tellers at gunpoint to put an 'extra ten dollars' in workers' pay envelopes. That is, the use of the means of the forces of reaction for progressive ends, a fusion of the criminal and the political that tacitly resolves Bill's dilemma. However, the scene ends with Von, without any 'progressive' mitigation, cleaning out a safe. The sequence continues with Von robbing a train's rich passengers and the group robbing a ticket-office. In short, they are shown engaging in, and profiting from, dispossession analogous to that which is condemned when perpetrated by the ruling patriarchy. This is complemented by the incidents' phallic reference. Von encourages the passengers to hand over their valuables with a pistol, while during the raid on the ticket-office the staff, the security guard and the McIvers are all impotent before the protagonists' firearms: an inversion of power underscored by a close-up of the McIvers divesting themselves of their shotguns.

As the text's 'progessiveness' is subsumed by its exploitative elements, so Bill's use of reactionary means for progressive ends is subsumed by the group's use of criminality for purely personal gain. Similarly, as Bertha seeks to quieten Bill's scruples about the 'honesty' of the protagonists' activities, so the text again seeks to dissimulate their negative implications for the spectator. The progressive connotations of the payroll-office scene tend to carry across the group's subsequent actions, even though at no other point in their criminality, or their discussion of it, does the issue of helping the working class arise. Further, apart from the enjoyment of seeing the forces of oppression bettered, the film invites us to share in the protagonists' delight in their successes: hence their noisy joy when Von joins the others on the train's rear platform after he robs the passengers. This echoes their earlier, childlike abandon when, having robbed the train, they detach and escape in its engine. The train robbery itself is represented as lacking premeditation. When the train stops, its guard asks, 'we get robbed?', almost inviting Von to raise a shotgun to his head and the rest of the group to 'vote' likewise.

Similarly disarming are Rake's 'tough-guy' antics during the ticket-office scene. Hat at an angle, he pushes past the McIvers before, wielding his pistols gunslinger-style, he forces the counter staff to lie on the floor; behaviour that renders the robbery an amusing game. Rake, however, is also shot from a low angle akin to that which lends an oppressive aspect both to the McIvers and the police when Bill addresses the strikers and to the McIvers when they shoot some strikers in a police cell. The ticket-office scene ends with Bertha taunting the McIvers by ordering them repeatedly to 'Sit down' and 'Stand up'. Yet not only is Bertha, too, shot from a low angle, but the scene cuts to Sartoris himself ordering the McIvers to 'Sit down'.

The paralleling of the protagonists with the dominant order continues during the raid on Sartoris's party. Rake and Bertha are driven to
the party by Von, who wears a uniform like that of the landowner's
chauffeur in the pre-credit scene. Rake wears a tuxedo, Bertha an
evening dress. Costume here serves as disguise, but also relates the
characters with those whom they rob. Moreover, Rake's complaint that
he is wearing a tuxedo instead of, like other guests, tails has a peevish-
ness that suggests less a fear of discovery than a desire for social
acceptance, while Bertha's adorning herself with stolen valuables
implies a censurable acquisitiveness. The latter is likewise critiqued by
the second sex scene, during which Bill's assertion to Bertha that
'there're no chains on you honey' is undermined by the sight of her
naked body 'enchained' by jewellery.

The raid on the party also further indicts Bill. He and Sartoris trade
versions of a passage from the gospels,[25] an exchange that Bill cuts
short by declaring, over a close-up of a pistol in his hand: 'This here's
my Bible.' Ideologically, the shot foregrounds Bill's adoption of what
the text places as the means of expropriation; underscoring which
Sartoris comments explicitly on Bill's compromised position: 'I
thought you was some sort of crazy bolshevik. But hell, you're just a
common crook.' Psycho-sexually, the shot implies Bill's assumption of
the phallus, a connotation that the situation lends a precise Oedipal
resonance. For if the generational difference between Sartoris and Bill
figures a father–son relation, it is an implication heightened by John
and David Carradine's actual father–son status.

The shot can be seen symbolically to condense the protagonists'
inability to operate outside the parameters of the dominant, patriarchal
order, to deny – in effect – their cultural conditioning. This suggests a
further link between *Boxcar Bertha* and *Who's That Knocking at My Door?*;
one, moreover, that implies a key authorial concern. With regard to this,
the prime figure of cultural determination in *Who's That Knocking at
My Door?*, the mirror motif, reappears in *Boxcar Bertha*, although in a less
foregrounded, more narratively integrated fashion. The motif is again
introduced before the film's main credits. Bertha looks at her reflection in
the bodywork of the landowner's car, upon which an italicizing, intra-
scene dissolve shows her mirrored image. In part this alludes to another,
very different film about poor Southern whites during the Depression,
Tobacco Road (John Ford, 1941), and the moment when Ellie May (Gene
Tierney) regards her reflection, minus dissolve, in the bodywork of Dude
(William Tracy)'s car. However, with the car in *Boxcar Bertha* a signifier of
the landowner's wealth and class status, the diminished reflection of
Bertha's figure implies her reciprocal, alienated social position.

The protagonists' suggested inability to overcome their determined situation is capped by the ending of *Boxcar Bertha* reflecting those of *It's Not Just You, Murray!* and *Who's That Knocking at My Door?* in implying cyclicity. The scene following the first set of main credits shows Bertha running alongside a train. The film ends with her running alongside the train that carries the crucified Bill. Both the parallels between the scenes and Scorsese's directorial implication are underscored by the incidents' precise formal patterning. As Bertha runs, each scene presents her in facial close shots and in shots taken from directly above her from near-identical overhead set-ups. Once more, the implied cyclicity has a negative inflection. At the beginning, Bertha manages to board the train, that enables her to find Bill. At the end, the train picks up speed and takes Bill from her. In turn, not only does the spike that Bill and his workmates hammer during the pre-credit scene find negative reflection in that which is hammered into Bill's hand, but the close-up of Bertha's hand as she clutches a hasp to hoist herself into a boxcar is translated into a close-up of the hand of the crucified Bill.

VII

Like other country thieves films, *Boxcar Bertha* follows the rise–fall structure of the gangster film. This is underlined by the inverse pairing of the sequence representing the protagonists' successful criminality and the scene of their failed kidnap attempt. In both Von is disguised, with contrasting effect, as a railroad steward, while the close-up of the McIvers divesting themselves of their shotguns is replayed when Rake moves to lay down his pistol. Rake, however, halts mid-motion and raises the pistol, upon which he is blasted from Sartoris's state car by one of the McIvers' shotguns. Rake's dead body lands on the train's rear platform, where Bill, on shouting a warning to Bertha, is beaten senseless. A site previously associated with the protagonists' joyous success thus becomes that of their painful defeat.

Bill's crucifixion completes his association with Christ.[26] It also, in terms of generic structure, constitutes the culmination of the protagonists' fall. As such, the incident typifies a split in the narrative's address that *Boxcar Bertha* once more inherits from the classical gangster film. Logically, Bill's death confirms the restored authority of the dominant order. Emotionally, just as the death of the gangster in classical examples of the genre effects, to quote Thomas Schatz, 'the consummate reaffirmation of his own identity' (1981: 90), so the cruel excess of Bill's killing apotheosizes both the character and the opposition that he embodies; a 'transcendence' that Bill's crucifixion explicitly figures.

Similar connotations attend the endings of other films in the country thieves cycle. Note, for example, the slow-motion end of Bonnie (Faye Dunaway) and Clyde (Warren Beatty) or the combination of massive police firepower and concluding frozen frames of Ma Barker and her dead sons in *Bloody Mama*. While the extreme force represented repeatedly in the overcoming of the protagonists of the country thieves cycle emphasizes the oppressiveness of the dominant order, it no less enhances the implied potency of the threat posed by the protagonists. Nevertheless, the concluding split of the films' logical and emotional address privileges neither, but rather brings them to a position of balance that effectively reconciles the texts' informing ideological oppositions. This is a characteristic common to genre narratives and relates to what – revisionism notwithstanding – has been posited to be genre's fundamental ideological function: that is, the expression and mediation of cultural contradiction.

In unpacking this function, critics have drawn an homology between genre and the model of myth outlined by Claude Lévi-Strauss; an adduction that is much more defensible theoretically than that of the *auteur*-structuralists.[27] However, if the expression of contradiction lends genre narratives a potential progressiveness, genre is – like myth – primarily concerned with cultural maintenance, not ideological challenge, with the containment of challenge as much as its articulation.

Containment, moreover, is what *Boxcar Bertha* finally purveys. For while the film repeatedly hints at the expression of a substantively progressive position, it is a promise that the film, on closer inspection, disappointingly – if not perniciously – fails, refuses or perhaps, given the context of its production, is unable to deliver.

5
New Hollywood Cinema: *Mean Streets*

I

Mean Streets made Scorsese's reputation. As an individual text, the film presents an intensively resonant correlation of style, structure and meaning. As an example of film authorship, it bodies forth the maturation of Scorsese's authorial discourse. The film, however, is no less paradigmatic of New Hollywood Cinema, and needs also to be discussed in relation to that particular phase of filmmaking and the debates that surround it.

Mean Streets returns Scorsese to New York and the narrative territory of *It's Not Just You, Murray!* and *Who's That Knocking at My Door?*. The film revolves around four young men in Little Italy: Charlie (Harvey Keitel), the central character, a collector for the local Mafia; Johnny Boy (Robert De Niro), his irresponsible friend; Michael (Richard Romanus), a small-time hustler and loan shark; and Tony (David Proval), who runs the bar in which many of the film's scenes take place. Charlie strives with increasing difficulty to balance his material desire for a restaurant, his sense of Christian obligation to Johnny and the demands of his affair with Johnny's cousin, Teresa (Amy Robinson). Johnny owes Michael $3000, a volatile situation that, despite Charlie's attempts to defuse matters, explodes when Johnny tauntingly threatens Michael with a gun. Charlie, Johnny, and Teresa try to escape New York by car, but are followed by Michael, who extracts bloody retribution.

Mean Streets began as *Season of the Witch*, a script written in 1966 by Scorsese and Mardik Martin. Rewritten by Scorsese in 1968, it was shelved following the difficulty in finding distribution for *Who's That Knocking at My Door?*.[1] The project was effectively revived by John

Cassavetes, who, on seeing a rough cut of *Boxcar Bertha*, urged Scorsese to move away from exploitation cinema and to make something that Scorsese 'really wanted to do' (Kelly 1992: 68). *Boxcar Bertha* was released successfully, and Roger Corman offered Scorsese the chance to direct one of two further exploitation films – either *I Escaped from Devil's Island*, a rip-off of *Papillon* (Franklin J. Schaffner, 1973), or *The Arena*, a female gladiators movie. Scorsese, however, set again to rewrite *Season of the Witch*.[2] Rewriting centred upon cutting down the script's religious allusions before the inclusion of 'neighborhood' incidents that Scorsese had told Sandra Weintraub, with whom he was living, and that she thought 'were far funnier than anything in it' (Scorsese 1981: 135). The title *Mean Streets* derives from Raymond Chandler,[3] and was suggested by Scorsese's friend, film critic Jay Cocks.

Drafts of *Season of the Witch* had been rejected by the American Film Institute's feature programme and by Joseph Brenner. The reworked script found it no easier to obtain backing. The majors passed, and Scorsese tried to put together a package with actor Jon Voight. Corman also, if somewhat bizarrely, expressed interest. Corman's brother Gene had produced a successful blaxploitation film, *Cool Breeze* (Barry Pollack, 1972), and Corman offered Scorsese $150 000 to shoot *Mean Streets* 'all black' (Thompson and Christie 1996: 39). 'To make money', Scorsese was meanwhile editing both another Corman production, *Unholy Rollers* (Vernon Zimmerman, 1972), and the documentary *Elvis on Tour* (Pierre Adidge and Robert Abel, 1972) 'at the same time' (Scorsese 1975: 10).

In the same week as Corman's offer, Cocks's wife, actress Verna Bloom, put Scorsese in touch with Jonathan Taplin, road manager for, among others, Bob Dylan and The Band, who wished to get into film production. After reading the rewritten script and viewing Scorsese's previous films, Taplin eventually got $175 000 from an acquaintance who had received an inheritance, E. Lee Perry.[4] The deal was underwritten by Corman agreeing to distribute the film. The inclusion of a clip from *The Tomb of Ligeia* (Corman, 1965) is, in part, a thank you. Another $125 000 was obtained through a deferment from the Canadian Film Institute laboratories.

With a budget of only $300 000, Scorsese turned to Corman's experienced associate producer, Paul Rapp, who had been production manager and assistant director on *Boxcar Bertha*. Rapp costed the film and informed Scorsese that he would have to shoot most of it in Los Angeles and depend on exteriors to underpin its 'New York feeling' (Scorsese 1975: 11). After ten days of rehearsals, Scorsese and a combination of film students and much of the crew from *Boxcar Bertha* spent six days shooting around the clock in New York. Footage of the Feast of San Gennaro had been shot earlier, prior to pre-production. Virtually all the film's exteriors were shot in New York. The exceptions were the climactic car crash, shot in downtown Los Angeles, and the scene in which Johnny blows up a mailbox, shot in San Pedro. Almost all the interiors were shot in Los Angeles. The only exception were the hallways: 'because we couldn't find a hallway to double. We shot those literally where the film takes place' (*ibid.*),

Under pressure of time and money, there were occasionally 'twenty-four set-ups a day' – 'thirty-six for the big fight scene in the pool hall' (Thompson and Christie 1996: 41). Individual scenes were in addition shot 'out of sequence', with all the shots lit 'one way' filmed consecutively (Scorsese 1975: 12); an approach that, in its difficulty for the actors, even Corman has declared to be 'perhaps, an *overly* efficient way to work' (Corman with Jerome 1990: 34). Shooting was completed in 27 days.

With *Mean Streets* combining New York exteriors, Los Angeles interiors, scenes shot out of internal sequence, as well as scenes set up by Scorsese but filmed, often simultaneously, by different units, Scorsese has compared the film to 'a jigsaw puzzle' (Scorsese 1975: 11). Although Sid Levin is credited as the film's editor, Scorsese again largely cut the film himself; a process that took five months.[5] Corman was not called upon to distribute *Mean Streets*. After being turned down by Universal and Paramount, the film – that went just over budget, mainly because of the cost of music rights – was bought as a pick-up by Warner Bros for $750 000. *Mean Streets* premiered at the New York Film Festival in November 1973 and enjoyed considerable critical and festival success. It was not, however, a commercial hit. While this has been attributed specifically to an inappropriate distribution strategy and Warners' inability to 'sell' the film,[6] it is a box-office failure not untypical of examples of New Hollywood Cinema financed and/or distributed by the majors in the seventies.

II

What exactly constitutes New Hollywood Cinema needs to be clarified. For Thomas Schatz New Hollywood 'has meant something different from one period of adjustment to another' (1993: 8), and he consequently uses the term to refer to the majors' contemporary, conglomerated practice. This is inexact. Historically, the term New Hollywood Cinema has a dual, but not reducible, institutional and textual meaning. What can be considered the institutional phase of New Hollywood Cinema can be conveniently periodized as commencing with the release and box-office success in 1967 of *Bonnie and Clyde*. The film earned $22.8 million at the box-office and, along with the even greater commercial success of *The Graduate*, that took $43 million in 1967–68, helped 1967 to show the first increase in American cinema attendance since 1947. Like *Bonnie and Clyde*, *The Graduate* was geared specifically toward the youth market, which thus appeared to hold the potential to arrest Hollywood's post-war decline: a prognosis added particular weight in 1969 by the analogous success of the low-budget ($375 000) *Easy Rider* (Dennis Hopper), that returned $19 million.[7] This led to the youth audience being courted with increased ardour, resulting in a period during which, in the words of Teresa Grimes, 'the normally conservative and intransigent' studios became briefly 'more flexible and responsive' and gave 'opportunities to film-makers who they thought could turn out a product suited to youth audiences' (1986: 54).

However, while the strategy resulted in some individual hits and instigated and/or consolidated some significant filmmaking careers, it failed massively in its express purpose of restoring Hollywood's fortunes. Instead, the encouragement of 'new' talent coincided with and contributed to the majors' deepest economic and institutional crisis. Between 1968 and 1972 losses totalled over $500 million. In 1969 United Artists lost $89 million, in 1971 Columbia, that had distributed *Easy Rider*, lost $29 million, while between 1969 and 1971 Twentieth Century-Fox lost approximately $183 million. In 1971 American cinema attendance dropped to a low of 820 million. By the time that Scorsese arrived in Hollywood in January 1971 what Brian De Palma has called 'the "give-the-kids-a-break" era' (Pye and Myles 1979: 151) was largely over; a situation that informs both Scorsese's eagerness to direct *Boxcar Bertha* and his difficulties in making and finding distribution for *Mean Streets*.

Nevertheless, that *Mean Streets* was eventually acquired by Warner Bros underlines that the majors continued to engage with New Hollywood Cinema. Yet this engagement became increasingly selective and, in a reflection of broader structural changes within the studios, commercially rationalized. Symptomatic was the removal of support for a number of semi-autonomous production operations through which some of the majors channelled financing of New Hollywood Cinema. In 1969 Warner Bros staked $3.5 million in Francis Ford Coppola's Zoetrope project. In 1971, after viewing a rough cut of the studio's first film, *THX-1138* (George Lucas, 1971), Warners demanded repayment of all monies, closing Zoetrope down.[8] 1973 saw the end of Ned Tanen's adventurous programme at Universal, while Columbia refused to renew funding for BBS at the earliest opportunity in 1974.[9] The latter had considerable symbolic significance – BBS were in effect the company that made *Easy Rider*.[10]

In retrospect, the majors' rush to exploit the youth market in the late sixties and early seventies smacks of commercially suicidal desperation. Even so, the period did give an 'impetus to an altered and, it can be argued, a more innovative form of film-making' (Grimes 1986: 54). This can once more be related to the films' target audience. If in 1970 three-quarters of 'frequent moviegoers' were between the ages of 12 and 29, 'fully three-quarters of that group had had some college education' (Schatz 1983: 190). Like many of the time's young directors, this audience 'had gleaned the grammar of screen narrative and learned film history from hours spent with television; and in their filmgoing they sought increasingly esoteric or sophisticated fare: foreign films, classic Hollywood movies, even the youth-marketed exploitation films' (*ibid.*).

Discussion of the textual attributes of New Hollywood Cinema dates mainly from the seventies and posits a broad consensus regarding its divergence from the norms of classical Hollywood filmmaking. Peter Lloyd identifies the dilution of narrative linearity and 'the gradual collapse of the efficacy of the heroic individual' (1971: 12). Developing these points, Thomas Elsaesser refers the formal correlation of unmotivated protagonists and narrative fragmentation to the 'complex interchange between European and American film-making' (1975: 19). Similarly, Robin Wood (1975) and David Bordwell and Janet Staiger (1985) call attention to New Hollywood Cinema's awareness of and borrowings from art cinema, while Steve Neale highlights the adoption of 'techniques and conventions' from 'two cinematic spheres: the New Wave and the ciné-vérité movement' (1976: 119).

This is reflected in the appropriation and interplay of *nouvelle vague* and direct cinema elements in Scorsese's early films. That this is continued and developed in *Mean Streets* is immediately implied by the pre-credit scene. Following the black screen that accompanies the opening voice-over, the initial shot, as it covers Charlie from bed to mirror and back to bed, evokes a number of technical and stylistic components of direct cinema: an 'actual', cramped location; seemingly natural light and the accordant use of grainy 'fast' film; shaky, intimate hand-held camerawork; a long take. However, on Charlie's head moving toward the pillow, the shot's 'documentary' effect, and its connotation of real time and space, are interrupted by a pair of rapid, successive jump-cuts that, as they repeat – in different scale – a shot of Charlie's head hitting the pillow, bring the character closer to camera and spectator. The second cut, moreover, is synchronized with the non-diegetic introduction of the urgent opening beat of The Ronettes' 'Be My Baby' on the soundtrack and followed by a third jump-cut, edited with like rhythmic impact upon the song's first off-beat. It is a disjunctive manipulation of image and sound that, as it forcefully fore-grounds film syntax, correspondingly proclaims the influence of the *nouvelle vague*.

As in *Who's That Knocking at My Door?*, the use of direct cinema techniques connects with Scorsese's desire to document his specific subcultural milieu. He has described *Mean Streets* as 'an anthropological or a sociological tract', an attempt to show 'what life was like in Little Italy' (Thompson and Christie 1996: 48). Complementing this is the film's articulation of a dilapidated, quotidian diegetic world. Anchored by the New York footage, this projects a convincing simulation of the Lower East Side. Moreover, the film's four main male characters are given defining introductory scenes, during which their names are, as Robert Phillip Kolker notes, 'flashed on the screen, in imitation of the way David and Albert Maysles introduce the characters in their documentaries' (1988: 169).

This 'documentary' impulse informs *Mean Streets'* episodic, elliptical narrative construction. In documentary, the linearity associated with classical narrative tends to be downgraded before an emphasis on the moment or situation that is characteristically motivated by an imperative to detail the minutiae of a particular subject or event. Hence the incidents in *Mean Streets* that, mainly redundant to the film's plotlines, demon-strate the specificities of Little Italy life. For example, the firecrackers episode, the fight in the pool hall or the extended exchange between Charlie and Johnny in the back room of Tony's bar; a scene that – as it centres on Johnny's engaging résumé of his gambling activities – predominantly affords insight into the character and the environment that he inhabits.

The film's narrative fragmentation likewise implies New Hollywood Cinema's claimed relation to European art cinema. For Bordwell, art cinema also differentiates itself from classical narrative through a 'linkage of events' that is 'looser, more tenuous' (1979: 57). Given that art cinema in part 'defines itself as a realistic cinema', this is, on one hand, often textually 'justified as the intrusion of an unpredictable and contingent daily reality' (*ibid.*: 57, 59). On the other hand, it is a relegation of linearity that can be referred to art cinema's stress on theme rather than plot. Both this – and, more especially, the parti-cularity of the divergence of *Mean Streets* from the classical mode – can be clarified via allusion to the five narrative codes outlined by Roland

Barthes in *S/Z*. Art cinema orders these codes with a differential emphasis to that of classical narrative. Classical narrative tends to be dominated by the interaction of the proairetic and hermeneutic codes – those of narrative actions and enigmas – a dominance that grounds the mode's linear transitivity. By contrast, art cinema tends to allow greater prominence to the cultural, symbolic and semic codes – respectively those of social knowledge, metaphoric groupings and the implied meanings through which thematic structures are generated.[11] In *Mean Streets* not only is narrative flow subordinated before narrative moment, but linearity is superseded by a cogent pattern of repetition with increasingly critical intensification that, operating at various levels of the text, becomes the narrative's chief organizing principle. Correspondingly, as the proairetic code is predicated upon recurrence before progression, so there is a downplaying of the hermeneutic before the symbolic and the semic, a comparative intransitivity that foregrounds theme before plot. Crossing this, the cultural code, as it articulates the text's 'anthropological' intent, can be ascribed a similar relative emphasis.

Nevertheless, as *Mean Streets* proceeds toward its conclusion, the previously marginalized hermeneutic code obtains greater weight as the narrative becomes increasingly focused upon the text's main plotlines: the conflict between Michael and Johnny and Charlie's 'inadmissible' investment in Johnny and Teresa. Through this the film adheres to classical narrative's familiar, ongoing concentration on and integration of a progressively limited number of plot strands. The narrative's increasing linearity is also heightened by its use of 'one of the most characteristic marks of Hollywood dramaturgy', the deadline (Bordwell 1985b: 46). Although a deadline is initially sketched when, near the end of the scene in the back room, Johnny promises to pay Michael 'next Tuesday', deadlines become foregrounded by Johnny's failure to turn up at Vietnam veteran Jerry (Harry Northup)'s party and by the tensions generated by his climactic appointment with Michael.

Such maintenance of certain elements of classical narrative reflects New Hollywood Cinema's textual status as ultimately a hybrid of Hollywood and alternative forms and styles. It has further been the source of New Hollywood Cinema's theoretical dismissal. Robert B. Ray, for example, berates New Hollywood Cinema for adopting 'only the New Wave's superficial stylistic exuberance' while 'leaving Classic Hollywood's paradigms fundamentally untouched' (1985: 287). Bordwell and Staiger concede New Hollywood Cinema's ability to 'explore ambiguous narrational possibilities' but assert that 'those explorations remain within classical boundaries' (Bordwell and Staiger 1985: 377). Implicit in these criticisms is an investment in a particular Marxist–post-structuralist position that, centred in the seventies upon the British journal *Screen*, postulates classical narrative's needful contestation by a more 'progressive', reflexive Brechtian mode.[12] Neale makes the terms of this position and its relation to New Hollywood Cinema explicit. Adducing Colin MacCabe's influential conceptualization of the 'classic realist text', Neale argues that New Hollywood Cinema's textual address is, like classical Hollywood narrative, governed by its narration, or narrative discourse, that, citing MacCabe, 'is placed in a situation of dominance with regard to the other discourses of the text' (MacCabe 1976: 98; quoted in Neale 1976: 120). The narration's efficacy as a metadiscourse, however, 'depends on a repression of its own operations' – that is, a denial of its own contingent, material status – that 'confers an imaginary unity of position on the reader from which the other discourses in the film can be read' (MacCabe 1976: 99; quoted in Neale 1976: 120). Following Christian Metz, this would locate New Hollywood Cinema within the discursive category of *histoire*, or history, that, as a discourse that 'effaces all marks of enunciation' (1975: 226), has been regarded as foundational to classical narrative's transparent, 'readerly' address and the consequent placement of the spectator in a dissimulated ideological position.[13]

Seemingly problematizing this is the credit sequence of *Mean Streets*. This affords a reflexive commentary on the film's realism, a tacit deconstruction of its documentary effect. Accompanied by the continuing 'Be My Baby', the sequence opens with a shot of an old-fashioned 8 mm projector, filmed with a looming portentousness as the camera tracks toward and then around it in an arc. Foregrounding the mechanics of mediation, the shot offers a reflexivity heightened by the projector's imposing representation, anachronistic appearance and by the way that it finally, in a mechanical return of the Look, shines directly into the camera. Reflexivity is upheld as the shot cuts to a frame-within-a-frame configuration, suggestive of an 8 mm frame within the 35 mm frame of *Mean Streets* itself, within which, following a piece of leader, we are presented with images that approximate those of a home movie. While the frame-within-a-frame and the display of leader respectively suggest the constructedness of the sequence and the materiality of the images, the latter's jagged editing and blurred and indistinguishable frames not only evoke the amateurism associated with home filming – itself 'confirmed' by the inclusion of actual home footage of a baptism – but again imply mediation and contrivance. Contrivance is likewise suggested by the 'actuality' that the images represent. For as some of the film's main characters are 'captured' within the Little Italy milieu, so they tend to act out an exaggerated, almost parodic imitation of the stilted posturing that is another feature of amateur filmmaking. In short, as we are presented with actors pretending to be 'real' people pretending to act, any impression that the images comprise objective, documentary realism is displaced by a sense of self-conscious projection and the mannered representation of Little Italy attitudes. Add the use of typewritten credits – a conventional signifier of reportage, that is here used to denote a fiction – and the sequence connotes a declaration of the text's formal appropriation of direct cinema techniques, inviting us to read it as a discourse upon a replicated actuality.

The reflexive relation of the credit sequence to the narrative proper is underscored when the narrative's first subsequent shot – the Feast of San Gennaro at night – initially appears within the frame-within-a-frame before moving out to fill the screen. Yet if this early reflexivity would seem to challenge New Hollywood Cinema's proposed readerly, realist address, it is not sustained. Bordwell notes, moreover, that in classical Hollywood narrative credit sequences and early scenes 'can reveal the narration quite boldly' (1985a: 26). However, 'once present in these opening passages, the narration quickly fades to the background' (*ibid.*: 27), as would appear to occur in *Mean Streets*.

Implicated in this is the text's articulation of its non-classical stylistics. On one hand, their direct cinema reference serves to enhance the text's status – discursively and socially – as history; the narration being underpinned, in this case, by an apparent 'factuality'. On the other hand, the latent reflexivity of the text's *nouvelle vague* tropes is contained by their diegetic integration as an expressionist manifestation of reflected subjectivity.

With respect to this, we can return to the jump-cuts that conclude the pre-credit scene. Although spatially and temporally disruptive, they intensify rather than explode the scene's diegetic and dramatic unity, functioning as a heightening objectification of the unease suggested by Charlie's self-regard in the mirror. Like connotations are offered, say, by the 'unmotivated', insinuating lateral tracks during Charlie's early scene with Michael and by the reverse angle slow-motion shots of Charlie and Johnny on Johnny's initial entry to Tony's bar. The former camera movements transmit Charlie's and the situation's increasing unease, while the latter temporal manipulation implies an externalization of Charlie's ambivalence toward his friend at this point. It is a connotation not only 'placed' by Charlie's knowledge of Johnny's failure to pay his debts and his voice-over 'conversation' with God ('We talk about penance, and you send this through the door …'), but stylistically under-scored by a counterpointing cutaway to a close shot of Tony laughing at Johnny's entry that is shot normal speed.

The glaring red lighting of the bar similarly invites expressionist interpretation. With the bar a site of drug abuse, drunkenness, assigna-tions, violence and, through its topless dancers, 'illicit' sexuality, the lighting conveys a lurid but alluring sense of degradation and danger. That Scorsese has related the lighting to the influence of the films of Michael Powell is a critical commonplace. More particularly, not only is emphatic colour apparent across Powell's work, but the specific use of red recurrently affords connotations analogous to those offered by the lighting of the bar in *Mean Streets*. Note, for instance, the climactic scenes of *Black Narcissus* (Powell and Emeric Pressburger, 1946) or 'The Tale of Giulietta' episode of *The Tales of Hoffmann* (Powell and Pressburger, 1951).[14]

Another commonplace is the debt that the no less striking use of extended tracking shots in *Mean Streets* owes to the films of Samuel Fuller. The hand-held takes that track the fight in the pool hall and, later, Johnny's frantic passage through the New York streets in addition under-line the film's fused documentary and expressionist address. In both instances a conventionally 'neutral', 'objective' direct cinema technique is used explicitly to project the 'subjective' emotion of the moment – a sense respectively of relentlessness and of desperation. A similar docu-mentary-expressionist dualism informs the film's use of music: a combi-nation of sixties rock and pop and Italian opera and traditional tunes. Diegetic or non-diegetic, the music complements the film's evocation of the Little Italy of Scorsese's youth; this whether one considers an individ-ual tracks – '"Be My Baby" was the song … that's 1963 or 1962 in New York' (Scorsese 1975: 7) – or its virtual and varied omnipresence: 'I was living in a very crowded area where music would be playing constantly from various apartments across the street, from bars and candy stores … you'd hear opera from one room, Benny Goodman from another, and rock'n'roll from downstairs' (Thompson and Christie 1996: 28). Moreover, the music's narrative integration continues and extends the intelligence and complexity apparent in the deployment of rock and pop in *Who's That Knocking at My Door?*.

Consider once more the pre-credit scene and Johnny's entry. While the rhythmic synchronization of the beginning of 'Be My Baby' and the pre-credit scene's jump-cuts reciprocally heighten the impact of music and editing – and, through this, the dramatic force and significance of the moment – the song's subsequent upbeat energy functions in an anempathetic fashion in relation to Charlie's apparent disquiet. This, to cite Michel Chion, characteristically reinforces 'the individual emotion of the character and of the spectator, even as the music pretends not to notice them' (1994: 8). As Charlie turns on his side in tight close-up, it is as though he writhes beneath the weight of the music's insensitivity. The choice of The Rolling Stones' 'Jumping Jack Flash' to accompany Johnny's entry is, by contrast, decidedly empathetic: the combination of the brash dynamism of the music and the defiant nihilism of the lyrics heralds the character perfectly.

As with the use of 'Be My Baby', the effect of 'Jumping Jack Flash' is enhanced by, as it enhances, the other elements constitutive of the episode: the glaring red lighting; the compelling slow-motion tracking shot; the gestural expansiveness of De Niro as Johnny, acknowledging greetings, and with a young woman under each arm, moves with unabashed delight along the bar's counter. Given both Charlie's flagged discontent and Johnny's textual centrality, the incident's comparative stylistic assertiveness in turn accords with its narrative import. It is, moreover, a mutually augmenting integration of style, performance and situation that, with consistent but consonant intensity, is apparent, virtually undiminished, throughout the film.

The realization of *Mean Streets* demonstrates a sizeable qualitative improvement upon that of Scorsese's previous features, comparing favourably both with the exploitative illogic of *Boxcar Bertha* and, especially, in the light of the films' similarities of style and subject matter, with the indulgence and over-statement of *Who's That Knocking at My Door?*. The contrasting control evinced by *Who's That Knocking at My Door?* and *Mean Streets* can be underlined by briefly comparing the films in terms of performance. Whereas performance in *Who's That Knocking at My Door?* often effects a rambling dissipation of interest, that in *Mean Streets* is considerably honed; this despite it both centring upon similarly repetitive exchanges and conveying a naturalistic sense of improvisatory freedom. However, only 'three or four scenes' in *Mean Streets* were 'really improvised' (Scorsese 1975: 4–5). Also, although some scenes – such as when Charlie and Johnny walk the night-time streets – were improvised during filming, Scorsese has emphasized that most improvisation occurred during the production's ten days of rehearsal and was carefully structured, with lines and scenes being 'taped at rehearsal and then scripted from those tapes' (Thompson and Christie 1996: 43).

Yet not only does *Mean Streets* improve stylistically upon Scorsese's previous features, but in the film's particular articulation of representational elements Scorsese's stylistic discourse shifts from the emerging and derivative to the achieved and defined. To borrow a concept from literary theorist Harold Bloom, *Mean Streets* evokes the rhetorical trope of *metalepsis*, or transumption, whereby previously limiting, antecedent figures become, through a process that Bloom relates analogously to the psychoanalytic mechanisms of introjection and projection, assimilated, constitutive elements of a 'strong' poet's established style.[15] At the very least, the film's intensive relation of, say, editing to camerawork to performance to music, and the attendant, distinctive expression of diegetic time and space, forcibly contests the highly tendentious assertion that New Hollywood Cinema exhibits an 'almost complete conservatism of style' (Bordwell and Staiger 1985: 375). Notwithstanding, with the signifiers of Scorsese's stylistic discourse diegetically integrated, it is still largely possible to read *Mean Streets* in a realist fashion, as an admittedly singular window on the world, without having to negotiate the fact of its constructed, authored status.

By contrast, the stylistic redundancy and frequent lack of control apparent in *Who's That Knocking at My Door?* could, through its presumably inadvertent foregrounding of the text's constructedness, allow the film to be considered formally a more 'progressive' text. Admittedly, such a claim veers on a parody of seventies '*Screen* Theory', but that it can be made reflects upon the formalism that shapes the latter's narrative prescriptions.[16] Which is not to propose a blanket dismissal of an extensive and multi-faceted body of theory, nor to deny the potential efficacy of reflexivity: although limited in textual extent, the reflexivity of the credit sequence of *Mean Streets* offers a critically resonant route 'into' the film. Nevertheless, the essentialism that informs '*Screen* Theory''s position regarding narrative effects a disabling refusal to engage with the determining actualities of contrasting production situations. With New Hollywood Cinema mainly financed and/or distributed by the majors, it is unrealistic to expect that it might, or even could, have constituted a Brechtian counter-cinema, as Hopper discovered to his cost when he made *The Last Movie* (1971). *Mean Streets* was initially rejected by the majors because of its narrative intransitivity.[17] This helps to clarify why New Hollywood Cinema deviates from, rather than breaks with, classical principles. Further, not only was *Who's That Knocking at My Door?* produced outside a commercial context, but its difficulty in finding distribution itself becomes suggestive.

III

If in *Who's That Knocking at My Door?* Scorsese's authorial discourse suffers from a lack of restraint, and in *Boxcar Bertha* is dispersed within the text, *Mean Streets* implies a more enabling balance between authorial freedom and production constraint. There is also the fact of Scorsese's increased filmmaking experience. Even so, Scorsese has complained about the sloppiness of *Mean Streets*, bemoaning the absence of time for rudimentary niceties, like establishing shots.[18] Against this, the exigencies of the film's pressurized production, and the demands that it made of Scorsese and his collaborators, can be seen to have had a generative influence on its claustrophobic intensity – 'the economics dictated the style, and the style just happened to work' (Thompson and Christie 1996: 47).

Through its combined documentary and expressionist address, *Mean Streets* transmits a mutual sense of physical and psychic, environmental and emotional oppression. This is underpinned both by the film's extensive use of cramped, unprepossessing and/or darkened interiors and by its camerawork and soundtrack. Typified by the (economically and situationally) determined use of hand-held cameras, that 'entrap' us spatially with characters and situation, the shooting strategy of *Mean Streets* denies any effective sense of expansiveness. In addition to its specific narrative connotations, the almost constant use of music contributes often foregroundedly to a cluttered and at times cacophonous sound mix that, as it variously combines vocal and instrumental music, dialogue and frequently jarring ambient noises, maintains a constant and occasionally discomforting aural tension.

Although *Mean Streets* is primarily an 'indoors' film, the sense of environmental oppression is upheld by its exterior shots and scenes. Witness, for example, the pair of jump-cut high-angle shots of Little Italy at night, that place it, illuminated by the Feast of San Gennaro, as an insignificant enclave within the dark mass of Manhattan, or the crowded shabbiness that marks the shots of the Feast taken in the streets. When Michael complains to Charlie about Johnny on a dingy sidewalk, not only are the characters shot from across the street, with their figures repeatedly blocked by pedestrians and parked and passing cars, but the use of a long-focus lens visually flattens them into their surroundings, an effect compounded by the camera zooming in.

The transmission of environmental oppression stylistically reciprocates the film's central thematic concern with cultural determination. Although *Season of the Witch* was conceived as a follow-up to *Who's That Knocking at My Door?*, *Mean Streets* is in many ways a refocused remake, a reiteration and reworking of a number of its precursor's concerns and situations. Played by the same actor, Charlie is very much an older version of J.R., with the character's continuing biographical relation to Scorsese 'admitted' textually by Scorsese at times speaking Charlie's voice-over, including the film's first words.[19] But just as *Mean Streets* demonstrates a stylistic refinement of elements apparent in *Who's That Knocking at My Door?*, so its restatement of common concerns and structures exhibits more layered, complex and resonant thematic compactness.

Considered intertextually, with reference to Scorsese' s previous films, *Mean Streets'* concern with determination is signalled by the pre-credit appearance of the mirror motif. This further and characteristically links determination with alienation. If, as noted, Charlie's self-regard – as he sighs, nervously rubs his cheek and his chin and looks wearily at his reflection – signifies personal unease, the very situation of his uncomfortable contemplation of his own image implies the notion of identity as estrangement that is foundational to Lacan's account of subject-formation. It is also an alienation that – like that of Murray, or of J.R., or of Bill Shelley – is related textually to an inability to reconcile antithetical positions and demands. When Charlie moves between bed and mirror, he twice passes a crucifix that is visually prominent upon the room's bare wall, while, when he stands before the mirror, a police siren is heard on the soundtrack. The elements figure the conflict between the religious and the secular, between Christian morality and material, largely illicit gain that informs Charlie's alienation through-out. Moreover, Charlie's desire to reconcile these oppositions is declared by his opening voice-over: 'You don't make up for your sins in the church. You do it in the streets. You do it at home. The rest is bullshit, and you know it.'

Yet if this asserts the necessity for the fusion of the religious and the secular, the semantic clash of the holy and the demotic and the words' tense, insistent delivery suggests a fundamental strain. This is under-lined by Charlie's introductory scene, that shows him in a church. The scene opens with Charlie walking toward the altar-rail, a shot accompanied by the sound of another police siren. A sound bridge from the preceding scene, and, once more, a signifier of criminality, the siren's situational unfittingness is underscored when, as its sound fades out, it becomes slightly distorted, as though caught discordantly within the church's echoing space. Similarly, as Charlie stands raptly before a *pietà*, his voice-over not only jars tonally in its colloquial, streetwise insistence, but again incongruously combines the religious ('penance', 'sins') with the demotic ('that shit'), capping which is the incorrigible claim, 'you don't fuck around with the infinite'.

The voice-over ends by describing the 'two sides' of the 'pain in hell': 'The kind you can touch with your hand, the kind you can feel in your heart, your soul. The spiritual side.' On the words 'your soul' there is a cut to a slow-motion track along the counter of Tony's bar. The contrast between the high, spacious, airy church and the cramped, crowded, red-lit bar – that, through the contrast, partakes of an infernal connotation – reinforces the disparity of the religious and the secular; a disjunction complemented by the dichotomy of Charlie's verbal reference to 'the spiritual' and the sight of a prime diegetic location of the carnal and the profane.[20]

The collision of the religious and the secular and illicit continues throughout, being also instanced via dialogue – Michael's 'Bless you' when Charlie pays him for some cigarettes, for example, or Johnny's swearing 'to Christ' that he will pay Michael next week – and the film's *mise-en-scène*. In addition to the street shots of the Feast of San Gennaro, witness, say, the encased statue of Christ in Tony's back room, the pictures of Pope Paul VI and Christ crucified in Giovanni's restaurant or the pronounced sight of a large white statue of Christ atop a yellow brick building. While this implies the residual influence of the Catholic Church on the Italian-American community, with the exception of the scene in the church, incongruity is invariably represented as stemming from the religious. Charlie's perceived religiousness is the source of jibes, hilarity and self-defensive humour. On seeing Charlie, the owner of the pool hall, Joey (George Memmoli), sarcastically proclaims: 'Saint Charles is here ... . Benedictions.' Charlie responds by jokingly 'blessing' Joey, his associates and the room's pool-playing accoutrements. Similarly, when Charlie enters Tony's bar for Jerry's party, he intones, with mock sententiousness, 'I have come to create order', has a 'J & B and soda' poured over his thumbs in a parody of communion wine and bandies a Biblical passage with Tony.[21]

Comic disparity is likewise implicit in the 'likes' that Charlie lists for Teresa at the beach – 'spaghetti in clam sauce, mountains, Francis of Assisi, chicken, lemon, and garlic and John Wayne'. The scene nevertheless underlines the strength of Charlie's sense of religious obligation. When Teresa irritably complains about Johnny, Charlie laments the loss of Christian fellowship: 'That's what's the matter. Nobody ... nobody ... tries anymore ... tries to, to help ... help people.' Charlie/Keitel's hesitant enunciation implies a sincere belief, as though he is digging within himself to find the right words. It also continues to suggest that Charlie's morality is out of step, that it lacks an expressive model; a connotation underscored both by Teresa's contrastingly instant and selfish riposte – 'You help yourself first' – and by the clash of the sacred and the profane yet again demonstrated by Charlie's reaction: 'Bullshit, Teresa. That's where you're all wrong. Francis of Assisi had it all down. He knew.' However, as Charlie's Christian conscience distinguishes him from other characters, so it is privileged ideologically by the text and, like the incongruousness of most of the film's other religious references, functions implicitly (or, as here, explicitly) to critique the encompassing meanness and venality – 'the whole idea was to make a story of a modern saint, you know, a saint in his own society but his society happens to be gangsters' (Scorsese 1975: 5).

Diegetically, it is a context that, given Charlie's Mafia links, seriously qualifies his putative 'sainthood'. As Teresa points out: 'Saint Francis didn't run numbers.' Read biographically, Charlie's situation evokes another virtual cliché of Scorsese's personal history: that his career choices in Little Italy were those of gangster or priest. Read in terms of the film's thematic structure, it heightens Charlie's alienated difficulty in mediating the religious and the secular. Compounding this is Charlie's desire for the restaurant that he expects to be bequeathed by his uncle and local Godfather, Giovanni (Cesare Danova). This depends, however, on Charlie keeping the closeness of his friendship with Johnny – and that he has 'signed' for Johnny's loans – a secret. The point is made explicit when he dines at the restaurant with Giovanni and his associate, Mario (Victor Argo). Giovanni observes that Charlie is 'still around that kid, Johnny Boy' and warns: 'Don't spoil anything.' In turn, when Johnny suggests that Charlie talk to Giovanni about his financial problems, not only does Charlie refuse, but his refusal expressly contradicts the moral position that he espouses at the beach and instead recalls Teresa's statement of self-interest: 'Oh that'd be ... really great for you, wouldn't it ... But not for me.'

This contradiction is consistent with the complex modulation of what the film represents as Charlie's disjunctive Catholic and Mafia determination. With respect to this, Charlie's interest in Johnny could be viewed as a compensatory expiation of guilt. Charlie's reference to Johnny in relation to 'penance' reflects his earlier voice-over in the church, 'if I do something wrong, I just want to pay for it my way, so I do my own penance for my own sins.' These words, however, follow his refusal to accept conventional absolution that is 'okay for the others' – 'ten Hail Marys, ten Our Fathers ... they're just words' – and imply a sinful pride that is similarly implicit in his apparently heartfelt expression of concern for Johnny at the beach: 'Who's gonna help him if I don't?' It is a moral pride that is also mirrored in the hankering for social and mob status that is latent in Charlie's desire for the restaurant. Likewise, his 'desire to "help" Johnny' may, to quote Jill McGreal, 'be a Christian act, but it may also be that Charlie wants to act out the Godfather role' (1993: 64). Certainly, while Charlie's well-groomed, smartly dressed appearance in the church is hardly that of a humble penitent, and even less conforms to the example of Francis of Assisi, it epitomizes Mafia 'respectability'. It is nevertheless intimated that Charlie is conscious of his prideful culpability. Hence, for instance, the scene's initial, voice-over admission of unworthiness: 'Lord, I'm not worthy to eat your flesh, not worthy to drink your blood.'[22]

Charlie's relationship with Teresa also has to be concealed from Giovanni. An epileptic, Teresa is crudely dismissed by Giovanni as being 'sick in the head'.[23] When pressed by Teresa to admit that he loves her during their sexual liaison at a hotel, Charlie responds 'with you I can't get involved'. The words are echoed by Giovanni at the restaurant when he complains about Teresa's parents confiding their concern regarding Teresa's desire to move outside 'the neighborhood'. He tells Charlie, who lives next door, to keep 'an eye open', but cautions 'don't get involved'. The formulation implies an ideology of detached, calculating control that clashes markedly with Charlie's statement of Christian fellowship. When Charlie argues with Michael about Johnny's debt, Michael observes that Charlie should have enough sense 'not to get involved'. Similarly, after refusing Johnny's suggestion that he approach Giovanni, Charlie bemoans: 'That's what I get for getting involved.'

Charlie's relationship with Teresa is likewise implied to be transgressive of his Catholic determination. When Teresa continues to press Charlie at the hotel about why he cannot love her, he brusquely declares: 'Because you're a cunt.' With Teresa a sexual single woman this implies an adherence to the madonna–whore dichotomy. The scene, moreover, begins with Charlie describing a dream in which he is about to have sex with Teresa and 'comes' blood: an account redolent of sexual guilt. The broader cultural reference of the madonna–whore dichotomy is hinted at by the film's establishing images of women comprising respectively the figures of the Virgin Mary of the altar-piece and the *pietà* seen during Charlie's introductory scene and of Mary Magdalene, also of the altar-piece, and Diane (Jeannie Bell), the black topless dancer at Tony's bar. That is, (literally) the Madonna and (explicitly/implicitly) a whore.

It is a female marginalization maintained throughout the text. Until Teresa appears in the third reel, *Mean Streets* presents no substantively realized female characters, and those that do appear can, by virtue of their situation and/or appearance, be largely related to the madonna–whore axis. Scorsese has claimed that both Teresa's lack of an introductory scene and her delayed narrative appearance were attempts to index Little Italy's masculine dominance.[24] Similarly symptomatic is the physical absence of Charlie's mother. 'Explained' by her being on Staten Island looking after Charlie's sick grandmother, this nevertheless has a suggestive symbolic significance, not least as her narrative function is limited to the supportive, domestic role of leaving money, clothes and notes for Charlie. Indeed, represented as dominated by the Catholic Church and the Mafia, the Little Italy of *Mean Streets* is an explicitly, and exclusionary, patriarchal society. Giovanni is intolerant of otherness. Impressing on Charlie that 'Honorable men go with honorable men', he not only dismisses Johnny as 'half crazy', but implicitly links Teresa's being 'sick in the head' with her desire for independence.

IV

The psycho-sexual connotations of Giovanni's representation are heightened by his symbolic position as Charlie's father–figure. Charlie's material ambitions are implicitly dependent upon his achieving an Oedipal identification with Giovanni, who intimates that Charlie will receive the restaurant if he is not 'impatient' – that is, like Giovanni, who himself owns a restaurant. As the restaurant thus affords Charlie a potential patriarchal position, its attainment can be considered to symbolize the assumption of the phallus. Giovanni's patriarchal authority is figured by his phallic cigars, the symbolic relation of which to his peremptory power is foregrounded when he decides the fate of the young assassin (Robert Carradine) who shoots a drunk (David Carradine) in Tony's bar. Giovanni states that the assassin must be sent to Miami for 'six months ... a year', and we are given a close-up of his hand, cigar erect, as it makes a dismissive gesture and the subtitled translation of his instruction, spoken in Italian, 'Get rid of him.'

The Oedipal implications of Charlie's relationship to Giovanni are plainly consistent with the text's concern with determination. They are also complicated by the sole, almost throwaway reference to Charlie's actual father. This is spoken disparagingly, if with regret, by Giovanni, and occurs suggestively between Charlie asking a facile question about Mafia operations and Giovanni's attack on Johnny: 'I said the same thing to your father twenty years ago. He didn't listen.' The implication would appear to be that Giovanni fears that Charlie is repeating what, for Giovanni, was his father's 'patriarchal' failure.

The suggestion of Charlie's unease with his secular and material desires – and, figuratively, his assumption of the phallus – is underscored by the film's fire and water imagery. The central fire motif is that of Charlie putting his right forefinger over flames. For Scorsese, this has a specific religious and biographical reference: 'That was something they used to make us do on religious retreat to help us imagine the pains of hell' (Carducci 1975: 12). Charlie places his finger over a votive candle in the church, over a lighted match in Tony's bar and over a naked flame in the kitchen of the restaurant that he covets. In each case the motif is related to Charlie's transgression of his Catholic determination, occurring respectively after his prideful voice-over contemplation of sin and penance, between his dancing with and sexualized regard of Diane and following his tacit acceptance of Giovanni's outlawing of Johnny and Teresa. Not only does the motif's phallic suggestiveness connect with the text's psycho-sexual connotations, but its repetition once more implies Charlie's guilty self-consciousness.

This similarly informs the figurative use of water during the scene in which Giovanni despatches the assassin. The scene cross-cuts between Giovanni, Mario and the assassin's father seated at a table in Giovanni's restaurant and Charlie in the adjoining washroom. A subtitled translation of Giovanni's rejection of the father's pleas on his son's behalf – 'Protect him? Why? I didn't tell him to do anything for me' – is superimposed over a close-up of Charlie, with obvious metaphoric implication, washing his hands. Charlie raises his head and stares at his reflection in the mirror over the wash-basin. Recalling Charlie's self-regard during the pre-credit scene, the situation in particular suggests the character's unease with his Mafia affiliations. Charlie proceeds to put his wetted fingers to his face, as though seeking alleviation through water's symbolically cleansing agency.

Charlie's implied alienation is counterpointed in *Mean Streets* by the representation of the other main male characters, that suggests differing acceptance of and/or tensions within their acculturation. The representation of Johnny foregrounds a denial of social convention and personal responsibility; this whether one considers his checking his pants at Tony's bar, his accumulation of debt, his reported absence from work or his lank hair and unkempt appearance, elements that contrast signally with Charlie's groomed smartness. All this combines with both the character's manic and frequently anti-social behaviour (like blowing up a mailbox, or throwing a lighted stick of dynamite into the street) and his reciprocal refusal of repression and inclination toward instant gratification (such as speaking out of turn at the pool hall, or buying a tie instead of paying his debts) to place Johnny, in terms of the text's psychoanalytic structure, as a personification of the id. Further to this is Johnny's shooting of a pistol from a roof; an 'unsanctioned' release of phallic energy that, as it offers a parallel with the assassin's shooting of the drunk, helps to account for Giovanni's animus. Not only do both shootings breach Giovanni's behavioural emphasis on detached, patient self-control, but they correlatively imply a refusal of Oedipal repression and its attendant symbolic castration.

Although Charlie rationalizes his concern for Johnny as an expression of Christian fellowship, Johnny can also be regarded as an embodiment of Charlie's repressed self. A connotation implicit in Charlie's closeness to and even indulgence of Johnny, it is underscored by their shared and largely delighted recollection of past experiences and transgressions. These are partly re-enacted when the characters 'fight' with trash-cans and take some bread from outside Giovanni's restaurant; a 'return' of Charlie's repressed that notably takes place in the dream-like social limbo of the deserted night-time streets. Likewise significant is Johnny's 'youthful' representation. Apart from the appellation Johnny *Boy* and Giovanni's reference to him as 'that kid', Michael calls him a 'punk kid' and Charlie at one point tells him to 'Grow up'. When Charlie refers to 'Season of the Witch' and 'William Blake and the tigers' at Tony's bar, Johnny reacts with childish, superstitious fright.[25] In turn, if Johnny can be considered a personification of the id, then Charlie implies an ego-figure, a split subject characteristically bombarded by the conflicting demands of the superego (the contrasting dictates of Giovanni, the Catholic Church and, possibly, Charlie's absent father), the id (figured both by Johnny and by Charlie's sexual desire for Teresa) and, as his attempts to reconcile his situation become increasingly fraught, external reality.

Tony is another ego-figure, albeit one that suggests what Charlie might become. Whereas Charlie waits on the restaurant, Tony owns the bar. Correspondingly, Tony is seemingly more accepting of his determination, with his representation implying a pragmatic acceptance and balancing of the forces and affiliations that tear Charlie apart. While his bar is a site of the illegal and the illicit, Tony is introduced 'morally' ejecting a junkie and a drug-pusher. He nevertheless both joins with Michael in the firecrackers scam and drives Charlie and Johnny to the pool hall, taking part in the ensuing fisticuffs. This in addition implies a balance of involvement and detachment that, further summarized by his dual status as colleague and bartender, finds a displaced parallel in his tacit verbal collapsing of the Catholic

Church and the Mafia when, criticizing Charlie's religious investment, he notes of the former, 'it's a business, it's work, it's an organization'.[26] Capping this, Tony asserts to Charlie: 'You gotta be like me. You wanna be safe.'

Even so, the forcefulness with which Tony speaks his advice hints at remaining tensions. This informs the strangest scene in *Mean Streets*, that in which Tony reveals his lion and panther cubs in the bar's back room.[27] Illegal (Tony does not 'have a licence for them') and dangerous, the caged cubs imply a metaphor for Tony's repressed impulses, that are similarly outside the law and, following the Freudian belief that what is repressed returns in a more destructive form, potentially threatening. Both the animals' figurative relation to Tony and the 'pull' of his repressed urges are underscored when Tony opens one of the cages and lovingly caresses the lion cub. The scene is complemented by suggestions that in Tony's coming to terms with his determination, in accepting his repression, there has resulted a certain diminution of character. His excessive anger and exasperation as he ejects the junkie and the pusher and then rails against the failure of his bouncer, George (Peter Fain), to keep the bar 'clean' suggests a longstanding frustration and insufficiency. The relation of this to his implicit Oedipal determination is intimated by the character's subsequently wearing a bandage on his right hand. While signifying that Tony is injured during the ejection, this functions symbolically to confirm his 'castration'. Character appearance is again significant. With his shoulder-length, centre-parted hair and tight seventies clothes, Tony presents a gauche modishness that itself evokes an uncomfortable cultural accommodation. In turn, when late in the film Charlie sets light to a glass of spirits, Tony hurriedly blows out the flames, as though guiltily not wanting reminders of moral retribution in his 'place'. By contrast, when Charlie and Johnny complain about the running of the bar and, by extension, 'attack' Tony's masculine/patriarchal authority, he loses his temper and almost comes to blows with Johnny.[28]

V

Tony's outburst is consistent with the overcompensatory masculine aggression that connects the seemingly discrete outbreaks of violence that punctuate *Mean Streets*. Witness the incidence of violence during the film's first half. Apart from Tony's over-assertive removal of the junkie and the pusher, the fight that breaks out suddenly and without apparent motivation behind Charlie and Michael at the bar can be read as a displaced expression of Charlie's increasing tension as they discuss Johnny's failure to pay his debt. When Michael, Tony and Charlie go to the cinema, not only are we shown a clip from *The Searchers* in which Martin Pawley fights Charlie McCorry (Ken Curtis) for the hand of Laurie (Vera Miles), but it is a 'fictional' dispute that is followed by a heard but unseen argument between three men in the darkened theatre, while the fight in the pool hall is predicated upon Joey's almost territorial reluctance to give ground.[29] The relation between violence and masculine assertion is foregrounded by the shooting in the bar. Not only does the phallic hardness of the youth's pistol contrast with the drunk's limp penis as he urinates slumped in the bar's toilet, but the shooting is retrospectively placed as a bid by the youth to attain status within Little Italy's patriarchal domain. Charlie explains to Teresa that the assassin acted upon the drunk's claimed insulting of Mario: 'The kid's a climber, not very bright. He kills a guy who insulted a big man, he gets a reputation, he thinks he's made.'

The linkage of these incidents is underscored by a series of narrative and formal parallels. The bar's toilet is also the place where Tony discovers the junkie shooting up, and in each case there is an analogous lateral track as Tony manhandles the junkie and the wounded drunk struggles with the assassin as they move through the bar's interior, past pool-table and illuminated bar decoration, to the same red-lit area from which Tony ejects the junkie and the assassin fires his final bullet. The casting of half-brothers Robert and David Carradine is noteworthy. Just as the extra-diegetic relationship between John and David Carradine enhances the Oedipal connotations of the encounter between Sartoris and Bill Shelley in *Boxcar Bertha*, so this supports the suggested difficulty of upholding within Little Italy the Christian fellowship, the belief in being 'thy brother's keeper', that Charlie espouses at the beach. It is a suggestion likewise implicit in the dispute between Tony and Johnny, who are normally friends, as are Martin and Charlie in *The Searchers*. The dispute is also, again like the killing of the drunk, motivated by perceived insult: Tony responds to Charlie and Johnny's comments about the bar by deriding the debt-ridden Johnny's eargerness to play cards, to which Johnny reacts by making an inciting hand gesture. Tony calls both the pusher and Johnny 'Scumbag'.

The representation of violence exemplifies the narrative's structure of repetition with critical intensification. Although recurrent, violence is not at first represented as particularly destructive or consequential. Despite the intensity of Tony's initial aggression, its purport is tempered by George's comic obtuseness when Tony confronts him. Similar comic leavening is apparent in the humour of the clip from *The Searchers*, in Tony and Charlie's amused reaction to the argument in the cinema and in the use of The Marvelettes' incongruously jolly 'Please Mr Postman' to accompany the fight in the pool hall. The fight is also bracketed by the comedy of Charlie and his companions' incomprehension when Joey calls Jimmy (Lenny Scaletta) 'a mook' and that of Joey's payment of 'car fare' to the cop, Davis (D'Mitch Davis); following which the sequence concludes with the farcical resumption of hostilities. In each case comedy leaches the violence of seeming effect, something similarly achieved when, after the fight behind Charlie and Michael, Charlie calmly returns, with a wink, to watching Diane. However, with the argument between Tony and Johnny, things change. Tony pushes over a table to get at Johnny and, although Charlie steps between them, an undertone of nastiness lingers. There closely follows the killing, during which violence is, for the first time, represented with messy, painful graphicness. On the first two gunshots, a wide-angled facial close-up foregrounds the drunk's agony, while as a third gunshot rips into his white shirt it is – significantly – the first time in the film that we see blood. It is an impactful moment, the resonance of which is compounded both by cutaways to the frightened reactions of the four male protagonists and by the chaos that ensues as killer and victim proceed through the bar and the rest of the clientèle fling themselves behind benches and the bar counter. No attempt is made to mitigate the incident through comedy, nor to deny its consequence. Moreover, as the incident clarifies the text's relation of violence to masculinity, so its revelation of the painful actuality of violence reflects back upon its prior, frequently entertaining representation, placing both it and, possibly, our preceding pleasure in a more critical perspective.

The killing sets the tone for the subsequent representation of violence. An edgy nastiness marks Jerry's seizing of a young woman (Julie Andelman) at his party as well as the clash involving Charlie and a woman (Lois Walden) and her date. Again, these incidents are informed by a network of parallels. The outburst of returned veteran Jerry implies the eruption of repressed sexual energy. It is filmed in an unbroken hand-held take that recalls those used at the pool hall. On the woman disagreeing with the date, who moves away, Charlie makes joky advances. When the date reappears, Charlie grabs hold of the woman and challenges the date to take her from him. This sustains the relation of violence to masculine overcompensation: Charlie's action indexes his increasing difficulty in controlling the Michael–Johnny situation. The date moves on Charlie, but is attacked and removed from the bar by Johnny. The woman follows her date, and Charlie throws her coat to her. This repeats Charlie's throwing of the coat of the woman who accompanies the man attacked behind Michael and Charlie as she leaves the bar. With Johnny symbolically positioned as Charlie's repressed self, the parallel not only underscores Charlie's displaced relation to the earlier attack, but typically partakes of a critical intensification, with Charlie's solicitous 'Miss ...' as he throws the first coat being replaced by his sarcastic: 'Maybe we'll meet at bingo some night.'

VI

The relation of violence to masculinity and patriarchal determination obtains further modulation through the representation of Michael. From the first, Michael's actions are represented as inept, inapt and/or ridiculous. Revealed in his introductory scene to have mistaken 'two shipments' of Japanese adapters for German lenses, Michael is later 'stiffed' by the kids in the firecrackers episode, gauchely interrupts Giovanni and Charlie as they talk and, upon Jerry's violence, is shown sitting, cigarette in hand, but spattered with cake, in a pose of farcical, exaggerated 'cool'. Michael's increasingly intemperate threats regarding Johnny and his charging him excessive interest once more imply masculine overcompensation; albeit this is deprecated by the impotence conveyed by Michael's constant, anxious insistence. Parallel connotations attend Michael's appearance and dress. With his dark suits, perfectly knotted ties and felt-collared overcoat, the character assumes the image of Mafia/patriarchal respectability. But as Michael's nervousness contrasts with Giovanni's calm ruthlessness, so it is an image that, in its stiff, uncomfortable formality, is – precisely – ill-fitting.

Michael's precious hairstyle and finicky smartness can further be read to suggest a rather clichéd encoding of gayness. The connotation is underscored narratively by the scene in which a gay couple, Benton (Robert Wilder) and Sammy (Ken Sinclair), claim a lift in Michael's car. Despite Michael's denials, the couple appear to know him. Moreover, whereas Tony and Charlie are amused by the argument in the cinema, Michael sits tight-lipped. A contrast 'explained' by Michael having been impressed upon to pay Tony and Charlie's admission, it also, given the dispute's homosexual overtones ('Keep your hands off me', 'He's a fruit', 'You're a fruit'), possibly implies an uneasy self-consciousness. With homosexuality patently inadmissible within the represented patriarchal environment, its denial is another factor implicitly impacting upon Michael's masculine insistence. The shooting in the bar once more serves a clarifying function. On entering the toilet, the youth unfurls long, 'feminine' hair from beneath his coat collar. The combination of the youth's feminized appearance, the incident's phallic connotations and the stereotypical 'homosexual' site of a men's toilet lends the killing a homophobic aspect, that of a coextensive admission and brutal denial of homoerotic attraction.[30]

Homophobia is also implied by the defensive body-language and comments of Charlie and Johnny when Sammy sits between them in Michael's car. When both Charlie and Johnny and Benton and Sammy exit the car, and Sammy, hip thrust forward, jeeringly inquires, 'You going my way?', Johnny shapes to hit him. The incident is, moreover, staged to imply a *doppelgänger* situation, that Benton and Sammy represent Charlie and Johnny's other selves. Apart from both 'couples' leaving Michael's car at the same time, their positioning as they stand on the sidewalk is mutually reflective, and as Charlie restrains Johnny, Benton restrains Sammy. As in *Who's That Knocking at My Door?*, homoerotic suggestion would here appear to be placed as an ironic obverse to emphatic masculinity. This is underlined by the subsequent scenes involving Charlie and Johnny. For while their antics and exchanges as they walk the night-time streets confirm the intimacy and longstandedness of their friendship, shifting perspective they can be read as a mutual assertion and displacement of attraction. With the characters at Charlie's apartment sharing the same bed, the scenes symptomatically suggest extended, metaphoric foreplay.

Yet if this implies a potentially subversive critique of Little Italy's patriarchal norms, it is compromised both by an unacknowledged homophobia analogous to that which is represented textually and by a reciprocal denial of that which is seemingly admitted. The representation of Sammy uncomfortably nears stereotype: witness the character's explicit, yellow-jacketed campness, implicit licentiousness (his leering regard of Charlie) and exhibitionist outrageousness (his hassling of prostitutes from the car). Likewise, Michael's overcompensatory assertiveness has a febrile vindictiveness that other characters lack.

Further, when Charlie and Johnny share the bed, it is but briefly – Johnny barely gets into the bed before Charlie gets up. In addition, whereas Johnny gets between the blankets, Charlie sits upon them. Despite its brevity, the incident is also a possible disavowal: that the characters can share a bed 'proves' their heterosexuality. Similarly, when Charlie jokingly asks Johnny as he lies in bed 'Did you say your prayers?', Johnny's sarcastic reply, 'why don't you tuck me in sweetie', again functions, in its self-conscious, mocking 'campness', to distance the characters from the 'inherently' camp Sammy. Charlie and Johnny's 'camp' exchange is in turn followed immediately by Charlie's spying on Teresa through her window as she undresses: a 'confirmation' of Charlie's heterosexuality that is completed by the scene cutting to Charlie and Teresa in bed at the hotel.

Once more, this invites an alternative reading: that Teresa enables a heterosexual displacement of Charlie and Johnny's homosexual complicity. Even so, the film's homoerotic suggestion veers uneasily between being an instrument and an object of criticism. A like contradictoriness infects the treatment of heterosexual relations.

VII

Charlie's spying on Teresa can be considered to reflect negatively upon the character's implied misogyny. Not only does his looking at the naked Teresa recall his earlier sexualized contemplation of Diane, but in both cases Charlie's objectifying and erotically fragmenting gaze functions with cinematic reflexivity to critique his actions; a connotation enhanced by Charlie's regard of Teresa being expressly voyeuristic. The power relation implicit in such looking is underlined at the hotel when, despite Teresa telling Charlie not to look, he peeks at her as she dresses, through his fingers as they mockingly 'cover' his eyes.

The 'transgressive' independence suggested both by Teresa's relationship with Charlie and by her desire to move uptown nevertheless makes her a potentially progressive character. As with the girl in *Who's That Knocking at My Door?*, Teresa's status as a sexually active but decent young woman reconciles and transcends the madonna–whore dichotomy.[31] The representation of her relationship with Charlie also reflects that of the relationship between the girl and J.R. in being shown comparatively to thrive outside their determining environment, at the hotel and at the beach.

Teresa, moreover, is the only character in *Mean Streets* who *wants* to leave Little Italy. This compares favourably with the implied insularity of the film's male characters. *En route* to the pool hall Tony's car stops at some traffic-lights and a vagrant, a figure of the 'alien' environment, wipes the windscreen. The reactions of Tony, Johnny and Charlie convey situational unease: Tony nervously glances at the tramp and makes an unfunny quip, Johnny bites his nails and Charlie looks anxiously for the lights to change. The ensuing exchange regarding the pool hall's whereabouts and Tony's admission that he does not know his 'way around' implies that once they leave Little Italy the characters become, literally, lost.

At the traffic-lights, two successive close-ups show Tony's finger pushing a button and the car's window closing.[32] This not only suggests the exclusion of otherness, but makes the car an extension of Little Italy's *protective* insularity. Despite its alienating oppressiveness, Little Italy is, for the male characters in *Mean Streets*, a site of the comforting and familiar; the regressive connotations of which intersect with both the environment's physical and psychic enclosure and Charlie's implied dependence on his mother. When at the beach Charlie refuses Teresa's invitation to move uptown with her, Teresa's response, 'What are you afraid of?', draws forth irritation, intimating that Teresa has hit on a weakness. As another instance of reactive male assertion, this returns us to the film's representation of masculinity; a link underscored when, as Charlie and Teresa argue in their tenement's hallway, her unanswered repetition of her question on the beach is closely followed by his upset refusal to admit his love. An unmasking of pathetic machismo, the moment suggests a neurotic fear of admitting need that, in a complement to the representation of violence as overcompensation, affirms aggressive masculinity to be a defensive denial of weakness, not an expression of strength.

Teresa's representation is not unequivocally positive. She is also suggested to be subject to the determining structures of Little Italy. The irreligious, secular outlook implied by her belief that you 'help yourself first' is reinforced when, as she flees Little Italy with Charlie and Johnny, Charlie speaks aloud to God: 'I guess you could safely say that things haven't gone so well tonight. But I'm trying, Lord, I'm trying.' An admittedly eccentric moment, it is nevertheless tendered as another heartfelt expression of frustrated moral striving, to which Teresa and Johnny react with laughter and ridicule. Granting that Johnny, as an id-figure, exists outside moral determination, this reflects critically upon Teresa, as does her racist nastiness toward a black chambermaid at the hotel. This is consistent with the racism displayed by most of the characters in the film. Hence Tony's upsetting of Michael when he derisively claims that he has seen a girlfriend of Michael 'kissing a nigger', or the same character's rationale for defining the woman whom Charlie 'propositions' as Jewish: 'She's in here every night with a different guy. You know how they are.' Racism likewise informs Charlie's voice-over as he watches Diane: 'She is really good looking.

But she's black... . Well, there's not much of a difference, anyway, is there? Well, is there?'. Yet Charlie does, typically, 'try', making a date with Diane, even though he does not keep it. Teresa's acculturation is in addition intimated by both her apparent acceptance of the necessity of keeping her relationship with Charlie a secret and her manifest difficulty in leaving Little Italy. Her nervous insistence at the beach that this time she is 'really gonna do it' betrays a residual guilt and unease. Similarly suggestive is her waiting for Charlie to leave with her, as though she needs his support.

More problematically, the *perspective* of the representation of Teresa and of her relationship with Charlie frequently becomes uncertain and tends to actualize the misogyny that the film would seem elsewhere critically to foreground. Consider Charlie's repeated threat to hit Teresa in the mouth. This first occurs 'playfully' at the hotel. It is reprised more aggressively when, following the scene at the restaurant with Giovanni, Teresa contests his decision not to see her 'for a while'. Although this can be related to the text's structure of intensifying repetition, as a pattern that clarifies Charlie's misogyny, the largely sympathetic emphasis on Charlie's personal dilemma tends to place Teresa's demurral as selfishly uncomprehending. The moment in effect rebukes the independent, 'uncontrolled' woman; further to which, Charlie's threat at the hotel is 'justified' by Teresa's racism. A like rebuke is implicit during the scene in which Michael accosts Teresa to enquire about Johnny's whereabouts. While Teresa's defiance – 'fuck you' and, after Michael spills her groceries, 'Would you just give me my fucking egg-plant' – typifies the character's outspokenness, Michael's riposte, 'you've got some mouth', attains, in the light of Teresa's language, a certain textual authority.

Almost unreadable in terms of perspective is the moment when Teresa, upon Charlie calling her 'a cunt', leaves the bed and stands, naked, before the hotel room's window. On one hand, her action possibly demonstrates her contempt for Charlie's opinion of her. On the other, it possibly substantiates it.

Teresa's epilepsy is another questionable element. A weakening of her strength and independence and, correspondingly, of her social and sexual threat, it is besides a somewhat distasteful limitation. We might likewise consider Johnny's insalubrious desire to watch Teresa 'have a seizure' and his asking Charlie what happens 'when she comes' – impulses redolent of denigratory objectification. Although in both cases Charlie seeks to 'correct' Johnny, we are tacitly invited, as throughout, to delight in Johnny's transgressiveness. A similar complicity is offered by other instances of the text's often self-consciously 'amusing' misogyny. For example, Johnny's off-hand dismissal of the young women at the pool hall ('You call those skanks girls?') or Tony's ironically obscene turning of the photograph of Michael's girlfriend upside-down as he drawls: 'I know this girl ...'. Here Johnny's symbolic status as Charlie's repressed self can be appropriated against the grain: he gives voice to what Charlie – and the text – cannot openly acknowledge. Indicatively, Johnny's impulse to climb into Teresa's apartment in his underwear and, hopefully, to see her having a fit is soon followed by Charlie, in his underwear, spying voyeuristically on Teresa.

The text, moreover, fulfils Johnny's desire to see Teresa have a seizure when she suffers an epileptic fit while trying to intervene as Charlie and Johnny fight on the tenement's landing. Once more implying the vunerability of Christian fellowship within Little Italy, the fight is similarly consistent with the relation of violence to reactive masculinity – having discovered Charlie and Teresa's relationship, Johnny declares that he is going to tell Giovanni, at which Charlie attempts to stop him physically. On Teresa's seizure, Johnny runs off, followed by Charlie, who precipitately and misogynistically leaves the still suffering Teresa with a neighbour (Catherine Scorsese).[33] With the exclusivity of the male couple ensured, homoerotic suggestion shifts from subtext to dramatic surface. After catching up with Johnny and slapping his face and pushing him against a metal shutter, Charlie tenderly asks 'Did I hurt you?', gently rubs his tearful friend's head and puts his arm around him as they move out of shot. Yet if this reflects upon Charlie's privileging of his relationship with Johnny, not only Charlie but *the film* would appear to forget Teresa. It is a textual exclusion that finds an ironic diegetic parallel in the misogynistic ejection of the woman whom Tony claims is Jewish: a repulsing of the racial other that analogously ensures the (temporary) male exclusivity of the bar.

Again, this invites a homoerotic reading: note Tony's grinning mateyness as he gives Charlie a congratulatory pat on the back. Nevertheless, the unacknowledged parallel of the textual and diegetic exclusion of the female is symptomatic of the (con)fusion of the critical, the complicit and the disavowed – of the explicitly problematized and implicitly embraced – that characterizes the treatment of sexuality and sexual politics in *Mean Streets*. This prompts consideration of Scorsese's own acculturation, and his seemingly still unresolved position as both Little Italy insider and filmmaking outsider; a consideration tacitly validated both by the biographical reference of *Mean Streets* and by its textual emphasis on determination. If this further lends a more negative inflection to the film's marginalization of women, it potentially accounts for a central thematic emphasis of Scorsese's authorial discourse: his films' stress on the tensions within *masculine* heterosexual identity. Moreover, the complex of the critical and the complicit heightens the interest and power of *Mean Streets* through providing a representation of Little Italy's masculine subculture that clarifies both its censurableness and its ambiguous lure.

VIII

The final scenes of *Mean Streets* bring the text to a resonantly inclusive climax. This again implies the links between New Hollywood Cinema and classical narrative, the resolution of which has been seen characteristically to result in an equilibrium 'on many codic levels' that produces an 'effect of harmony – almost in a musical sense' (Neale 1976: 120).[34] The Michael–Johnny plotline comes to a head at Tony's bar. Having incitingly spent most of the money that Charlie has given him to assuage Michael on 'a few rounds of drinks', Johnny tenders a $10 bill. Michael throws the bill back at Johnny, who sets light to it while speaking a scornful diatribe. Michael snaps, and grabs for Johnny across the bar's counter. Johnny pulls a (derisively unloaded) pistol and, with a stream of abuse, forces Michael back and then out of the bar.

The burning of the $10 bill continues the metaphoric relation of fire to Charlie's moral retribution for his secular desires. Fire here destroys the means by which Charlie had hoped to pay off Michael, and hence to keep his involvement with Johnny under wraps and his hopes of getting the restaurant intact. The fires of hell in turn fill the screen via the extract from *The Tomb of Ligeia*; a film that Charlie and Johnny are shown watching as they lay low.

When Charlie (finally) 'phones Teresa from the cinema lobby, a pistol in a poster for *Point Blank* (John Boorman, 1967) points toward his head. This foreshadows events to come, but also contributes to the suggestion of Charlie's increasing loss of control. While this is marked overtly by Charlie's failure to keep the lid on the Michael–Johnny situation, it is concisely underscored by a nice narrative transition. Charlie tells Teresa that he intends driving Johnny to 'Greenwood Lake'. Teresa asserts 'I'm coming with you'; Charlie disagrees – cut to a shot of Teresa sitting between Charlie and Johnny in the front seat of the car that Charlie has borrowed from Tony.

The climactic sequence of *Mean Streets* completes the film's repetition–intensification structure, bringing the text to a forceful and jarringly clarifying conclusion. As Charlie drives Johnny and Teresa out of New York, the desperation suggested by the speed of their progress and his touchiness is compounded when he jumps a red light; another signifier of uncontrol. Prior to and complementing this, both Johnny and Teresa question Charlie's knowledge of their route: insularity has become endangering. Tension is augmented aurally by the introduction on the soundtrack as they cross into Brooklyn of the empathetic electric energy of '"Live Cream, Volume Two"' (Scorsese 1975: 7). Another car pulls alongside from behind, forcing that driven by Charlie to its left and drawing an angry response from Johnny. There follows an intensive, and intensifying, flurry of close shots: of Michael, revealed to be the driver of the other car; of the hitman Shorty (Scorsese), as he fires a pistol; of Johnny, suffering from a gaping neck wound; of Teresa, cowering with fear; and of Charlie, trying to control the car with blood pouring from his right hand. Johnny half-leans, half-falls out of the speeding car in agony, while on the soundtrack his groans are mixed with Teresa's cries, Charlie's shouts of 'Johnny' and the wailing acceleration of the music, that 'renders' the situation's exigency.[35] The unsettling passage concludes with four rapidly edited medium shots that, interspersed with another close shot of Charlie struggling for control, show, disjunctively, the car hitting other parked vehicles, mounting the sidewalk and crashing into a fire hydrant – at which there is a sudden, counterpointing silence.

The scene's graphic forcefulness crowns the text's progressively negative representation of violence, functioning structurally as a heightened and conclusive restatement of the salutarily shocking painfulness of the shooting in the bar. The scene also completes the critical relation of violence to overcompensatory masculine aggression. Reflecting previous violent outbursts, the situation involves if not friends, then associates, and is predicated upon insults. Apart from the slight that is the $10 bill, Johnny proclaims Michael's previously intimated insufficiency, asserting that he can borrow money from Michael without having to pay it back. If Michael's lunge toward Johnny implies a reactive bid to refute Johnny's words, then Johnny's pulling of the phallic pistol makes the situation's psycho-sexual connotations relatively explicit. This is complemented by the sexualized tenor of Johnny's verbal insults ('I fuck you right where you breathe', 'fuck face', 'motherfucker'). These further contain what is, given Michael's representation, a marked homosexual implication ('asshole', 'I'll put this [the pistol] up your ass' and, as Johnny gestures with his groin, 'This is for you asshole'). Likewise noteworthy is Johnny's repeated use of 'jerk-off'. A term redolent of sexual inadequacy, it comprises another accumulatively significant motif. The term is first used by Michael at the bar when he describes Johnny as 'the biggest jerk-off around', an attack that – signalling pertinence – Charlie sharply contests. Later, Michael rhetorically asks Charlie as they argue 'What do I look like, a jerk?', while Charlie stresses to Johnny the need at least to meet Michael at the bar because: 'This way he doesn't think that you're trying to make a jerk-off out of him'. Finally, when Michael's car pulls alongside, Johnny shouts 'Hey, jerk', an insult answered with gunfire. However, while the incident 'proves' Michael's potency, it is Shorty who wields the pistol. It is also Scorsese who shoots his own *alter ego*.[36]

That Charlie is shot in his right hand actualizes the desired retribution implicit in his repeated placing of the same hand over flames. Symbolically, the wound suggests castration, an apt punishment both for Charlie's inability to give up his morally compromising secular/patriarchal desires and for his 'transgressive' relationship with Teresa. Although Teresa is not shot, after the car crashes her blooded right hand is shown lying outside its shattered windscreen. That Teresa is injured through Michael's phallic imposition recalls the moment at the hotel when Charlie holds (significantly) his right hand in a pistol shape and, accompanied by the superimposed sound of a pistol, 'shoots' her. As this foreshadows the film's climax, so it underscores Charlie's implication in her pain. Yet as Teresa's hand injury mirrors Charlie's wound, so it implies an analogous 'castration' as punishment for her sexual 'transgressiveness'. Moreover, if during the climax gunfire metonymically replaces hellfire, so the water that floods the area from the hydrant sustains that element's symbolic cleansing function.

In addition to its Freudian connotations, Charlie's wound visually evokes the close-up of the sculpted right hand of Christ, upon which lies a red flower, that forms part of the *pietà* before which Charlie stands in the church.[37] The implied association between Charlie and Christ *crucified* contributes to the suggestion that Charlie's climactic agony constitutes a kind of martyrdom.[38] In plot terms, Charlie's wound is conditional upon his refusal to abandon Johnny, to deny his Christian obligation, no matter how compromised. Another parallel is invited between Charlie and San Gennaro, the Neapolitan saint and martyr who is celebrated throughout the film.

Raymond Williams writes: 'Martyrdom now is defensive ... there is not a renewal of our general life, but often a positive renewal of our general guilt' (1966: 157–8). Such moral reflection would appear to be sought by Charlie's suffering. Not only does Charlie's wound imply a mutual moral and pragmatic 'correction', but the climactic incident, as it results in Johnny's and Teresa's suffering, and implicitly problematizes his obtaining of the restaurant, derails both his Christian and his sexual and material inclinations and desires. The situation is, moreover, attributable tacitly to Charlie's inability to choose between or reconcile his warring impulses. The painful consequences of this suggest a pair of complementary connotations that consummate the text's 'Christian' perspective. On one hand, as the scene conclusively declares the impossibility of fusing the religious and the secular within Little Italy, it invites us to reflect critically both upon the represented milieu and, as it implies the culpability of Charlie's moral indecisiveness, it invites us to reflect critically upon the character.

As Charlie's wound evokes the scene in the church, so we are similarly returned to the beginning of *Mean Streets* by the sound of a siren as a police car arrives at the crash. Specifically, the sound occurs during the pre-credit scene and the introductions of Michael, Johnny and Charlie – that is, in those scenes representing the male protagonists involved in the film's climax. Thus placed as a foreshadowing device, the siren retrospectively evokes a sense of fated inevitability; albeit this is once more implicitly consequent upon Charlie's irresolution. Notwithstanding, the suggested fatedness is reciprocated by the recollection of the opening formally implying the narrative cyclicity common to Scorsese's early films. It is, moreover, a cyclicity that has a decidedly negative inflection. First seen rising from his bed, Charlie ends up on his knees, while whereas early on Johnny is seen running gleefully from the exploded mailbox in daylight, he is last seen staggering in agony down a darkened alley. By contrast, at the beginning Michael is embarrassingly inept, at the end he is destructively effectual.

Cyclicity is underscored by the film's closing montage sequence. This intercuts shots of the scene of the crash with shots of the Feast of San Gennaro and of Tony, Giovanni, Diane and Michael and Shorty. The implication is that Little Italy life goes on unchanged, regardless of what has happened to Charlie and the others. As Giovanni watches television, we are given a clip from *The Big Heat* (Fritz Lang, 1953) that shows Dave Bannion (Glenn Ford) pulling his dead wife, Katie (Jocelyn Brando), from the wreckage of their car. A 'fictional' situation reflective of diegetic events in Brooklyn – where the injured Teresa is shown being helped from the crashed car by firemen – its provision of dismissive irony is heightened by Giovanni's relaxed, domestic comfort (floral wallpaper, easy chair, glass of spirits, shirt sleeves ...). That Giovanni smokes yet another phallic cigar again signifies his patriarchal dominance and contrasts with Charlie's 'castration'. The shots of Tony in the bar's toilet and of Michael's car parked on some wasteground beside a flyover evoke cyclicity by returning the characters to the sites where they were first seen. That Tony washes his hands maintains his implied difference from Charlie. Not only does it contrast with Charlie's troubled washing of his hands as Giovanni despatches the assassin, but the logic of the editing implies a characteristically pragmatic abandonment of his friends. Tony's control over water suitably reverses Charlie's helplessness before the hydrant's flood. Diane is shown, alone, sitting in a café outside 'the neighborhood', still marginalized because of her race and gender. The shots of the Feast of San Gennaro represent the singing of the song 'O Marienello': 'It ended every fiesta on the streets... That meant "go home"' (Macklin 1975: 27). Go home, of course, to return the next year.

IX

When the car hits the hydrant, a spout of water shoots vertically upward. This recalls a similar car crash during the gang-war sequence of *Scarface* (Howard Hawks, 1932). Moreover, with Charlie represented as caught between criminal materialism and Christian morality, his dilemma suggests a central ideological opposition of the gangster film. More particularly, Charlie's situation implicitly replays the gangster–priest conflict explicitly played out between Rocky (James Cagney) and Jerry (Pat O'Brien) in *Angels with Dirty Faces* (Michael Curtiz, 1938). Extending this, *Mean Streets* contains numerous other elements of the gangster film genre, whether one considers iconography (suits, guns, an often night-time urban setting ...), characters (Giovanni as godfather, Charlie as 'family' heir, Shorty as hitman ...), narrative situations (meetings, deals, threats, shootings, a car chase ...), or its 'Mafia dynasty' subplot.

Such generic reference has been seen to work with New Hollywood Cinema's posited 'conservatism of style' to 'swallow up art-film borrowings' and hence to tame their formal 'disruptiveness' (Bordwell and Staiger 1985: 375). Undoubtedly, genre is another way through which the 'difference' of New Hollywood Cinema was commercially circumscribed. No less than the attacks on New Hollywood Cinema's formal recidivism, however, criticism of its generic status is contextually inexpedient. For much New Hollywood Cinema genre provided a framework within which ideological and formal challenge could be both expressed and contained within familiar, commercially acceptable boundaries.[39] It is a challenge embodied specifically in the generic revision noted in relation to the country thieves cycle: that is, a critical reworking of generic conventions that, correspondingly, problematizes their implicit ideological assumptions. Symptomatic of the USA's contested historical situation, it is a development that extends the formal debt that New Hollywood Cinema owes to the *nouvelle vague*. Moreover, as genre thus moves from being predominantly a means of representation to being, in part, an object of representation, the generic revision of New Hollywood Cinema has been seen to comprise – in another sidelight upon its theoretical dismissal – the most extensive and coherent phase of reflexive and intrinsically modernist filmmaking in Hollywood's history.

Mean Streets transposes the ideological emphasis of the classical gangster film by representing the Mafia not as a criminal 'other' but as the dominant, patriarchal norm. Accordingly, Charlie's Christian conscience is – in generic terms – unwontedly placed as transgressive. In turn, instead of morality overcoming gangsterism, *Mean Streets* ends with Charlie in effect defeated by Little Italy's criminal mores.

Generic revision further intersects with the film's other formal qualities. On one hand, its documentary emphasis strips gangsterism of its generic glamour before a revelation of its shabby, workaday actuality.[40] On the other, *Mean Streets* tends to shift stress from gangster action to a reflection upon, and questioning of, its connotations; a shift attributable to the reciprocity of its comparative narrative intransitivity and indecisive central character.

The goal-directed, cause–effect logic of classical narrative is perceived to reflect certain ideological premises. Namely, it implies 'a fundamentally affirmative attitude to the world it depicts' whereby 'whatever the problem, one can *do* something about it' (Elsaesser 1975: 14). That this was an attitude increasingly difficult to sustain during the sixties and early seventies suggestively informs New Hollywood Cinema's assumption of art cinema's looser narrative form. For if this privileges theme before plot, so 'plot-linearity and its corollary, the goal-oriented hero' becomes 'replaced by narrative fragmentation and troubled, introspective protagonists' (Neale 1976: 117). As embodied by Charlie in *Mean Streets*, this troubled introspection in addition demonstrates a textually specific shift from Hollywood's customary melodramatic approach to a tragic aesthetic. In short, instead of a unified (melodramatic) character who unreflectively responds to external forces in a divided, manichaean world, we are given, as Charlie disastrously defers decisive action, a (largely tragic) figure who is torn between – and ruminates upon – internalized, divergent impulses and desires.[41]

This heightens the potential progressiveness of *Mean Streets*. Melodrama has a facility – as Hollywood cinema widely demonstrates – for expressing and mediating ideological changes, conflicts and contradictions, but its characters remain *subject* to external forces. By contrast, tragic dividedness 'implies moral choice' (Walker 1982: 29). This is, it suggests *subjective agency*, the possibility of acting upon the world. Consequently, 'tragedy here emerges as a progressive form' (*ibid.*). Moreover: 'Important tragedy seems to occur, neither in periods of real stability, nor in periods of open and decisive conflict. Its most common historical setting is the period preceding the substantial breakdown and transformation of an important culture' (Williams 1966: 54).

If this proposed setting once again evokes the ideological context generative of New Hollywood cinema, it is precisely figured by the representation of Little Italy in *Mean Streets*. In a modulation indicative of broader social developments, the cultural contestation implicit in J.R.'s relationship with the girl in *Who's That Knocking at My Door?* is in *Mean Streets* suggested to be much more pervasive. It is also, in a reflection of both the country thieves cycle and much other New Hollywood Cinema, predicated upon a generational split. Whereas the names of the older characters are Italian, those of the younger characters are Anglicized: this despite Giovanni remarking that Johnny is 'named after me'. Similarly, whereas the older characters tend to speak Italian, the younger characters invariably speak English – this obtains even when Giovanni speaks in Italian to Charlie. It is a generational opposition mapped on to the film's intensive use of music. Rock and pop is associated with the younger characters and with actions and attitudes that challenge Little Italy norms. Italian opera and traditional music is associated with older characters and with actions and attitudes indicative of established Italian-American mores. Generational difference likewise informs Teresa's desire to move uptown, a decision contended (explicitly) by her parents and (tacitly) by Giovanni. Further, whereas the 'disruptive' female in *Who's That Knocking at My Door?* originates from outside Little Italy, that in *Mean Streets* comes from 'the neighborhood'.

Implicit throughout, these generational connotations accumulatively create a resonant sense of a dominant culture in a condition of embattled flux. Nevertheless, it is still a culture that, as the film's conclusion confirms, is difficult successfully either to challenge or to escape. While Michael's retribution is textually consistent with the established pattern of masculine aggression, it also conforms to the no less reactive and overcompensatory violence by which the dominant order, across New Hollywood Cinema, conclusively reasserts its authority. Apart from the examples furnished by the country thieves cycle, one might cite the endings of, say, *Easy Rider* or *Butch Cassidy and the Sundance Kid* (George Roy Hill, 1969). Once more, this can be considered testimony to the perceived threat posed to the dominant order. However, although the 'substantial breakdown and transformation' of the dominant American ideology seemed, during the sixties and early seventies, a distinct possibility, it was precluded. Discussing this, Wood has noted that while American society 'appeared to be in a state of advanced disintegration', no alternative and 'coherent social/economic' – and necessarily socialist – 'programme emerged' (1980: 26). This lack can be adduced as another, and less affirmative, influence upon New Hollywood Cinema's downgrading of linearity and goal-orientation, not to mention many of its films' assertively irresolute endings.[42] Moreover, as the ideological challenge of the sixties and early seventies was, by the end of the seventies, largely recuperated, so there can be charted an analogous recuperation of New Hollywood Cinema.

6

Into the Mainstream: *Alice Doesn't Live Here Anymore*

Alice Doesn't Live Here Anymore beings with a prologue that shows Alice as 'a young girl' (Mia Bendixsen) defiantly declaring that she can 'sing better than Alice Faye'. Cut to Socorro, New Mexico, and Alice (Ellen Burstyn) '27 years later', a housewife in her mid-thirties with a boorish husband, Donald (Billy Green Bush), and a precocious 11-year-old son, Tommy (Alfred Lutter). Donald is killed in a truck crash, and Alice takes to the road with Tommy with the aim of returning to her childhood home of Monterey, California, and of rekindling her brief singing career (one date at a hotel). Lack of money forces Alice to seek work *en route*, and she gets a job as a bar singer in Phoenix, Arizona. This ends when Alice and Tommy have to flee the violence of Ben (Harvey Keitel), with whom Alice had become sexually involved. Alice and Tommy drive to Tucson, where Alice has to work as a waitress. Through this she meets David (Kris Kristofferson), a rancher. Although an argument threatens their relationship, David offers to take Alice to Monterey himself. The film ends with a scene between Alice and Tommy in which Alice admits her decision to stay in Tucson with David.

II

The script for *Alice Doesn't Live Here Anymore* was written by Robert Getchell. Originally sent to Shirley MacLaine, it was next optioned by producer Peter Thomas, before David Susskind paid $1500 for a three-month option. Warner Bros, meanwhile, were eager to build on the success of Burstyn in *The Exorcist* (William Friedkin, 1973), for which she had been nominated for a Best Actress Oscar. The studio offered Burstyn the chance to select a project for which, if 'not extremely expensive' (Thompson 1976b: 142), she could choose the director and have script approval. Burstyn's agent contacted Thomas, who suggested Getchell's script.

Asked by Burstyn about 'the best young filmmakers', Francis Ford Coppola suggested that she see *Mean Streets* (Howard 1975: 22). On viewing the film, Burstyn got Warner Bros' production chief John Calley to send the script to Scorsese, despite reservations about what, on the evidence of *Mean Streets*, Scorsese 'knew about women' (Kelly 1992: 83).[1] During production Scorsese drew upon the experience of a number of women employed on the project. Apart from Burstyn and the other actresses, Sandra Weintraub, who is credited as associate producer, production designer Toby Carr Rafelson and editor Marcia Lucas were present during shooting, 'and when a line or response rang false, these women were free to criticize and suggest alternatives' (Rosen 1975: 42).

Lucas was the first editor since Thelma Schoonmaker to be employed substantially on a film directed by Scorsese. Having largely cut *Boxcar Bertha* and *Mean Streets* himself, Scorsese nevertheless supervised the editing closely, discussing any changes and even cutting some scenes himself – 'the music scenes, the violent scenes, the kitchen scene' (Howard 1975: 26). During post-production Scorsese was also involved in setting up his documentary on his parents, *Italianamerican* (1974), and in discussing a project about Native Americans with Marlon Brando. The first of Scorsese's films to be financed by a major, *Alice Doesn't Live Here Anymore* evinces a markedly greater scale of production than any of this preceding work. Consider the film's prologue. For two minutes' screen time the scene cost $85 000, excluding crew salaries; that is, nearly twice the overall cost of the extended production of *Who's That Knocking at My Door?*.

With the exception of the prologue, that was the last scene 'to be shot on the old Columbia sound-stages on Gower Street' (Scorsese 1981: 137), *Alice Doesn't Live Here Anymore* was filmed in and around Tucson over eight weeks in the spring of 1974. Initially budgeted at $1.6 million, the final negative cost was between $1.7–2 million. Overage accrued from a combination of the addition of a week's shooting to film and refilm three or four extra scenes and Scorsese falling ill during post-production. Before filming there was a three-month pre-production period, including two weeks of intensive rehearsal immediately prior to shooting.

Again this compares favourably with the variously pinched and frenzied production of Scorsese's previous projects. However, the making of *Alice Doesn't Live Here Anymore* was attended by other institutional pressures. Warner Bros forced the film into production without a finalized shooting script; a move attributable to the need to ensure that the film, to be eligible for the 1974 Oscars, be completed and shown theatrically before the year's end. Lucas was present on location to enable Scorsese to start editing during shooting. Despite this, the initial cut ran a commercially unacceptable 196 minutes. This had to be cut drastically to allow the film 'to fit in the two-hour times-lot in regular theatres so most people from ages twelve to eighty could see it' (Macklin 1975: 16). Cuts were in particular made to the early scenes representing Alice's marriage, an emphasis informed by the responses of preview audiences.[2]

Alice Doesn't Live Here Anymore was released in a cut running 112 minutes. Unlike *Mean Streets*, it was carefully distributed. After an initial Los Angeles release in December 1974, the film was opened in 60 cities in January 1975, with an emphasis on suburban theatres: 'Get the house-wives to go first and that sort of thing' (Scorsese 1975: 13). The approach paid off – *Alice Doesn't Live Here Anymore* was a box-office hit.

III

The concern with the film's accessibility reflects its market status as a commercial, mainstream product. Moreover, *Alice Doesn't Live Here Anymore* was made as the majors sought to re-establish their economic stability following the disastrous period 1968–72, and can be considered – institutionally, formally and ideologically – in relation to the recuperation of New Hollywood Cinema. Not that New Hollywood Cinema was ever more than a part of Hollywood's output; even during its 'heyday' many of Hollywood's box-office successes were formally and ideologically conservative – witness the likes of *Barefoot in the Park* (Gene Saks, 1967) or *True Grit* (Henry Hathaway, 1969). Nevertheless, David A. Cook has claimed that it was the 'enormous popular success in 1970 of two conventional formula films, *Love Story* (Arthur Hiller) and *Airport* (George Seaton)' that 'restored Hollywood's faith in the big-budget, mass-appeal feature' (1996: 933).

The reversion to more conventional filmmaking was in addition informed by the delayed structural ramifications of the majors coming under conglomerate ownership. Although conglomeration dates from 1952, and Decca's acquisition of Universal, it came to a head in the mid-to late sixties. By 1974, all but two of the majors were part of larger corporate bodies, and the exceptions – Columbia and Twentieth Century-Fox – were in the process of becoming media conglomerates themselves. Warner Bros, for example, had in 1967 merged with Canadian-based film sales company Seven Arts to form Warner-Seven Arts. This was taken over in 1969 by Kinney National Services, with the company changing its name to Warner Communications in 1971.[3] As a business strategy, conglomeration seeks to diminish risk through diversification. For the economically embattled majors, the belief was that conglomeration would maintain their cash flow during periods of downturn. In return, the often unglamorous parent company sought to partake of the reflected celebrity of Hollywood – in 1969 Kinney National Services' interests were 'primarily in car rentals, car parks, construction and funeral homes' (Maltby 1998: 31–2).[4] However, by the early seventies corporate parents had become concerned about the size of the majors' losses and determined to set their finances on a firmer footing.

The corporate rationalization of Hollywood involved changes in studio management. Instead of the instinctive, 'charismatic' control of the legendary studio heads – a trend maintained by interim successors like Mike Frankovich (Columbia 1963–67) – there was installed a newer breed of 'professional', more business-minded executives. Frequently recruited from outside the film industry, these executives have been represented as being motivated primarily, or even solely, by the need to make profits to keep their jobs. Which is not to claim that the majors have not always been interested in profits. There was, however, a definite shift of emphasis, attributable, according to Chris Hugo, to 'the dictates of con-glomerate economic thinking, which demand ... lower risks and steadier profit curves' (1980: 49). Undoubtedly the reforms helped to salvage the majors financially, but their longer-term effects have in general been bemoaned: 'The phantom promise of "artistic freedom" offered when the old Hollywood structure collapsed has turned into something of an economic nightmare where costs, salaries, profits, and reputations are juggled and manipulated, with the film itself all but disappearing in a mass of contracts and bookkeeping' (Kolker 1988: 6).

The shifts in management style have been complemented by changes in management structure. The period saw the introduction of much top and middle management, 'layer upon layer of decision-making' (Laskos 1981: 32). This affords another check against spontaneous, and perhaps commercially ill-advised, decisions, further lessening the possibility of 'untoward' projects. It has also been seen to have contributed to what has been perceived to be the virtual interchangeability of both the majors and their product; a corporate 'anonymity' hardly mitigated by the heavy and frequently incestuous turnover of executives since the early seventies. A complaint of older executives was that conglomerate owners appeared to believe that filmmaking could be reduced to the 'impersonal' efficiency of other corporate divisions.[5]

The rise of the package as the majors' preferred mode of film financing accords with such rationalization. Projects have come to be chiefly developed through the combination of various 'elements' (star, property, director, producer and so on) into a potentially bankable 'package' that it is hoped will attract studio interest. The package constitutes an attempt to control box-office unpredictability by predicating projects upon the elements' track records: gambles are taken upon proven commercial power. The centrality of the package has been instrumental to the increasing influence of agents within Hollywood: 'Since the early sixties when the old studio system disintegrated, the agent has been in a prime position of power. Representing writers, directors, and actors, he can put together the nucleus of a project even before the studio chief sees a treatment' (Monaco 1984: 46). This has led to agents 'crossing over' to become executives and studio heads. Among the first to do so was Ted Ashley, head of Warner Bros, 1969–80. During the fifties and sixties Ashley had seen his Ashley Famous Agency become one of the most successful agencies in Hollywood and, upon Kinney National Services taking over Warner-Seven Arts, he was hired as the man whom it was believed – correctly – could make the studio profitable.

As a package, *Alice Doesn't Live Here Anymore* presents some characteristic features. That it was founded, in the first place, on Burstyn's bankability reflects the central importance to most packages of stars, the elements that are usually the main box-office draw. Getchell's script brought together Burstyn and Susskind; who, by virtue of his option, became the film's co-producer (with Audrey Maas). The package became especially attractive when Scorsese was approached to direct: '*Mean Streets* was going to open. They had no idea how good or bad it was going to do financially but we got incredible reviews at the time' (Scorsese 1975: 3). While in package philosophy there is 'general agreement that two strong elements are enough to close a deal', the combination of 'a hit star and a hit director form the perfect equation' (Pirie 1981: 47).

IV

Writing of New Hollywood Cinema, Steve Neale states that 'the "package" system' sees the director being 'more overtly institutionalised in a role analogous to author' (1976: 118). This returns us to New Hollywood cinema's art-cinema antecedents, and, specifically, to art cinema's implication with Romantic ideologies of personal expression. Not only is art cinema 'marked at a textual level by the inscription of features that function as marks of enunciation – and, hence, as signifiers of an authorial voice' (Neale 1981: 13–14), but it is mainly sold via *auteur* name. Timothy Corrigan describes this 'auteurist marketing of movies' as guaranteeing 'a relationship between audience and movie in which an intentional and authorial agency governs, as a kind of brand-name vision that precedes and succeeds the film, the way that movie is seen and received' (1991: 102). This relationship has served to differentiate art cinema as 'personal' statement from the 'industrialized' product of Hollywood; a differentation appropriated by New Hollywood Cinema.

Conglomerated Hollywood has also 'bought the idea' of authorship 'in many ways', an investment that has been related to the consequences of the studios' structural reorganization: 'Part of the reason why Hollywood itself appeared to go for the idea may be that the disappearance or decline of any distinguishing studio identities for films ... left a kind of vacuum which director identity helped to fill' (Hillier 1993: 4). Nevertheless, conglomerated Hollywood's embrace of authorship is very much a commercial decision that, while it plays off notions of film as individual 'artistic' expression, is founded primarily upon the author's market function. Indicative of this dissimulative interplay is the director interview. The practice 'might be described according to the action of promotion and explanation: it is the writing and explaining of a film through the promotion of a certain intentional self; it is frequently the commercial dramatization of self as the motivating agent of textuality' (Corrigan 1991: 108). In promoting *Alice Doesn't Live Here Anymore*, Scorsese engaged in what was (for the time) a heavy interview round, during which we can perceive the establishment of certain elements of Scorsese's 'star image'.[6] For matters at hand, there is significantly an emphasis on Scorsese's necessary personal engagement with his filmmaking in general and with *Alice Doesn't Live Here Anymore* in particular.[7] Scorsese, however, has subsequently dismissed *Alice Doesn't Live Here Anymore* as 'a business proposition' (Ehrenstein 1992: 42) – 'I needed to do something that was a major studio film for a certain amount of money and to prove that I can direct women. It was as simple as that' (DeCurtis 1990: 108).

If this foregrounds the tendentiousness of the author as commercial construct, Scorsese's dismissal of *Alice Doesn't Live Here Anymore* itself suggests the adduction of a 'preferred' *oeuvre*. *Alice Doesn't Live Here Anymore* has, moreover, been proposed as one of the 'very few' cases 'on which the totality of a film can be laid at the door of the star' (Dyer 1979: 175). Apart from selecting the project and its director, Burstyn 'was very active in the casting' (Thompson 1976b: 142), suggesting Lelia Goldoni and Diane Ladd as well as bringing Scorsese's attention to Jodie Foster. One of Burstyn's reasons for asking Scorsese to direct was that in *Mean Streets* the 'level of acting was consistently high all the way' (Gardner 1975: 34). *Alice Doesn't Live Here Anymore* can be read as a showcase for Burstyn's acting talents, a series of set-pieces that demonstrate her versatility as she plays Alice as oppressed housewife, as wisecracking mother, as bar singer, as reluctant waitress, as tipsy lover and so on.

Diegetically, the relative ostensiveness of Burstyn's role-playing in each of these situations can be referred to her character's status as a would-be or actual performer.[8] Textually, it reflects the dualism of the naturalistic and the actorly that characterizes Method performance. Burstyn is associated with the Actors Studio, as are Keitel, Bush, Goldoni, Ladd, Lane Bradbury and Vic Tayback. The making of the film in addition saw an extension of the structured improvisation used in relation to *Mean Streets*. Another influence on the film's emphasis on the performative, improvisation began during casting and continued during both rehearsals and shooting. It can further be considered a factor on the film entering production without a settled script: improvisations were videotaped and sent to Getchell, who integrated them into the screenplay. Burstyn's performance secured her the Best Actress Oscar that she failed to obtain for *The Exorcist*. Getchell was nominated for Best Original Screenplay and Ladd for Best Supporting Actress.[9]

V

As the promotion of *Alice Doesn't Live Here Anymore* evokes auteurism's commercial appropriation, so the film can be seen stylistically to approach Robert B. Ray's contention that the mainstream 'quickly co-opted the power of all but the most radical departures' of the *nouvelle vague* by 'converting' them 'into mere cosmetic flourishes assimilable by Hollywood's conventional forms' (1985: 294). The *mise-en-scène* of *Alice Doesn't Live Here Anymore* lacks the mutual documentary-expressionist connotations of that of *Mean Streets* and instead presents a more normative location-based realism. Expressionist connotation is, likewise, largely absent from Scorsese's by now familiar employment of certain *nouvelle vague* tropes and techniques (jump-cuts, 'unmotivated' camera movement, elliptical sequence construction). Consider the scene in which Alice learns of Donald's death. As Alice talks in her back yard with her neighbour and friend, Bea (Goldoni), they are filmed in a series of slow, vaguely unsettling, 'unmotivated' lateral tracks. Alice goes inside to answer the 'phone and, as she is told of Donald's accident and begins to weep, three jump-cuts bring her abruptly into close-up. In *Mean Streets* similar tracking shots and jump-cuts transmit Charlie's subjectivity. Here they solely constitute narration. The lateral tracks work as a foreshadowing device that, providing a portentousness excessive to the immediate situation, is fulfilled by the news of Donald's death, while the jump-cuts dramatically heighten the moment of Alice's agony. In short, the correlated first- and third-person perspectives of *Mean Streets* are replaced by a more customary third-person narration; a point of view defined by George M. Wilson's notion of the 'implied film maker' (1986: 134). Scorsese's narration in *Alice Doesn't Live Here Anymore* typically '*asserts* the existence of certain fictional states of affairs by showing them to the audience demonstratively ... we feel ... a constant guidance and outside direction of our perception toward the range of predetermined fictional facts which we are meant to see' (*ibid.*: 133).[10]

Notwithstanding, *Alice Doesn't Live Here Anymore* does occasionally veer toward the expressionist. Witness the three scenes in which Alice plays the piano and sings. During these the camera tracks repeatedly around her, conveying a sense of her involvement and release as she gets 'into' the music. The first of the scenes, in which Alice practises prior to taking to the road, opens with an unsteady hand-held medium shot of Alice sitting at her piano. When she starts to sing, the camera cuts closer and begins to track around her. While initially jerky, as Alice grows in confidence the camera, too, starts to flow. The overall movement, across shots, matches Alice's progression from apprehension to engagement, an engagement shared by the spectator *via* the camerawork. A similar approach marks Alice's audition in a bar. During this the tracking picks up speed in tune with both the tempo of her medley and her increasing conviction, with character and spectator becoming 'lost' in the music. The tracking is again repeated when she sings 'I've Got a Crush on You'. The scenes are among those edited by Scorsese himself.

As a film directed by Scorsese, *Alice Doesn't Live Here Anymore* once more makes extensive use of various popular musics. However, with the exception of the scenes of Alice singing, their textual integration, while intelligent, tends to lack the particular intensiveness that distinguishes the use of music in *Who's That Knocking at My Door?* and *Mean Streets*. Music helps to define different characters. Alice is associated with romantic standards, Tommy with seventies pop and David with country music not dissimilar to that performed, extra-diegetically, by Kristofferson. Individual songs in addition supply specific lyrical and/or tonal commentary. When Alice and Tommy take to the road we hear Elton John's 'Daniel' ('Daniel is travelling tonight …'), while when Alice rehearses she plays Richard Rodgers and Lorenz Hart's 'Where or When', a song whose lyrical concern with *déjà-vu* reflects her attempt to revive former aspirations. The song's wistful tone empathetically reinforces the sense of the ressurection of past dreams, a tonal function differentially exemplified by the deployment of the rasping rock of Mott the Hoople's 'All the Way from Memphis' to establish familial tensions in the first Socorro scene.

VI

The narrative of *Alice Doesn't Live Here Anymore* would appear to trace a linear and affirmatory trajectory: Alice moves from her unfulfilling marriage, via her entanglement with Ben, to a relationship with the more prosperous and grounded David. This nevertheless splits into a coherent 'three-act' structure. Roughly conforming the film's beginning, middle and end, each act centres upon a different location – Socorro, Phoenix and Tucson – and in each Alice's relationship with a different man is matched by her friendship with three different women – Bea, (briefly) Rita (Bradbury), Ben's wife, and fellow waitress Flo (Ladd). Through such parallels the acts become mutually reflective, creating patterns that problematize the film's 'positive ' development.

The three acts exhibit a shifting generic emphasis. The first act implies the melodramatic sub-genre of the woman's film. Historically, the woman's film stems from Hollywood's attempt to serve the large female audiences of the thirties and forties. Maria LaPlace lists some of its defining elements: 'The woman's film is distinguished by its female protagonist, female point of view and its narrative which most often revolves around the traditional realms of women's experience: the familial, the domestic, the romantic – those arenas where love, emotion and relationships take precedence over action and events' (1987: 139). Specifically symptomatic is the incident in which Alice dispiritedly leans her head against her dining-room's French doors before banging her hands against them in a fit of frustration and poking her head outside defiantly to shout: 'Socorro sucks'. For Mary Ann Doane, within the woman's film: 'images of women looking through windows or waiting at windows abound. The window has special import in terms of the social and symbolic positioning of the woman – the window is the interface between inside and outside, the feminine space of the family and reproduction and the masculine space of production' (1987: 138). As Alice subsequently crosses this interface and enters the 'masculine space of production', so the film suggests a familiar woman's film plotline; that of a woman striving for success and independence within a patriarchal environment, an attempt that is within the woman's film usually, if variously, recuperated.

The woman's film informs *Alice Doesn't Live Here Anymore* throughout (hence the film's credits – red 'handwriting' over a light blue satin backdrop). However, in the third act the influence of the woman's film both crosses with and is at times subordinated to that of screwball comedy. This is especially apparent during the scenes in Mel and Ruby's Café, a setting for often frenzied and farcical comedy that, with generic typicality, fuses the physical (for example, the almost slapstick incompetence of the waitress Vera/Valerie Curtin) and the verbal (Flo's ribald repartee).

The second act of *Alice Doesn't Live Here Anymore* privileges the film's relation to the road movie. This is foregrounded stylistically by the sequences that show Alice and Tommy travelling from Socorro to Phoenix and from Phoenix to Tucson – 'we cut several times within each sequence from inside the car to long shots of the car moving through landscape, while the soundtrack consists of casual conversation and a rock song' (Geraghty 1976: 42). Although the road movie has, in various guises, a longstanding cinematic history, it attains a particular prominence within New Hollywood Cinema. Apart from the country thieves cycle, numerous other examples of New Hollywood Cinema – including *Easy Rider*, *Two-Lane Blacktop* (Monte Hellman, 1971) and *Vanishing Point* (Richard C. Sarafian, 1971) – can be characterized as road movies.[11] This is unsurprising. The road movie's loose narrative structure and frequently vague or nominal goal-orientation epitomizes the posited relationship between New Hollywood Cinema's formal difference and its refusal of ideological assent. Steven Cohan and Ina Rae Hark, moreover, write: 'Key moments in the history of the road movie tend to come in periods of upheaval and dislocation, such as the Great Depression, or in periods whose dominant ideologies generate fantasies of escape and opposition, as in the late 1960s' (1997: 2). However, whereas previous road narratives recurrently represent women as part either of a heterosexual couple (as in, for instance, *It Happened One Night* (Frank Capra, 1934) or the outlaw-couple cycle) or a larger peripatetic grouping (as in *The Grapes of Wrath*, John Ford, 1940), and while such tendencies are continued by the country thieves films, the post-*Easy Rider* road movie predominantly centres upon male protagonists unencumbered by explicit romantic, domestic or communal ties. Not only in most seventies road movies are women 'lucky to be mere bodies, way stations where the heroes can relieve themselves and resume their journey', but rarely 'is a woman, let alone a wife, permitted to explode against the inequities of her situation or embark on her own journey of liberation' (Haskell 1974: 336). By contrast, *Alice Doesn't Live Here Anymore* puts a widow with a son behind the wheel.

The gendered and formal difference that is implicit in the second act of *Alice Doesn't Live Here Anymore* is nevertheless enclosed by acts that, generically, position Alice in more conventional female spaces and, formally, conform to more plot-driven development. The second act's relation to the formal looseness of the road movie is also tempered by the increasing focus on the Alice–Ben subplot. Further, while the placing of Alice behind the wheel invites consideration as a positive response to the rise of feminism, it no less carries commercial connotations; namely, the interplay of standardization and differentation that is fundamental to capitalist commodity production and, thus, to generic longevity. This and the film's cross-generic reference imply generic self-consciousness. Getchell has stated both that he 'set out to write a vehicle for a woman' and that, 'quite consciously', it 'could fit into the road movie genre, the woman's vehicle genre, several more' (Thompson 1976b: 142).Yet unlike the generic articulation of much New Hollywood Cinema, such self-consciousness in *Alice Doesn't Live Here Anymore* lacks a revisionist impulse. Similarly, whereas *Easy Rider* and its progeny present an anti-hegemonic vision of a fragmented USA, *Alice Doesn't Live Here Anymore* recalls what Hark describes as 'a reintegrative tradition' popular in thirties and forties road narratives wherein 'the protagonists, having learned important lessons along the way, reenter mainstream society' (1997: 224). It is, moreover, a 'tradition' that not infrequently sees road plots integrated with screwball comedy – apart from *It Happened One Night*, witness, say, *Love on the Run* (W.S. Van Dyke, 1936) or *Sullivan's Travels* (Preston Sturges, 1941).

VII

Despite such generic implications, *Alice Doesn't Live Here Anymore* on its release received praise as a 'feminist' film. This needs to be contextualized in relation to different strands within seventies feminism. Simplifying, there is a tension between a desire to improve women's situation within existing social structures and a desire to change the social structure itself. Critically, it is a contrast reflected by two different schools of feminist film practice that are broadly defined by national and methodological differences. On one hand, there is criticism informed by the American Women's Movement that, from a liberal-humanist perspective, in general seeks to ratify representations of female personal experience and positive female images. On the other, there is predominantly British/Eurocentric feminist criticism that, theoretically founded upon a combination of Marxism and Freudian and post-Freudian psychoanalysis, seeks to relate the structural and ideological positioning of female characters within texts to the positioning of women in society. It is mainly from a Women's Movement position that *Alice Doesn't Live Here Anymore* has been considered to be 'progressive'. The film can nevertheless be seen to offer a no less progressive reading from a Marxist-psychoanalytic perspective.

Central to the claimed progressiveness of *Alice Doesn't Live Here Anymore* is Alice's representation. This reflects what Pam Cook sees as a longstanding feminist imperative 'to destroy old patriarchal myths and replace them with new images of women as active subjects' (1976: 123). Slightly overweight, and unglamorous in jeans and ill-fitting dresses, Burstyn's Alice openly exhibits female tensions, desires and frustrations. As Christine Geraghty notes: '*Alice Doesn't Live Here Anymore* ... [is] very much concerned with the creation of a central female character who is meant to be seen as "real". ... The film encourages this interpretation by presenting Alice as a character who makes decisions, initiates action and changes her mind' (1976: 39). But if Alice is hence a potentially validating identification figure for (at least a part of) the female audience, her energies are frequently spent on placating patriarchy. For example, she seeks to mollify Donald by cooking lamb the way he likes it, and makes herself 'sexy' – that is, has a perm and buys a short, tight dress – to seek employment in Phoenix.

Switching critical perspective, the latter can be regarded as reflecting the reciprocal economic and psycho-sexual dominance of the male bar-owners. This is foregrounded when a bar-owner (Dean Casper) asks Alice to 'turn around' for him. Alice retorts 'I don't sing with my ass' and storms out. While the moment, in its combination of female defiance and unladylike language, 'confirms' the film's feminist credentials, Alice's alternative job-seeking tactics – her flirtatiousness with the hick barman of Joe's & Jim's (Harry Northup) and the tears and sob story that impel the paternal Jacobs (Murray Moston) to give her a chance – no less signal, in their necessity, and despite their sympathetic reception, her gendered subordination.

The sequence of Alice's job-hunting highlights the sexualization of the female within the public, masculine realm. Moreover, in becoming a bar entertainer while seeking and, indeed, in order to fulfil her responsibilities as a mother, Alice's representation fuses 'types which are normally kept separate' (*ibid*.: 40), and while Alice capitulates sexually to Ben as a singer, she is guiltily reticent about it as a mother.

Although Alice's 'sexy' appearance is consciously assumed, the text also places it – with directorial implication – as culturally determined. This serves further to contextualize Alice's gendered subjection. When the 'transformed' Alice returns to her motel room, the camera pulls back to cover the room's door from a close-up of a beauty advertisement in a magazine read by Tommy. Alice ironically announces herself as 'Diana Ross' and, when Tommy opens the door, presents herself for inspection in an exaggerated pose. Filmed in a single hand-held take, the shot fixes Alice's sexualized 'new self' as a culturally mediated construct; a connotation reinforced when the camera tracks from a television set showing Johnny Carson to Alice shaving her legs in the motel room's cramped bathroom. As she does so, she talks of getting 'one of those fancy negligées' and 'a pair of gold, high-heeled slippers' and shaving her legs 'like all those ladies on television do'. Later, there is a cut from the scene in which Ben first 'hits on' Alice to a shot of another television set as it shows a scene from *Coney Island* (Walter Lang, 1943) in which an annoyed Kate Farley (Betty Grable) has her dress ripped, and made more revealing, by Eddie Johnson (George Montgomery) before she sings 'Cuddle Up a Little Closer, Lovey Mine'. This presents parallels with Alice's situation. Not only does Kate, like Alice, find herself with an importunate man, but she performs for the mainly male gaze of an audience while bearing an image that is determined (explicitly, in Kate's case) by masculine demand.[12]

The contingency of Alice's sexualized public image is also suggested in terms of performance. Thus the shift from the smiling invitingness of her 'public' self as she sings 'I've Got a Crush on You' to her frostiness when, having finished her set, she is first approached by Ben. In the third act, Flo similarly switches from arguing bitterly with café-owner Mel (Tayback) to welcoming the café's morning customers with warm friendliness. The café is another public, masculine space. Male-owned and having a mainly male clientèle, it is likewise another site of sexualized female accommodation. While this is implicit in Flo's welcome, it is both foregrounded by Flo's introductory monologue about Alice, which points up Alice's 'big tits' and warns against 'grab-assing', and underlined when Flo advises Alice to unbutton her uniform in order to get 'more tips'.

Alice's waitressing implies a public reflection of her married life that, as represented, centres upon the provision of food. Conventionally, the domestic may well be 'the feminine space of the family and reproduction', but Alice's home situation is suggested to be no less patriarchally constrained than public space. It accordingly 'demands' that she adopt a compliant, subordinate role. Hence Alice's ingratiating sweetness when, having quietened Tommy, she informs Donald that dinner will be 'ready in about thirty minutes'. Donald responds with gruff off-handedness and Alice's 'mask' slips, revealing an expression that momentarily hints at defiance. Alice's 'performance' of her wifely part is highlighted during the scene in which she serves her pacifying lamb dish. Dressed in demure white, Alice attempts to engage Donald in dinner-table conversation. Failing, she acts out a mock dialogue that, as it comically exaggerates Donald's machismo and her preceding, 'womanly' chattiness, reflects upon the latter's assumed status.

Alice's taking of different and contradictory feminine roles can once more be related to the call for non-stereotypical female figures: 'Alice's confusion is ... important in the creation of her as a character who is recognisably real. The assumption seems to be that film reflects life and that if Alice is to avoid being a stereotype, then she must reflect our confusions and uncertainties' (Geraghty 1976: 40). During the seventies the accepted negativity of female stereotyping was challenged by Marxist-psychoanalytic feminism that argued, from a Lacanian-inflected position, that it instead presented a material expression of women's subjection that could 'be used as a short-hand for referring to an ideological tradition in order to provide a critique of it' (Johnston 1973: 210). A similar critique is implicit in the suggestion of Alice's adoption of a series of patriarchally delimited roles.

VIII

Patriarchal constraint is further intimated by the marginalized spaces allowed interpersonal female contact. Apart from the scene in which Alice talks with Bea in her back yard, that in which she talks with Rita takes place in a functional motel kitchen and those in which she talks with Flo are set in a wind-blown lot and the café's cramped outside toilet.

These scenes of female accord again flag the woman's film: 'One of the most important aspects of the genre is the prominent place it accords to relationships between women' (LaPlace 1987: 139). The scenes are sites for the expression of female subjectivity – the characters share confidences and perceptions and delight in 'transgressive' desires. Thus Alice and Bea's discussion of Robert Redford's 'build' or Flo's offer to 'fix' Alice up, both of which exchanges end in hilarity. The scenes also carry a more defensive connotation, suggesting mutual understanding in the face of gendered oppression. Alice's sympathy toward Rita when she reveals Ben's adultery is immediate and indicative: mutuality is predicated upon a recognition of common female and, especially, maternal cares. Alice mentions to Bea her worry concerning Donald's anger toward Tommy, while Rita and Flo refer to 'medical treatment their children need and which they cannot afford' (Geraghty 1976: 40). This indicts their partners' fecklessness. Rita talks of Ben 'missing work' since meeting Alice and Flo observes that her 'old man' has not spoken to her 'since the day Kennedy got shot'. Paternal negligence is similarly implied when Audrey (Foster), the androgynous girl whom Tommy meets in Tucson, speaks of her father having left her and her mother. She likewise characterizes him as a 'bastard' who used to whip her with his belt. This again implicates Donald, whose own belt is, in one scene, in view on the family dinner-table.

David is initially suggested to be different. First shown reassuring Alice when she is embarrassed by Flo's monologue, he is subsequently represented as a model of a more responsive and responsible masculinity. In a contrast to Donald's irascibility and Ben's importunity, David's wooing lacks overt sexual aggression – he even offers to shave off his beard. He finally makes a successful play by taking Tommy riding; an act through which he presents himself as that most unusual of things – an interested father-figure. David also compares favourably to Donald and Ben in terms of appearance, manner and situation. Whereas Donald is lumpen and irritable and Ben somewhat 'klutzy' and grinningly immature, David is ruggedly handsome and apparently affable. Likewise, whereas Donald drives a truck and Ben fills 'bullet cases with powder', David owns his ranch; the natural openness of which might be seen to mirror his character. David's positive representation culminates with the post-coital kitchen scene with Alice. His quizzical response to Alice's admission that she 'kind of liked' Donald's peremptoriness because it embodied her 'idea of a man, strong and dominating' serves as both commentary and another marker of his 'difference'. The scene ends with David responding laughingly to her sexual suggestion; a ready assent that contrasts with

Donald's sullen refusal of Alice's earlier and notably more tentative desire for intimacy.

Yet it is also revealed that David is divorced and that his ex-wife has custody of their children. The character is further problematized by the sequence that follows the kitchen scene. He is irritable when pestered by Tommy, then – in a stereotypical clash of male demand and female loquaciousness – interrupts Alice's news about a robbery to tell her first to see to his order. David discovers that his truck has an oil-leak and calls off his and Tommy's fishing trip, but leaves it to Alice to pass on to Tommy his blunt rationale, that 'he can't ruin his truck so you can catch a fish'. Tommy wearily responds: 'Sounds familiar.'

Indeed, David's apparent difference is compromised by a number of parallels with Donald and Ben. When Tommy asks Alice why she married Donald, she answers: 'Because he was a great kisser.' Although this is said with irony, the film dissolves from a kiss between Alice and Ben to a shot of them in bed together and cuts from Alice kissing David to the post-coital kitchen scene. Both Ben and David first make an impression by making Alice smile – Ben through a quip, David by 'ordering' a 'big smile' – and both are shown looking at Alice as she works.

Most significantly, all three male characters are shown to act with analogous violence. Donald reacts to Tommy's prank of switching sugar for salt by confronting Tommy menacingly and lunging aggressively, if unsuccessfully, toward him as he runs from the house. Ben smashes his way into Alice's motel room, forces Rita out at knife-point and threatens to 'bust' Alice's jaw. David 'succeeds' where Donald failed, and ends an argument with Tommy by sending him sprawling from a slap to his backside. All three incidents occur after meals – dinner, breakfast and Tommy's twelfth birthday party – and in all three Tommy flees the immediate situation. Sites of familial communion and celebration hence become diegetic sites of familial discord, for which masculinity is once more culpable.

All three incidents are in addition filmed with hand-held cameras and present, to varying degrees, forceful editing. This contributes to a stylistic intensity that bears close scrutiny. Consider the scene involving Ben. The most extended and brutal of the three incidents, it begins with the sounds of Ben shouting and banging the front door interrupting Alice and Rita's *tête-à-tête*. A series of shots establish Ben's fury and the women's and Tommy's fear. Tension is heightened by repeated cuts between Alice and Tommy, standing in the space between bedroom and kitchen, and Ben, framed by the door's glass pane. A

wider shot of the door from above and behind Alice and Tommy prolongs the tension, that is shattered when Ben punches through the
glass pane and opens the door from the inside. The shot cuts forcefully, mid-motion, to a closer, lower angled shot that emphasizes Ben's
force and anger as he enters. The shot continues – with unbroken,
tense jerkiness – to follow Ben as he strides into the kitchen, grabs and
shakes Rita and half-pushes, half-throws her against a wall and on to
the floor of the bedroom. This cuts, somewhat disjunctively, to a
reverse angle, cluttered close shot, in which Ben prevents Alice helping
Rita, and then, again reversing angle, to a medium shot of Ben, who
flicks open a switch-blade. Cut back to a wider shot of the bedroom,
with the camera following Rita as she scrambles, on all fours, out of the
room, her passage speeded by Ben's kick at her backside. The take
becomes a medium scale two-shot, with Alice and Ben positioned at
the edges of the frame, as a brief, strained respite ensues. Alice suggests
that Ben 'calm down' and 'go home'. A medium shot of Ben sweeping
her belongings from the dressing-table cuts to a reaction shot of Alice
cowering before flying objects. Cut back to Ben, who walks toward
both Alice and the camera, with the shot becoming a tight over-the-
shoulder close shot as he grabs her robe with one hand and threatens
to hit her with the other. This cuts to a reverse close shot and then to a
two-shot as Ben releases the robe. The reverse angle close shots are
twice repeated – in reverse order – as Ben, comparing himself to the
scorpion figured on his tie, again threatens Alice. There is a cut back to
the two-shot before the camera covers Ben as he walks to the door and
leaves.

The incident has been called a 'Scorsese signature piece' (Taylor
1981: 338). Like the scenes of Alice singing, those of masculine violence were among those that Scorsese cut himself; an intimation of
personal investment that is complemented by the engagement implicit
in what is, within the context of *Alice Doesn't Live Here Anymore*, the
episodes' heightened integration of style, incident and performance. As
demonstrated by the scene of Ben's violence, this integration is intimately attuned to the modulations of Keitel's tense and frighteningly
sustained aggressiveness; a focus that is reflected in the scenes involving Donald/Bush and David/Kristofferson.

The emphasis accorded these scenes has broader connotations regarding Scorsese's authorial discourse. For all that *Alice Doesn't Live Here
Anymore* centres upon a female protagonist, the scenes suggest that
Scorsese's authorial interest remains with the masculine. Moreover, as in
both *Who's That Knocking at My Door?* and *Mean Streets* the scenes relate

aggression to masculine overcompensation. Ben's edgy violence implies a frantic attempt to assert a patriarchal control 'threatened' by Rita's appeal to Alice – he holds his expressly phallic knife at groin level, and as he responds menacingly to Alice's 'calming' advice he repeats: 'Don't tell me what to do.' Similar connotations attend the scenes involving Donald and David. The disrespect implicit in Tommy's salt-for-sugar prank suggests Donald's lack of achieved paternal authority; a connotation similarly evoked by his angry, but ineffectual, complaints about Tommy's loud playing of Mott the Hoople. These are paralleled by David's anger when Tommy loudly and defiantly plays a T. Rex record. Tommy's defiance here carries significant Oedipal implications. Tommy's playing of the record compounds his refusal of David's attempt to teach him a particular guitar chord. Suggesting, symbolically, a denial of Oedipal identification, this also reflects Tommy's declining of Donald's offer to say grace, that Donald then says himself. Tommy's protest that the chord hurts his fingers and David's slap correspondingly carry intimations of symbolic castration.

When Tommy flees Donald's anger, Donald blames Alice for their son's insubordination– 'if you'd show a little respect around here it just may rub off on him'. Not only is Alice and Tommy's relationship founded upon their shared, joky irreverence, but it is introduced as a jointly supportive alliance: Alice does not so much admonish Tommy for his disruptive playing of Mott the Hoople as appeal to him conspiringly.

This raises further, and complementary, Oedipal connotations. These are, with psycho-sexual logic, more particularly developed after Donald's death, when Alice and Tommy take to the road together. Upon Alice gently kissing a sleeping Tommy, the opening chords of her performance of 'I've Got a Crush on You' are introduced on the soundtrack. Apart from creating a suggestive sound–image correlation, the music also functions as a sound bridge to the sequence in which she meets Ben, Alice's relationship with whom is signalled to be a displacement of that with Tommy. Ben's initial, almost child-like appeal to Alice, 'I'm lonely', both seeks to play on her (maternal?) sympathy and reflects Tommy's complaints about his solitary, motel room existence. Not only does Ben's relative youth give Alice pause, but when he makes a juvenile quip about her name she compares him to someone 'under twelve' – Tommy only turns twelve in Tucson. Moreover, the shot of Alice and Ben in bed together dissolves to a shot of Alice in bed with Tommy. The intimations suggest another factor in Alice's guilt regarding Ben.

Tommy's asking of Alice why she married Donald implies a reciprocal sexual jealousy that is maintained with regard to Ben. Tommy spies
on Alice and Ben as they talk outside the motel, makes knowing comments ('Should I call him Uncle Ben?') and even asks Alice: 'Did you
sleep with him?'. Later, at David's ranch, Tommy approaches Alice and
David as they cuddle on a settee, draws a toy pistol and 'shoots' them
with a loudly shouted 'BANG'. The suggestion of Tommy's (suitably
phallic) aggression toward Alice's relationship with David is plain;
complementing which, Alice and David's embrace implies the primal
scene.[13]

Yet if Alice's relationship with Tommy implicates her in familial and
psycho-sexual transgression, it can be considered a contained and con-
taining transgressiveness that, functioning as both safety-value and
emotional comfort, enables her to endure her position. The relationship is an index of her discomfort rather than a consciously enacted
violation – her collusion with Tommy against Donald is, at most,
implicit. Further, when Alice enters into her apparently fulfilling relationship with David, there is an acquiescence in the even encouragement of Tommy's 'correct' Oedipal identification. Hence the birthday
present of Tommy's cowboy outfit, that Tommy is first seen wearing
when reflected in Scorsese's figure of determination – a mirror.
Moreover, in the two scenes in which David teaches Tommy the guitar
Alice is initially set apart – and seemingly accepting of her separation –
in the 'proper' maternal space of David's kitchen.[14]

Alice's 'enduring' discontent implicitly informs the narrative
necessity of Donald's death to release her from her marriage. This has
drawn criticism. Teena Webb and Betsy Martens write: 'It's not the
kind of act that we can be expected to admire and emulate. She never
left her husband, she never confronted him, and she is freed from him
only by his accidental death' (1975: 4). The patterning of Alice's subsequent experiences invites an alternative, psychoanalytical reading.
Alice's propensity to fall for 'great kissers' evokes a form of repetition
compulsion. Psychoanalytically one of the most common symptoms of
neurosis, repetition compulsion describes obsessively repeated
behaviour that marks an uncontrolled return of the repressed 'which
over-rides the pleasure principle' (Freud 1920: 293). Further, the
compulsion to repeat 'can also be observed in the lives of some normal
[that is, non-neurotic] people': 'Thus we have come across people all of
whose human relationships have the same outcome' (*ibid*.: 292).[15] If
we accept the applicability of this to Alice's representation, then the
kitchen scene implies a figure of the psychoanalytic process. With

David a gently probing 'therapist', the scene conveys a situation of relaxed (if alcohol-fuelled) trust, within which Alice is able to 'free associate' about her past. While this characteristically involves recollections of her childhood (of her brother teaching her how to kiss, of their youthful stage act), her comments about Donald comprise an admission of her internalization of subordinating patriarchal norms: 'It seems probable that the compulsion can only express itself after the work of treatment has gone half-way to meet it and has loosened the repression' (*ibid.*: 290). With her fixation brought to consciousness, Alice's compulsion to repeat is effectively removed. Consequently, when David hits Tommy, Alice for the first time confronts a male partner. Contesting David's claim that Tommy 'needed' hitting, and questioning his parental record ('Where are your children?'), Alice challenges heretofore accepted patriarchal dominance. The scene ends with her leaving, unlike previously, of her own volition.

Alice's enabling release from her compulsion is underscored during the toilet scene with Flo. Having earlier defended Donald against Bea's claim that he is 'mean', Alice can now admit 'I was so scared of Donald', and – in a retrospective, liberating self-criticism – that, although she felt that Donald looked after her, 'he didn't, I just felt like he did, just 'cause he was there'. She also affirms 'it's my life ... not some man's life that I'm gonna help him out with'.

The scene in addition amends Alice's boast to Bea that she could easily live without male company. On the evidence of the intervening narrative, Alice's tearful 'I don't know how to live without a man' seems valid. Its apparent complication of her other statements might likewise be seen to maintain the 'realistic' confusion of her representation. However, it is also an admission that can be related to the film's 'needful' recuperations.

IX

The third act of *Alice Doesn't Live Here Anymore* represents Alice's psychic and ideological emancipation, but simultaneously implies the need for her to re-embrace patriarchal authority. This centres on criticism of Alice as a mother. For much of the film Alice's unconventional motherhood is rendered unproblematic. On one hand, her indulgent, wisecracking and mutually supportive relationship with Tommy is largely allowed to stand as an example, in unpropitious circumstances, of creditably open parenting. On the other, the problems that arise from Tommy being left alone when Alice sings are glossed over. True, Tommy is shot watching *Coney Island* alone and while 'entrapped' by the *noir*-ish shadows cast by the motel room's venetian blinds. Yet when Tommy raises his neglect openly – 'What am I supposed to do all the time?' – it is both dramatically overwhelmed by the scene's focus on Alice's delight at getting a 'job as a singer' and comically disavowed by Alice's quick-fire banter and Tommy's antics with a fan.

Much in all this is tactically disingenuous – the film is seeking to keep Alice sympathetic. No less partial and disingenuous are the criticisms made of Alice during the third act. These are initially channelled through David, whose representation lends them an authority that, say, the attacks of Donald lack. Witness David's respectively surprised and interrogative facial reactions to Tommy's crude remarks at the diner and as he milks a cow at the ranch. In each case David looks toward Alice. Not only does her embarrassment lend the tacit criticism of David's responses further weight, but when at the ranch she essays a guiltily unconvincing excuse, 'I just don't know where he gets that language', it is sarcastically undermined by Tommy: 'Think real hard, it'll come to you lady.'

When David and Alice argue, he makes his criticisms explicitly: 'he's got the foulest mouth on any kid I've ever seen. ... You spoil him rotten. That kid thinks he can do whatever he wants to do, whenever he wants to do it, wherever he wants to do it.' Given Tommy's often irritating precociousness, this articulation of Alice's faults has a certain aptness; this despite Alice's own attacks on David, that are themselves hardly invalidated by David's claims. The contradiction lends the scene a sense of lived complexity. The film, however, undertakes Alice's denigration. Driving home, Alice and Tommy argue. Losing patience, Alice pushes Tommy out of the car to walk the 'last mile'. Although Tommy's brattishness makes this understandable, the issue of Alice's parenting is maintained. Moreover, Tommy does not return to the motel but gets drunk with Audrey, leaving Alice to endure a night of desperation.

Adding little of narrative substance, the sequence mainly suggests a vindictive punishing of Alice's independence. This is compounded by Tommy and Audrey being arrested: a reassertion of patriarchal authority that is not only implicitly redemptive but markedly both sympathetic (charges are not going to be pressed) and caring (the police have replaced Tommy's cowboy outfit, over which he has been sick, with a sweatshirt). At the police station Alice comes face to face with Audrey's mother, whom Karyn Kay and Gerald Peary pungently describe as 'a bleached

1 *Who's That Knocking at My Door?*: The final meeting – J. R. (Harvey Keitel) and the girl (Zina Bethune).

2 *Boxcar Bertha*: The outlaw group – Bill (David Carradine), Bertha (Barbara Hershey), Von (Bernie Casey) and Rake (Barry Primus).

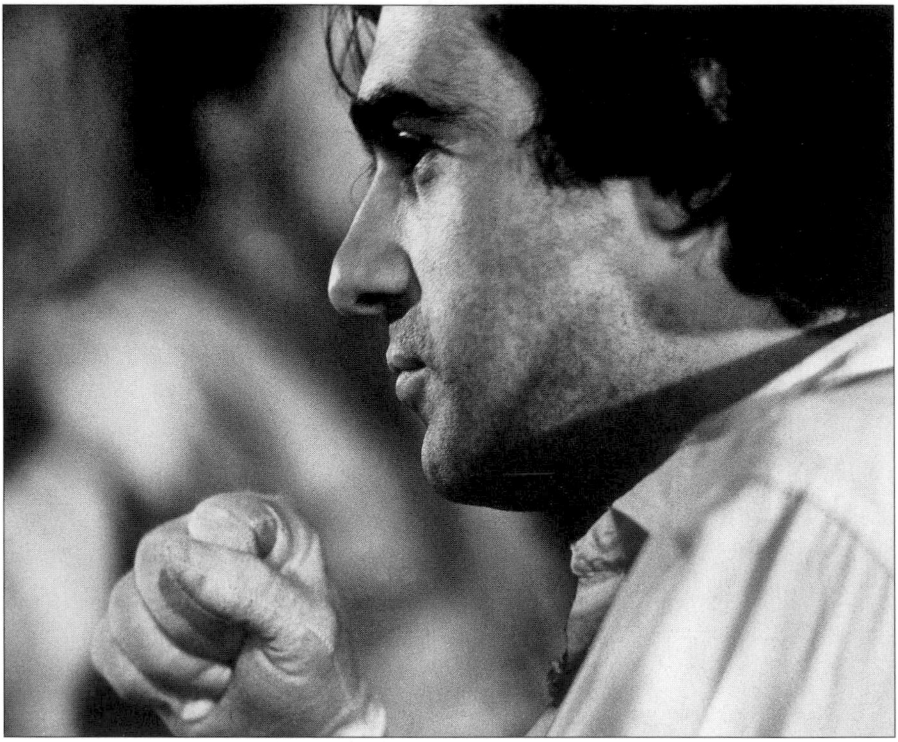

3 Scorsese directing *Mean Streets*.

4 Mean Streets: The shooting in the bar (Robert and David Carradine).

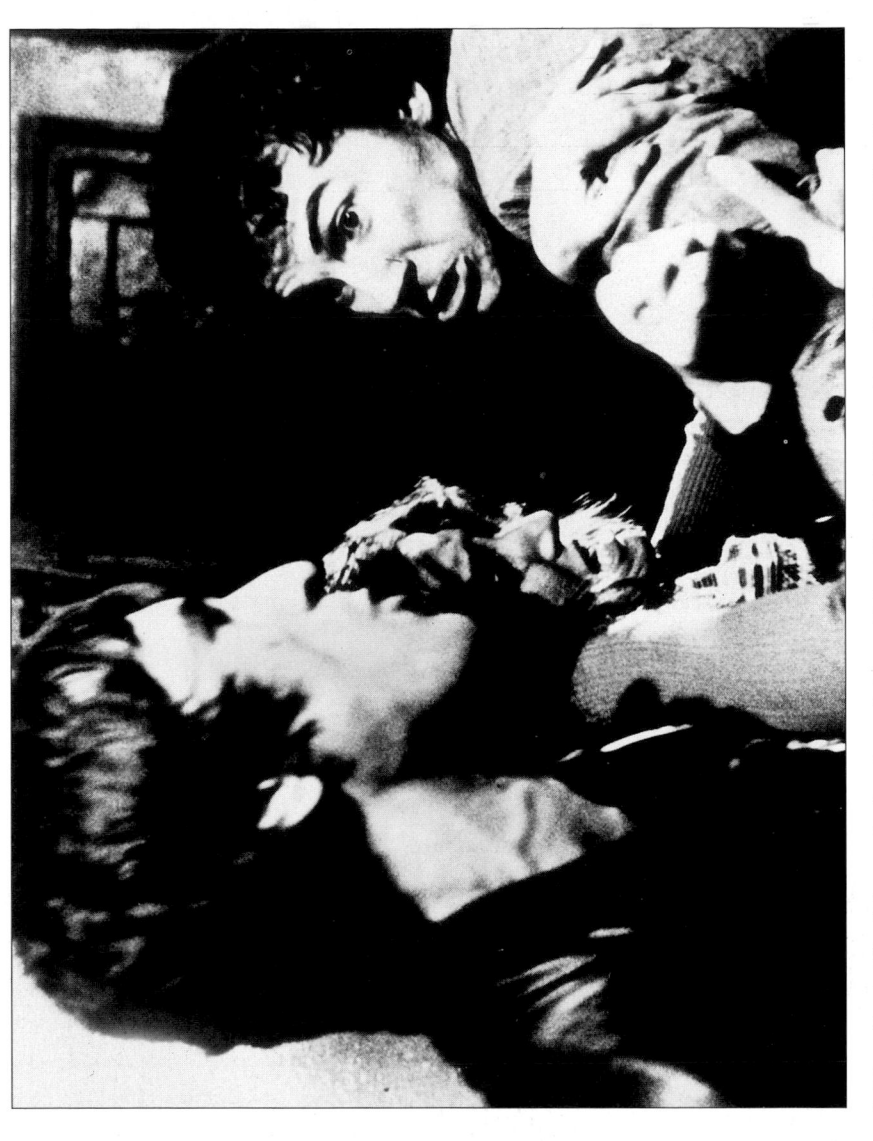

5 *Mean Streets*: The fight on the landing – Johnny (Robert De Niro), Teresa (Amy Robinson) and Charlie (Harvey Keitel).

6 *Alice Doesn't Live Here Anymore*: Another great kisser . . . – David (Kris Kristofferson) and Alice (Ellen Burstyn).

7 *Taxi Driver*: Travis (Robert De Niro) 'romances' Betsy (Cybill Shepherd).

8 *Taxi Driver*: Travis and woman #2 – Travis (Robert De Niro) and Iris (Jodie Foster) have breakfast.

9 *New York, New York:* The Up Club – Jimmy Doyle (Robert De Niro) attacks Paul Wilson (Barry Primus).

10 *New York, New York*: Minnelli as Francine as Garland as Minnelli – Francine Evans (Liza Minnelli) sings 'Theme from New York, New York'.

blonde caricatured prostitute in a tight, clinging green-flowered pantsuit' (1975: 6). Audrey's mother embodies the independent woman as tart and bad mother, being responsible – along with the absent father – for Audrey's 'weirdness': Audrey explains to Tommy that she could have 'a troop of bare-assed eagle scouts in for the afternoon' and her mother 'wouldn't even blink an eye'. It is also Audrey who get Tommy drunk and who leads him to shoplift. Placed as Alice's negative *alter ego*, Audrey's mother is a 'jarring example of lapsed parenthood' for character and spectator: 'The lesson is learned. No longer can Alice be indolent or unclear in her motherly duty' (*ibid.*).

The third act further seeks to 'rectify' Alice's illusions regarding Monterey and her singing career. Her need to work at Mel and Ruby's Café reverses her proud assertion at Joe's & Jim's: 'I'm not a waitress. I'm a singer.' In the kitchen scene, David asks, 'Do you want to go home or do you want to sing?', and suggests that they are not necessarily the same thing. As a challenge to the credibility of Alice's ambitions, this is once more lent force by David's established solidity, against which Alice's giggling, tipsy desire for 'both' seems somewhat vacuous.

We might here consider the film's prologue. Like the film's credits, this is presented within an Academy ratio frame that, masked with black, stands within the film's actual frame. With the accompanying music, Alice Faye singing 'You'll Never Know', continuing, the credits dissolve to an overtly artificial, studio-bound exterior of a country road and farm buildings.[16] These stand before an orange and purple backdrop and are lit, in a simulation of a Technicolor sunset, by exaggerated reds and golds. The set specifically evokes a singular combination of a sky from, say, *Gone With the Wind* (Victor Fleming, 1939) or *Duel in the Sun* (King Vidor, 1946) with buildings that imply *Tobacco Road* and the Kansas scenes of *The Wizard of Oz* (Fleming, 1939). The young Alice is an imperfect reflection of Dorothy (Judy Garland). Blonde instead of dark, and wearing bunches instead of plaits, she nevertheless wears a similarly styled dress and, like Dorothy, sings, trying her own version of 'You'll Never Know' when Faye fades from the soundtrack.

The scene is a self-consciously nostalgic evocation of a *filmic* time and place – a reflexivity enhanced, as during the credits of *Mean Streets*, by the frame-within-frame device. Placed 'somewhere between memory and fantasy' (Stern 1995: 123), the scene would appear to seek correspondingly to weigh our perception of Alice's subsequent plans: unlike Dorothy/Garland, the young Alice also sings off-key. The prologue's illusoriness is further underlined by the transition to the narrative proper. In a combination of devices that imply the tornado from *The Wizard of Oz*, the camera cranes back, the word 'now' is repeated with echo, the image recedes into the frame and there is a straight cut to a full-frame shot of Socorro. But this time we move from 'dream' to 'reality'. Within Socorro, Alice's 'memory' of Monterey is reduced to a mural of a country road on her dining-room wall.

The prologue's pre-emptive dismissal of Alice's ambitions is neverthe-less complicated by the scene's stylistic vividness. Not only does this lend Alice's 'memories' a ratifying appealingness, but it once more suggests a no less validating authorial investment. Apart from the almost lovingly detailed set,[17] much of the scene is filmed in a combination of crane and tracking shots that are characteristically unmotivated and insinuating. Scorsese's relation of the prologue to Alice being 'really hung up on movies' (1975: 6) is, moreover, evidently applicable both to Scorsese and to his films. Indeed, allusiveness continues upon the transition to Socorro. The camera cranes along and toward white houses and, via a dissolve, past a tree and into a window to show Alice, who sings as she sews. This reworks the opening of *Summer Stock* (Charles Walters, 1950), at which the camera cranes – in another link to the prologue – through a studio farmyard and, via a dissolve, past a tree and into a window to show Jane Falbury (Garland), who sings as she showers.

X

By the end of Alice's scene with Flo, the film would appear to have reached a narrative and ideological impasse. For as Alice both affirms her autonomy and yet yearns for David, so the film has both charted her liberation and declared the desirability of her recuperation, while David has been both panegyrized and problematized. The subsequent café scene attempts to resolve these tensions. After Alice seemingly rebuffs David's attempted reconciliation, he moves to leave, but halts at the café door. A grandstanding argument follows. Alice states that she does not want to hear David and Tommy 'fighting for the next ten years'. David responds: 'That's between me and Tommy.' An expres-sion of patriarchal authority, this goes pointedly unanswered by Alice, who instead notes that anything she does from 'now on' has to include singing. After Alice avoids David's questioning of how good she is, he suddenly says that he will take her to Monterey, that he does not 'give a damn about that ranch'. This jars against not only David's earlier proprietorial pride ('It took me six years to get this place'), but his more immediate challenge to Alice's desire to return to Monterey when he exclaims, exasperatedly: 'You were a little girl in Monterey.' David's solution to Alice's predicament is implausibly over-convenient: Alice obtains a perfect balance of dependence and independence, gets her man and her career. The effect is one of forced closure that, in its unconvincingnes, foregrounds, rather than resolves, the narrative's ideological contradictions.

Implausibility is heightened when, at the scene's finish, the characters embrace and applause appears to come from behind as well as in front of the camera. As this appears consciously and reflexively to highlight the situations's constructedness, it could be read as an attempt to achieve 'Brechtian' distanciation.[18]

We must be careful here. Alice and David's argument is itself stagy, being replete with cutaways to reaction shots that, in their 'interested' commentary, further signal the scene's factitiousness. Such, however, is hardly *critically* reflexive. Neale has noted that 'Regimes of verisimilitude vary from genre to genre', and that generic verisimilitude can 'ignore, sidestep, or transgress' wider social and cultural verisimilitude (1990: 46, 47). Further: 'Comedy always and above all depends upon an awareness that it is fictional' (Neale 1980: 40). This places the recurrently 'theatrical' orchestration of the third act's verbal and physical humour, as well as the comparatively broad characterization of, say, Mel, Vera or even Flo. It likewise accounts for Alice's twice explicit acknowledgement of the camera, the latter of which sees her respond to Tommy's enumeration of David's virtues with a knowing, ironic look. The aim is not estrangement, but amused complicity.

Alice and David's applauded embrace has, in turn, been described as 'something straight out of the romance comedies of the 'thirties' (Taylor 1981: 339). The moment offers a dual reading: as an example both of comic factitiousness and of critical reflexivity. This imbrication of the critical with the comic once more evokes the film's mainstream acceptability. Warner Bros, moreover, demanded a 'happy ending' – that is, the restoration of the heterosexual couple – much to the disgust of Burstyn: 'Marty and I worked on the script and handed the rewrites to John Calley... . John said, "We love the whole thing except for the ending. She has to end up with the guy. We just did a movie with an unhappy ending and it didn't sell"' (Kelly 1992: 84).[19] This further suggests what Robin Wood has termed, in relation to seventies Hollywood, 'the limits of the ideologically acceptable, the limits that render feminism safe' (1986: 202–3). Burstyn interprets the climax as Scorsese's reaction against this: 'The end they wanted was a *movie* ending, not a *real* ending – which was why Marty had everybody in the restaurant applaud, because that was *his* way of acknowledging that this was the *movie* ending' (Kelly 1992: 84–5).

The climax, however, is only the culmination of the discordance that affects the third act. This further implicates Warner Bros, and their decision to speed *Alice Doesn't Live Here Anymore* into production – from the first Scorsese felt they needed to 'change the third part' (Thompson and Christie 1996: 49). Symptomatic of the contradictions, and their generation, are the various endings proposed for the script. Getchell's first draft, before Scorsese was involved, had Tommy committing suicide. Subsequent drafts saw Tommy running away to Monterey, but returning to Tucson with Alice, Alice and David happily reconciled and, in the climax drafted by Burstyn and Scorsese, Alice leaving David.[20] The filmed climax was suggested by Kristofferson, who 'sprung' it on Burstyn 'during rehearsal' (Kelly 1992: 85).

But Scorsese would appear to have the last word. The final scene not only modifies the film's 'ideal' resolution before Alice's more 'realistic', if recuperative, acceptance of David and Tucson, but intimates continuing, unresolved tensions. Tommy rationalizes Alice's decision by saying: 'You always said you could fight with somebody and still like 'em.' A reference to Alice's earlier explanation of her relationship with Donald, this again pairs David with Donald, hinting that nothing has really changed. That the film concludes with Alice and Tommy also restates their transgressive, compensatory closeness.

The scene's final shot shows Alice and Tommy walking away from the camera. Filmed with a long-focus lens, its flattened perspective makes it appear that the characters are going nowhere. Monterey has become, simply, a sign, the word appearing in shot, denoting a shopping area.[21]

Even so, with David a preferable option to either Donald or Ben, the ending avoids the downward spiral that inflects the endings of previous Scorsese fictions. Further, while the logic of the text, as it suggests the seeming untenability of existing heterosexual relations, is toward separation, the initial scenes of Alice and David's relationship hint at the possibility of a more equal, accepting and workable model for heterosexual coupling. It is, moreover, a possibility that, while marginalized by the film's later scenes, is not utterly denied.

7
An Italo-Judeo Production:
Taxi Driver

I

Taxi Driver is probably Scorsese's most discussed film. Analyses have varied from close formal and thematic exegesis (Bliss 1985, Kolker 1988, Friedman 1997) to studies of the film as, for example, as 'incoherent text' (Wood 1980), the culmination of Hollywood's 'certain tendency' (Ray 1985), a domestic relocation of the experience of Vietnam (Fuchs 1991), a pre-eminent instance of seventies 'apocalyptic art' (Sharrett 1993) and a 'recasting' of *The Searchers* (Stern 1995). In adding another reading to the densely documented terrain of *Taxi Driver*, this chapter will strive to negotiate a path between existing accounts of the film and, hopefully, to open up some fresh ground.

Taxi Driver concerns Vietnam veteran Travis Bickle (Robert De Niro), a cab driver appalled by New York's depravity. Amidst 'the scum' he spies Betsy (Cybill Shepherd), a campaign-worker for presidential candidate Charles Palantine (Leonard Harris), and a woman whom Travis perceives as pure. On their only date Travis inexplicably takes Betsy to a porno cinema. Rebuffed, Travis buys some guns and begins a regimen of exercise and target practice. He stalks Palantine, and becomes obsessed with the welfare of Iris (Jodie Foster), a 12-year-old prostitute, whom he seeks to save from her pimp, Sport (Harvey Keitel). After failing to assassinate Palantine, Travis storms Iris's block, killing Sport, Iris's timekeeper (Murray Moston) and a mafioso (Robert Maroff). A coda shows Travis – who has returned Iris to her family and who has been hailed as a hero – apparently readjusted and able to drive Betsy without reaction.

Written by Paul Schrader in 1972, the script for *Taxi Driver* was optioned by producers Tony Bill and Michael and Julia Phillips. With only a single credit, the unsuccessful *Steelyard Blues* (Alan Myerson, 1973), they found the project – with its violence, teenage prostitution and racism – difficult to sell. The majors passed, as did actor Al Pacino, before Columbia offered to make the film with actor Jeff Bridges and director Robert Mulligan, who was bankable following *Summer of '42* (1971). After seeing a rough cut of *Mean Streets*, Schrader felt that *Taxi Driver* ought be made with De Niro and Scorsese; a view shared by Julia Phillips upon being shown Scorsese's film. Following the success of *Mean Streets* at the 1973 New York Film Festival, Warner Bros proposed then withdrew from a deal to make *Taxi Driver* with De Niro and Scorsese for $750 000. Columbia offered $800 000 for a summer 1974 shoot. This was postponed because of Scorsese's involvement with *Alice Doesn't Live Here Anymore* and De Niro's involvement with *The Godfather, Part II* (Francis Ford Coppola, 1974) and *Novecento* (Bernardo Bertolucci, filmed 1974–75, released 1976). The hiatus proved beneficial. Apart from the success of *Alice Doesn't Live Here Anymore*, De Niro won the 1974 Best Supporting Actor Oscar for *The Godfather, Part II*, Schrader sold his script for *The Yakuza* (Sydney Pollack, 1975) for $325 000 and Bill/Phillips Productions, in combination with Richard Zanuck and David Brown, scored a hit with *The Sting* (George Roy Hill, 1973).[1] While this raised the profile of those involved in *Taxi Driver*, the film was again almost delayed, and even put in doubt, by Scorsese's involvement in *New York, New York* and his project with Marlon Brando, *Bury My Heart at Wounded Knee*. In the event, *New York, New York* was postponed, and Scorsese withdrew from *Bury My Heart at Wounded Knee*.[2] *Taxi Driver* entered production in June 1975 with a budget from Columbia of $1.3 million: small, but undoubtedly boosted by the participants' increased stature.

The difficulty in obtaining financing for *Taxi Driver* reflects the majors' corporate rationalization and recourse to 'safer', more mainstream filmmaking. By 1973 Columbia had debts of $223 million and was kept in business only by the banks arranging a 'revolving credit' of $120 million (Pye and Myles 1979: 47). In 1973 Wall Street investment bankers Allen & Co. took a controlling interest and diversified Columbia's interests into adjacent media areas. This was characteristically combined with the introduction of more business-orientated management. Alan J. Hirschfield, a former vice-president of Allen & Co., was appointed President and David Begelman became studio head. Begelman was another ex-agent, the co-founder, with Freddie Fields, in 1960 of Creative Management Associates. As if to symbolize Columbia's new regime, one of Begelman's first acts was to cease Columbia's financing of BBS.

Financially, Hirschfield and Begelman restored Columbia's fortunes. Until their demise in the 'Begelman Affair' of 1977–78, they cut Columbia's debt to $35 million, increased the company's net worth from $6 million to $140 million and turned an earnings deficit of $50 million into a profit of $80 million.[3]

Within this context, *Taxi Driver* was clearly an 'aberrant' project – hence its constant low-budget status. Begelman, moreover, personally hated it.[4] However, with its 'hot' star, director, scriptwriter and producers, *Taxi Driver* was finally too persuasive a package to refuse. Even so, De Niro was – typically – the key: without him the Phillipses would not have let Scorsese direct.[5]

Schrader's script also presented some seductively presold features: elements that, 'guaranteeing' success, were already 'etched in the public consciousness' (Monaco 1984: 16). On one hand, the script self-consciously evoked the persona and confessions of Arthur Bremer, who attempted to assassinate Governor George Wallace in 1972. Bremer's diary enjoyed magazine serialization before being published as *An Assassin's Diary*.[6] On the other hand, the script suggested a variation of the successful urban western cycle.

II

Commencing with *Coogan's Bluff* (Don Siegel, 1968), urban westerns transplant the lone western hero into a corrupt, dangerous and usually big-city setting.[7] This he proceeds – implacably – to 'clean up'. Primarily set in New York and San Francisco, the American cities with 'the most radical images' (Ray 1985: 306), urban westerns are the ideological obverse of much New Hollywood Cinema, proffering a patently reactionary mediation of the time's social and political turmoil. This the films relate – expressly and negatively – to the rise of alternative and oppositional cultures. The psychotic villains of *Coogan's Bluff* and *Dirty Harry* (Siegel, 1971), Ringerman (Don Stroud) and Scorpio (Andy Robinson), are long-haired, wear vaguely hippy clothes and act in a flaky manner that implies drug-use; a trend that culminates in the clownishly stereotyped youths who kill the wife and rape the daughter of Paul Kersey (Charles Bronson) in *Death Wish* (Michael Winner, 1974). In *Coogan's Bluff*, Coogan (Clint Eastwood) has at one point to negotiate a red-lit, 'psychedelic' dance floor of sexually aggressive, sometimes barely-clad young people before overcoming a stoned, switch-blade-wielding black (Albert Popwell). This reflects the racism that is a constant of the cycle – the majority of the victims of Kersey's vigilantism are black (the others are either young or drug addicts).

In New Hollywood Cinema the source of discord is commonly the represssiveness of social and legal institutions. In urban westerns it is, by contrast, the weakness of the law (in all its senses) that is the cause of social breakdown; a perspective that evokes that of the Nixonian Right. Either protagonists are frustrated by 'liberal' legal niceties or the law is 'too soft' and ineffectual. In *Coogan's Bluff*, Coogan's extradition of Ringerman is hampered by the suspect's treatment for an LSD trip experienced while *in* custody; while in *Walking Tall* (Phil Karlson, 1973) the legal system's insufficiency and corruption has allowed a *female*-headed confederation of criminals to take over a small Southern city. In *Death Wish*, not only are the police able to offer Kersey little hope of arresting his family's attackers, but New York's muggings only decrease upon Kersey's vigilante revenge. Violent masculine retribution is central to each of the films, whether embodied through 'Dirty' Harry Callahan (Eastwood)'s. 44 Magnum or Buford Pusser (Joe Don Baker)'s club in *Walking Tall*. This is complemented by the repeated demolition of liberal 'sophistry' by upright 'common sense'. Hence the rationale for gun-ownership given to New Yorker Kersey by Tucson property-owner Jainchill (Stuart Margolin): 'Unlike your city, we can walk our streets and through our parks at night and feel safe.'

The urban western protagonists are further validated by the films' western allusions, that lend their actions an 'historical' pretext. Coogan is an actual western deputy and wears a western suit, cowboy hat and cowboy boots throughout the film. Both Coogan and Callahan are, moreover, extensions of the 'The Man With No Name' whom Eastwood had played in Sergio Leone's spaghetti western trilogy.[8] *Walking Tall* contains 'nearly every standard western convention' (Ray 1985: 308) and in *Death Wish* Kersey recognizes 'himself and his "destiny"' (*ibid*.: 325) while watching a staged western shoot-out. He later explains his killing as 'the old American social custom of self-defence'.

However, *Taxi Driver* does not so much continue the urban western cycle as subject it to a disabling generic revision. It in particular can be read as a response to *Death Wish*, a film that unexpectedly became one of 1974's biggest box-office successes.[9] Indeed, if as a package *Taxi Driver* met the needs of the newly conglomerated Hollywood, as a text it is – stylistically, formally and ideologically – a prime example of New Hollywood Cinema.

III

The collabroation of Scorsese and Schrader brings together two of modern Hollywood's major *auteurs*. Like Scorsese, Schrader is a self-confessed 'personal' filmmaker whose work is informed by his experiences and beliefs and whose scripts and films are often admitted means of working through certain problems. He has related *Taxi Driver* to a disturbed period in his life. Out of work, in debt and with his first script rejected and his first marriage over, Schrader – gun-obsessed and prey to suicidal fantasies – found himself 'living more or less in my car in Los Angeles, riding around all night, drinking heavily, going to porno movies because they were open all night, and crashing some place during the day' (Kelly 1992: 89). Hospitalized for a stomach ulcer, Schrader was 'hit' by the script's key metaphor – 'I was like a taxi driver, floating around in this metal coffin in the city, seemingly in the middle of people, but *absolutely, totally alone*' (*ibid.*). While in hospital, two other experiences 'tied the project together': hearing Harry Chapin's song 'Taxi', 'in which an old girlfriend gets into a guy's cab', and Bremer's shooting of Wallace (Thompson 1976a: 11). During shooting, De Niro, when in character, wore Schrader's shirt, boots and belt.

Continuing through *Raging Bull* (Scorsese, 1980) and *The Last Temptation of Christ* (Scorsese, 1988), Schrader and Scorsese's collaboration would appear to be underpinned by some suggestive biographical parallels: 'we both have essentially the same moral background – a kind of closed-society Christian morality, though mine is rural and Protestant and his is urban and Catholic; mine is North European and his is South European' (Jackson 1990: 117).[10] Schrader was brought up in a Calvinist environment in Grand Rapids, Michigan, and did not see his first film until he was 17. Aiming to be a minister, Schrader entered the denominational Calvin College, but a burgeoning interest in cinema led him to become a film postgraduate at UCLA and a critical fellow at the American Film Institute. After writing film criticism for the *L.A. Free Press* and editing the magazine *Cinema*, he abandoned a (Pauline Kael-sponsored) career as a film critic to write his first script.[11] There is at times nevertheless a seemingly close relationship between Schrader's criticism and his filmmaking; a virtual creation of context that recalls the example of the *Cahiers* critics-become-filmmakers. The relation of *Taxi Driver* to his article 'Notes on Film Noir' has become a critical axiom. However, a more extensive correlation between Schrader's criticism and his filmmaking is grounded in his conceptualization of transcendental style.

In *Transcendental Style in Film* Schrader describes transcendental style as a trans-cultural form through which a sense of the transcendent is created for the spectator. Its elements include the denial of rational or psychological causality, a stress on 'sparse means' rather than stylistic expressiveness and a de-dramatized narrative progression. The aim is an 'intellectual' instead of an emotional engagement, a sense of formal, abstract motivation amenable to the suggestion of spiritual agency. Transcendental style has three narrative stages. There is an initial concentration on the 'everyday', *'a meticulous representation of the dull, banal commonplaces of everyday living'* (1972b: 39). This is disturbed by 'disparity', the representation of 'out-of-place emotion'(*ibid.*: 43) that suggests 'something deeper than [the characters] and their environment' (*ibid.*: 71), and that culminates in 'decisive action'. Formally a moment of rare stylistic excess, 'decisive action' is 'an outburst of spiritual emotion totally inexplicable within the everyday' (*ibid.*: 43) that allows the final stage of 'statis' – 'the quiescent, frozen, or hieratic scene' that ends the film with the suggestion of 'the oneness of all things', 'the Transcendent' (*ibid.*: 82–3).

Schrader exemplifies transcendental style through analyses of the films of Yasujiro Ozu, Robert Bresson and Carl Dreyer. It is, however, Bresson's prison cycle (*Journal d'un curé de campagne*, 1950; *Un Condamé à mort s'est échappé*, 1956; *Pickpocket*, 1959; and *Le Procès de Jeanne d'Arc*, 1962) that provides the template for Schrader's attempts at transcendental style. These span films that Schrader has directed – especially *American Gigolo* (1980), *Mishima: A Life in Four Chapters* (1985) and *Light Sleeper* (1992) – and scripts that he has written for other filmmakers – including *The Yakuza*, *The Last Temptation of Christ* and, not least, *Taxi Driver*.[12] Although *Taxi Driver* contains allusions to *Un Condamné à mort s'est échappé* and *Pickpocket*, its Bressonian model is largely *Journal d'un curé de campagne*. References range from the discrete – such as the parallel between Travis's meal of bread, milk and peach brandy and the Curé d'Ambricourt (Claude Laydu)'s secular communion of bread and cheap wine, or Travis noting, like the Curé, that he thinks he has 'stomach cancer' – to the narratively more substantive and integrated. Both films centre upon 'a man and his room' (Jackson 1990: 163), both are first-person narratives, a perspective reinforced by a reflective use of diaries and voice-over, and both films' protagonists are alienated from and disturbed by surrounding corruption and sexuality, from which they seek 'suicidal' release.

This stress on the first-person, on the protagonist's apartness and on his desire to vindicate quotidian reality also connects with the tradition of European existential narratives. Schrader cites the influence of a triad of novels – Albert Camus's *The Outsider*, Jean-Paul Sartre's *Nausea* and Fyodor Dostoyevsky's *Notes from the Underground*.[13] Scorsese had read *Notes from the Underground* 'some years before' and 'wanted to make a film of it' – '*Taxi Driver* was the closest thing to it I'd come across' (Thompson and Christie 1996: 62).[14] Scorsese, moreover, felt as though he had almost written the script himself and that he 'had to make it' (Schrader 1990: xix).

Scorsese, however, has attributed *Taxi Driver* to Schrader: '*Taxi Driver* really is Paul Schrader's. We interpreted it' (DeCurtis 1990: 108). Schrader concurs, 'everything I intended is on the screen' (Thompson 1976a: 14). The film has nevertheless been described as presenting 'a relatively clear-cut conflict of *auteurs*' (Wood 1980: 26). More specifically, Scorsese's 'interpretation' of *Taxi Driver* is less a 'neutral' adaptation than a discursive appropriation through which the text not only inscribes Scorsese's stylistic and thematic emphases, but would appear seriously to compromise the script's implicit spiritual and redemptive trajectory.

IV

Even with its increased budget, the completion of *Taxi Driver* ultimately depended on the commitment of those involved. The above-the-line costs for the producers, Schrader, Scorsese and the principal cast were only $150 000. De Niro, who was paid $35 000, reputedly turned down a $1/2 million part to play Travis. Filming occurred during a hot, humid summer, in some of the New York's less salubrious areas and amidst a garbage workers' strike. Four days were lost to rain, much to the ire of a nervous Columbia. After Scorsese abandoned the tenth day of shooting when rain disrupted the street background to the coffee-shop scene between Travis and Betsy, the production was briefly put in doubt. The situation was defused by Michael Phillips who, as line producer, spent much of his time mediating the mutual antagonism of the studio and Scorsese.[15] It is indicative of the film's institutional context that Scorsese feels that Columbia 'would have cut the violence out completely, and emphasized anything that, in their view, would have made it more – "appealing"' (Ehrenstein 1992: 115). Scorsese, however, stood his ground, not least because of the studio's limited financial commitment: '$1.3 million. I was going to compromise over that?' (*ibid.*).

To enable release in February 1976, Columbia demanded a rough cut four weeks after shooting. Editing was supervised by Marcia Lucas, who was assisted by four other editors. There were censorship problems. These centred on two areas, the climactic violence and a pair of incidents involving 13-year-old Jodie Foster: Sport's graphic description of Iris's sexual prowess and the sound of Iris undoing Travis's zipper in her room. Initially, the Motion Picture Association of America (MPAA) gave *Taxi Driver* an X rating. The filmmakers were contracted to deliver an R-rated film. Scorsese made the violence acceptable by cutting some frames and desaturating the scene's colour, so that the blood appeared a 'less realistic' reddish-brown. The Foster problem was solved by 'a friendly call from a Power Broker' (Phillips 1991: 252).[16] Released with an R-rating, *Taxi Driver's* final negative cost was $1.9 million.

The score for *Taxi Driver* was composed by Bernard Herrmann. Herrmann's first film score was for *Citizen Kane* (Orson Welles, 1941). Although a diverse career followed, our collective view of his work has tended perhaps to be defined by his collaboration with Alfred Hitchcock, for whom he scored *The Trouble With Harry* (1955), *The Man Who Knew Too Much* (1956), *The Wrong Man* (1956), *Vertigo* (1958), *North by Northwest* (1959), *Psycho* (1960) and *Marnie* (1964).[17] Herrmann's scores for these films typically combine variously rich and oppressive low registers and often extreme dissonance to create a potent and characterizing mix of dark romanticism and disquieting tension. This is echoed by his score for *Taxi Driver*, that hypnotically and edgily fuses rich romantic tones, ominous percussion and lush jazz saxophone.[18]

Prior to *Taxi Driver*, Herrmann scored two films directed by Brian De Palma, *Sisters* (1973) and the Schrader-scripted *Obsession* (1976).[19] Both comprise modernist reworkings of Hitchcock films: *Sisters* of *Psycho* and *Rear Window* (1954), with further allusions to *The Man Who Knew Too Much*, and *Obsession* of *Vertigo*, with further allusions to *Rebecca* (1940), *Notorious* (1946), *Dial M for Murder* (1954) and *Marnie*. As they replay and parody incidents, dialogue and camerawork, both films reinflect the themes and ideological concerns of their predecessors. It is a perspective summarized in *Obsession* when Sandra (Genevieve Bujold) talks to Michael (Cliff Robertson) about the difficulty of deciding whether to restore a great painting or to reveal another work found beneath: 'Should they remove and destroy a great painting ... to uncover what appears to be a crude first draft ... Or should they restore the original, but never know for sure what lies beneath it?'. The suggestion of the interplay of surface and depth, re-creation and analysis reflexively implies the films' engagement with Hitchcock's *oeuvre*. Herrmann's scores are central to this project. His music for *Sisters* implies a number of his Hitchcock scores, while his score for *Obsession* reworks that of *Vertigo*. Like so much New Hollywood Cinema, the films suggest a *nouvelle vague* (or, specifically, post-*nouvelle vague*) antecedent: François Truffaut's similarly Herrmann-scored and often playfully deconstructive rearticulation of the Hitchcockian mode, *La Mariée était en noir* (1967).

Herrmann's music for *Taxi Driver* was the first orchestral score for a Scorsese film. This links with the film's formal reflection of the modernist address of *Sisters* and *Obsession*. Expanding the allusiveness of Scorsese's previous films, *Taxi Driver* re-presents incidents, elements and structures from numerous forerunners. Apart from its allusions to *Journal d'un curé de campagne*, the most extended and integrated references are to *The Searchers*, *Psycho* and *Peeping Tom* (Michael Powell, 1960). On one level, *Taxi Driver* asks to be read – in part through such allusions – as a self-consciously and critically reflexive text; with respect to which, Herrmann's score at times replicates that of *Psycho*. However, like *Psycho*, and a number of other Hitchcock films, much of the text's reflexive self-criticism only becomes apparent retrospectively, or even on a second viewing.[20]

This is a corollary of the identification that the text encourages with Travis. Stylistically, this centres upon a cogent elaboration of the expressionist devices noted in *Who's That Knocking at My Door?* and *Mean Streets*. Through a combination of an expressive use of colour and the systematic deployment of non-classical camerawork and editing (slow-motion, jump-cuts, intra-scene dissolves) *Taxi Driver* represents New York as refracted through Travis's reflected subjectivity. Add the dominance of the character's frequently voyeuristic point of view, the use of voice-over and his presence in, and reflected perception of, all but a few scenes, and we, too, are made to share Travis's perception.

This commences with the film's first shot: a yellow Checker cab, filmed from a low-angle and in slow-motion, moves toward and past the camera, leaving the title credit in its wake. Accompanied by percussive, militaristic music, the shot is ominous, but also intriguing and impressive. The cab and steam connote New York, but – as Robert Phillip Kolker points out – the shot effectively defamiliarizes the familiar.[21] A concept coined by Russian Formalist Victor

Shklovsky, defamiliarization (*ostranenie*) describes the way that art 'makes strange' and renews our perception of existence – 'art exists that one may recover the sensation of life; it exists to make one feel things, to make the stone *stony* . . . to impart the sensation of things as they are perceived and not as they are known' (1917: 12). Reflecting this, the opening shot of *Taxi Driver* presents an affective, highly particularized vision that immediately draws us within the film's stylized point of view.

It is a point of view that the rest of the credit sequence concretizes and more specifically locates. The opening shot dissolves to a close-up of Travis's eyes, coloured by the glare of red, white and blue lighting. This dissolves to a reverse shot of a rain-spattered windscreen, that dissolves to a shot of a neon-lit, rain-slicked, night-time city street. Framed by the windscreen, and distorted by slow-motion and multiple exposure, the shot dissolves to a shot of couples crossing the street amid red- and blue-lit steam. A dissolve back to Travis's eyes, that are lit by a deepening red, places this as Travis's point of view. The close-ups of the eyes are filmed in slight slow-motion (36 frames per second), contributing an enigmatic, if virtually subliminal, intensification.[22] For Kolker, the sequence's continuing, defamiliarizing stylization establishes 'a kind of perceptual state of mind that diffuses itself over the film' (1988: 188). It is also a perception that the sequence assigns to Travis, and within which we are further fixed by the shot-reverse shot pattern.

Following the more 'mainstream' stylistic approach of *Alice Doesn't Live Here Anymore*, the expressionism of *Taxi Driver* implies an enabling correlation of modest budget, personal engagement and relative (and seemingly asserted) autonomy. The opening also marks a divergence of Schrader and Scorsese's authorial discourses. Neither stylistically 'sparse' nor denying of emotive apprehension, the sequence is disregarding of transcendental style. Accepting the acknowledged sources of Scorsese's established style, it is a contrast that has been referred further to the difference-within-similarity of Schrader and Scorsese's religious backgrounds; to the disparity between the rigorous asceticism of Dutch-American Calvinism and the sensuous ritualism of Italian-American Catholicism. Schrader has likened Scorsese's realization of his script to 'the story of a Protestant kid from the snow country who wandered into a cathedral in the middle of New York' (Jackson 1990: 117). The 'conflict of sensibilities' (*ibid.*) is acknowledged by the name of the film's production company: Italo-Judeo.

V

Early in the film we see Travis in his room, writing in his diary. His voice-over speaks what he writes, a description of his daily routine: 'I'm working long hours now. Six in the afternoon to six in the morning, sometimes even eight in the morning. Six days a week, sometimes seven days a week'. In illustration, the scene cuts to a sequence of Travis's cab moving through night-time, downtown New York, an environment of whores, street people, more steam and diffused and garish red and green lighting. Over a tracking point-of-view shot, taken from the cab, of a crowded, gaudily lit street, Travis's voice-over resumes: 'All the animals come out at night. Whores, skunk pussies, buggers, queens, fairies, dopers, junkies, sick, venal.' As the words anchor the image, which reciprocally 'validates' Travis's strident, illiberal comments, so the sequence, with its expressionist colour and the use of point of view and voice-over, heightens our identification with Travis. Once we 'enter' Travis's cab, we share both his perceptual *and* ideological space.

In their combination of situation, subjective voice-over, point-of-view editing and a Herrmann score, the scenes of Travis's night-time cruising reflect those of Marion Crane (Janet Leigh)'s journey to the Bates Motel in *Psycho*.[23] Both characters drive into a 'corrupted' world, and as Travis's point of view dominates *Taxi Driver*, so that of Marion dominates the first half of *Psycho* – with Marion in every scene we are locked into her experience. Moreover, one of the most subversive aspects of *Psycho* is the film's prompting of identification with transgressive, criminal characters: Marion, who steals, and Norman Bates (Anthony Perkins), who kills.

Robin Wood has termed Travis's vision of New York as that of 'The Excremental City' (1980: 28). Travis's New York both maintains the melodramatically conventional representation of the city as corrupt that is apparent throughout American culture and implies more specific antecedents. While Scorsese's expressionist use of red continues the  influence of Powell's filmmaking, the street scenes in especial recall the garish Eastmancolor of *Peeping Tom*, a film that likewise represents a city, London, seemingless obsessed with sex. A similar vision of the city is a repeated element of urban westerns. Whether the disco scene of *Coogan's Bluff* or the downtown San Francisco of *Dirty Harry*, such sequences 'prove' counter-culture decadence. Reflecting this, not only is Travis's vision dominated by open prostitution and porno houses, but the people that he sees are mainly young and wear seventies fashions.

The representation of the city in urban westerns is indebted to that of *film noir*. *Taxi Driver* foregrounds the link: the film's particular incorporation of claustrophobic, expressionist lighting, voice-over, neon-lit and rain-slicked streets and a jazz-tinged score implies a self-conscious updating of *noir* stylistics. The film is in addition informed by certain *film noir* structures.

As Travis writes in his room, we also hear: 'Thank God for the rain which has helped wash away the garbage and the trash off the sidewalks.' Following his 'moral' diatribe and the tracking shot of the sidewalk, his voice-over asserts: 'Someday a real rain'll come and wash all the scum off the streets.' This suggests that the 'trash' is human and that the rain is symbolic and retributive: '[Travis's] statement is especially interesting given the absence of the first person singular pronoun: it is not a statement of intent, for there is no human subject undertaking the action, but rather the prognostication of an intervention on the part of some unspecified transcendental agency' (Weaver 1986: 14). As Travis's cab moves through the streets, we are given three successive close-ups of its rain-spattered body: shots of a back side window, its gas-tank cover and a wing mirror. If this offers the cab as a vehicle of retribution, its visual fragmentation not only augments its presence but – in a particularly 'Catholic' suggestion – lends it an iconic, sacramental status. While these religious suggestions are in part (literally) Travis's, they add force to his 'moral' judgements. The need for retribution is further 'justified' by two directly subsequent scenes. First, Travis drives a middle-aged businessman (Peter Savage) and a black hooker (Copper Cunningham). Then, after he drives through 'cleansing' water spouting from a hydrant, Travis parks the cab in the garage, pops some pills, takes a cloth, straightens his back and ducks into the cab's back seat. His voice-over intones: 'Each night when I return the cab to the garage, I have to clean the come off the back seat. Some nights I clean off the blood.'

Travis's 'morality' is, however, problematized when he enters the Show & Tell. This bears out his admission to the personnel officer (Joe Spinell) that he visits porno theatres, but also evokes the 'Fascination' sign prominently in shot before the hood of his cab near the beginning of the night-time sequence. The suggestion is of Travis's mutual denial and attraction, that, desiring what he consciously rejects, he is caught in a compulsive return of the repressed: as he rails against 'the animals', his view of the sidewalk focuses upon and follows a hotpants-clad woman. Travis, too, comes out at night and, for all his claims that he drives 'all over' New York, seems only to work in the most sordid areas.

With Travis thus caught between and unable to reconcile conflicting impulses, his representation reflects that of previous Scorsese male protagonists, suggesting another split, and here agonizingly alienated, subjectivity: 'Twelve hours of work and I still can't sleep .... Days go on and on, they don't end.' As Schrader proposes, Travis's situation as a taxi driver – amongst people, but apart – perfectly figures his condition. So does his room. Established via a circular tracking shot, the room is dingy and uncomfortable, with cracked paint, bare plaster, rudimentary furniture and barred windows. As much a cell as a room, it suggests – on one level – the rooms/cells of the protagonists of Bresson's prison cycle. On another, it implies an externalization of Travis's psychological and emotional state, expresses his repression and alienation. Yet even in Travis's room what is repressed has returned. Not only is the room littered with what appear to be pornographic magazines, but it is soiled and untidy: as Travis's voice-over speaks of 'the garbage and the trash', the camera tracks past squalid cooking facilities.

When Travis joins some fellow cabbies in what the script identifies as a 'greasy spoon' his alienation is reflected through the framing of shots. Sitting at the edge of the others' table, Travis is shot either in a front-on medium shot, that stresses his apartness, in close one-shots or as a slightly out-of-focus presence in the foreground or background of the two-shots of Wizard (Peter Boyle) and Doughboy (Harry Northup). The suggestion of Travis's repressed desire is maintained as Travis listens, fascinated, to Wizard's sexual fantasy about a fare who changed her pantyhose in his cab. Given this, Wizard's bantering greeting that Travis is a 'ladies' man' and Doughboy's joky query, 'How's it hangin'?', have ironic aptness. Travis responds to Doughboy's words with a combination of alienated incomprehension and embarrassment, as if he has been 'caught out'. As in *Peeping Tom*, in which various characters are implicated in illicit activities, the sexual preoccupation of Wizard and Doughboy, who ends the scene by trying to get Travis to sell a piece of Errol Flynn's bathtub, marked by three bathers, extends and personalizes the film's representation of 'depravity'. The connotation is of a determining cultural context, the relation of which to Travis's disjunction is underscored when, upon Doughboy's question, and as though to change the subject, Travis notes that a driver has been 'cut up' on '122nd Street'. Wizard comments 'Fuckin' Mau Mau land'. Travis uneasily looks left and there is a cut to a portentous, slightly slow-motion, forward tracking point-of-view shot of a pair of sharply-dressed, aggressive-looking blacks; a look that is interrupted only by Doughboy enquiring, insistently, whether Travis carries 'a piece'. The incident implies Travis's racism, but equally figures an 'instant' conditioning: it jars against both his voice-over's earlier (albeit 'unconsciously' unreliable) contrasting of self with drivers who 'won't even take spooks' and his racially untroubled attempt to pick up the black Show & Tell concession girl (Diahnne Abbott). The latter, moreover, can itself be read as foreshadowed and 'determined' by his driving of the businessman and the black hooker.

The scene with the concession girl in addition foreshadows Travis's rejection by Betsy. Although Travis's approach to the concession girl is seemingly friendly rather than openly sexual, his repetitive insistence, the accompanying groans of a porno film and the very setting of the dark, seedy lobby combine to lay bare his 'inadmissible' desire. Similar situational intimations attend Travis's taking Betsy to a double bill of *Sometime Sweet Susan* and *Swedish Marriage Manual*. He also overcomes Betsy's hesitation ('This is a dirty movie') with like nervous, repetitive insistence: 'No, no ... this is a movie that a lot of couples come to. All kinds of couples go here.' The increasingly irritated concession girl – 'wise' to Travis's intent – eventually calls to the manager, and Travis reverts to an overcompensatory innocence ('Do you have any ju-jubes?'). This is replayed by Travis's naïve, confused response when Betsy exits the porno theatre ('I don't know much about movies ...'). She, too, is 'knowing' about his motivation: 'Taking me to a place like this is about exciting to me as saying "let's fuck"'.

VI

Betsy is first seen in slow-motion as she enters Palantine campaign headquarters from the street. Her movements are accompanied by Travis's voice-over: 'She was wearing a white dress. She appeared like an angel, out of this filthy mess.' The combination of slow-motion and voice-over, with its awkward rhyme, again locates the vision as Travis's. Implying mental effort, the voice-over hesitantly ends, 'They ... cannot ... touch ... her', and the shot dissolves to the same words written in clumsy print in his diary. This visual repetition of the voice-over reflects Bresson's combination of voice-over and shots of the Curé d'Ambricourt writing in his diary in *Journal d'un curé de campagne*. It is through such techniques – what Schrader, following Susan Sontag, terms 'doubling'[24] – that Bresson creates the 'disparity' that Schrader considers vital to transcendental style: 'his narration does not give the viewer any new information or feelings, but only reiterates what he already knows ... because the detail is doubled there is an emotional queasiness, a growing suspicion of the seemingly "realistic" rationale behind the everyday' (1972b: 72). But while Scorsese's use of 'doubling' follows Schrader's script, its contextualization more specifically evokes the reworking of Bresson's use of voice-over and diary in *Pierrot le fou* (Jean-Luc Godard, 1965), in which the scheme functions to foreground the contingency and constructedness of Ferdinand (Jean-Paul Belmondo)'s romantic viewpoint. The moment exemplifies the text's dual expressionist-reflexive connotations. Placing Travis's vision of Betsy as a romantic idealization, it can be seen to switch the text's address from expressionist defamiliarization to 'Brechtian' distanciation. Scorsese himself, moreover, is shown sitting before Palantine headquarters, eyeing Betsy as she passes. Inserting himself, Hitchcock-like, into the shot's chain of looks, Scorsese's presence heightens the scene's reflexivity by suggesting the source of the *film's* point of view.

Travis's idealizing of Betsy is in turn compromised diegetically by the following scene, one of the few that is represented as occurring outside Travis's perception. Instead of an angel, Betsy, as she talks with fellow campaign worker Tom (Albert Brooks), appears to be a self-possessed, if unexceptional, individual, whose stress on pushing Palantine before his policies implies a certain cynicism. With his useless advances and unfunny quips, Tom is almost a figure of fun. Indeed, throughout *Taxi Driver* Travis appears to have an upright seriousness lacking in the film's other characters, who seem to be variously asinine, facile and/or corrupt(ed). Again this evokes the identification strategy of *Psycho*, wherein Marion and Norman are sympathetically preferable to the film's 'normal' characters.

When Travis enters Palantine headquarters and 'romances' Betsy, his words comprise a collection of clichés ('you are the most beautiful woman I have ever seen ... I think you're a lonely person ... I think you need something ... you can call it a friend'). This reinforces both the suggestion of his romantic idealization of Betsy and, through this, that of his cultural determination. Travis's dialogue and attitude also differ utterly from those in other situations; compare, say, his sententiousness when he writes in his diary or his 'gabby cabby' routine when Palantine rides in his cab. However, the self-consciousness that informs Alice's adoption of contrasting feminine roles in *Alice Doesn't Live Here Anymore* is, with regard to Travis, somewhat and increasingly uncertain. As the film proceeds, the implication is that Travis's subjectivity is not just split, but radically decentred.[25] Intrigued and flattered by Travis's attention,

Betsy accepts his hackneyed invitation to join him for 'coffee and pie'. This implies an indulgence of the myth of the romantic outsider: as Travis relates to his image of Betsy, she can only relate him to a 'song by Kris Kristofferson ... "He's a prophet and a pusher, partly truth, partly fiction, a walking contradiction"'. The alienated Travis has not heard of Kristofferson and gets irritated at being called 'a pusher', implying that Betsy has hit a nerve regarding Travis's 'corrupt' self: we have, after all, seen him popping pills.

The suggestion recurs when Travis declines gun-salesman Easy Andy (Steven Prince)'s offer of drugs with a slightly troubled 'I'm not interested in that stuff.' However, the scene also cuts to Travis in his room doing push-ups, lifting extemporized weights and doing chin-ups on a bar while his voice-over intones: 'There'll be no more pills, there'll be no more bad food, no more destroyers of my body.' This is the beginning of an extended preparation sequence that, centred upon Travis's room, is divided into three segments. It culminates with Travis practising drawing his guns in a series of shots that all show mirrored reflections. Travis ejects a .25 Colt automatic from the gun-slide he has constructed and points it at his image. This he addresses – while, out of shot, he replaces the gun – as if he were challenging an assailant. He then again ejects the (unloaded) pistol and 'fires' it at his reflection. Travis replaces the Colt, and there follows the film's most quoted piece of dialogue. Standing sideways to the mirror, Travis speaks at his reflection: 'You talkin' to me? You talkin' to me? You talkin' to me? Then who the hell else are you talkin' ... You talkin' to me? Well I'm the only one here. Who the fuck do you think you're talkin' to? Oh yeah? Huh? Okay?'. Travis half turns away only to turn back and yet again eject the gun and point it at his reflection. Read in terms of Scorsese's authorial discourse, the scene's reiteration of the mirror motif not only underscores Travis's suggested determination, but compounds the Lacanian connotations that attend the motif in Scorsese's preceding films. The mirror here explicitly relates determination and alienation: Travis's assumption of a new, violent image is – as he threatens and 'shoots' himself – intimately linked to a repression of the self. Scorsese has described the scene as 'the key to the picture' (Goldstein and Jacobson 1976: 30).

As we share Travis's contemplation of self, the mirror shots uphold identification. Yet as Travis speaks to and threatens himself, he also speaks to and threatens us, proffering a possible estrangement. This duality is sustained by the remainder of the sequence, that cuts from Travis's reflection to a half-profile medium shot of him standing, arms folded, in the centre of his room. Defying classical convention, this dissolves to a close shot, that dissolves to a reverse close shot, filmed from behind Travis's left shoulder. As Travis turns his head, in slow-motion, toward the camera, his voice-over resumes: 'Listen you fuckers, you screwheads, here is a man who would not take it anymore, who would not let ... '. The voice-over abruptly stops, then restarts, with Travis repeating his opening words and the scene jump-cutting to a reprise of the shot of his head turning. On one hand, the non-classical editing and camerawork reflects and keeps us 'inside' Travis's perception. On the other, they mark Travis as unhinged. This is heightened when Travis's voice-over again affirms 'here is a man who would not take it anymore', and there is a cut to an overhead shot of Travis disconcertingly lying on his back on his bed like a broken doll. The voice-over continues: 'a man who stood up against the scum, the cunts, the dogs, the filth, the shit. Here is someone who stood up.' On the first 'stood up' Travis turns on his side into a foetal position. While this sound–image dichotomy is itself potentially distancing, there follows a cut, as Travis's voice-over says 'Here is ... ', to the same words written in his diary. This cuts to another reflection shot of Travis, in which he once more ejects the pistol and points it at himself, and us, before saying: 'You're dead.' Fleetingly 'removing' us from Travis, the shot of the diary, like that before, offers a brief distanciation. This italicizes the succeeding mirror shot, presenting Travis, like Betsy before, as discursively constructed.

The preparation sequence is markedly allusive. The shots of Travis exercising replay a sequence in *Murder by Contract* (Irving Lerner, 1958), a low-budget feature that Scorsese has dubbed 'the film that has influenced me most' (1978: 66). During the sequence's second segment, Travis practises drawing his guns, constructs the gun-slide from a drawer-rail, tapes an army knife to his boot, practises drawing the knife and indents the tips of bullets, making them dumdums. Largely filmed in comparatively long takes, the detailed representation of these actions evokes Bresson's assiduous representation of Fontaine (François Leterrier)'s escape preparations in *Un condamné à mort s'est échappé* and Michel (Martin La Salle) practising pickpocketing in *Pickpocket*. This is accentuated not only by the way that Travis, like Bresson's protagonists, acts alone in his room/cell, but also by the segment's sound, that consists mainly of ambient street noises.[26] These are mixed with the insistent sound of a clock ticking. Implying, expressionistically, that Travis is a 'time bomb', this creates a tension that, combined with our 'sharing' of Travis's preparations, enhances our

involvement with the character. The sound is also another allusion to
Murder by Contract.

Through such allusiveness, *Taxi Driver* achieves a formal – and,
again, implicitly reflexive – homology with the suggested psychology
of its protagonist. For as Travis is represented as a decentred personality, differentially determined by and acting out a variety of clichéd,
mythic roles, so the text analogously reworks a plurality of filmic
influences. Indeed, the protagonist of *Murder by Contract* – Claude
(Vince Edwards) – is an assassin, while not only are the shots of
Travis's reflection preceded by Travis twirling a .38 snub-nose western
fashion, but his 'You talkin' to me?' speech recalls an exchange
between Shane (Alan Ladd) and Calloway (Ben Johnson) in *Shane*
(George Stevens, 1953):

> *Shane*: You speaking to me?
> *Calloway*: I don't see nobody else standing there.[27]

Similarly note the reverse tracks of Travis staring into a glass of Alka
Seltzer at the greasy spoon. Occurring after Travis's racist 'conditioning' and as Doughboy talks about getting him a 'real nice deal'
on a firearm, the moment refers to the renowned coffee-cup incident
in *2 ou 3 choses que je sais d'elle* (Godard, 1966) and can be read as both
an expression of Travis's seething, alienated frustration and as an
allusive admission of the text's constructedness.

VII

Scorsese makes a second diegetic appearance as a fare who, with manic
insistence, gets Travis to look up at a brightly lit second-floor window,
in which stands a silhouetted woman. The fare tells how the woman is
his wife, but that it is not his apartment, 'A nigger lives there', and that
he is going to kill her: 'did you ever see what a .44 Magnum pistol can
do to a woman's face? I mean, it'll fuckin' destroy it.' Then, with
phallic displacement: 'Did you ever see what it can do to a woman's
pussy? That you should see. That you should see what a .44 Magnum's
gonna do to a woman's pussy you should see.' Throughout the scene,
Travis sits almost petrified, with his back to the fare, and hardly says a
word.

So far the narrative of *Taxi Driver* has been largely episodic.
Approached in terms of transcendental style, this could be seen to
conform to the notion of the 'everyday'; in relation to which Travis's

alienated intensity might evoke the next stage of 'disparity'. But whereas transcendental style relates 'disparity' to inexplicable transcendental agency, in *Taxi Driver* Travis's behaviour has been afforded apparently materialist determination. Further: 'Expressionism is an anathema to transcendental style .... It "interprets" reality, assigning to it a comprehensible (though irrational) psychological reality' (Schrader 1972b; 118). The film's rough cut, edited 'according to Schrader's script', was, in the words of Julia Phillips, 'a disaster' (1991: 237). The film was recut following Travis's voice-over. Correspondingly, whereas narrative events are linear, narrative logic tends to be associational and symbolic, presenting a subjective structure that invites interpretation via Sigmund Freud's model of the dream-work.

Considered thus, the fare's bringing together of sex, racism and phallic violence suggests a condensation and displacement of the concerns of the scene in the greasy spoon. The scene with the fare also immediately follows Travis's rejection by and of Betsy. This has been accompanied by the first intimations of his violence – his rough handling of Betsy outside the porno theatre, his threatening of Tom at Palantine headquarters – incidents that imply a harmful displacement of thwarted sexual energy. The fare can hence be seen to be giving expression, in a kind of dream-distortion, to Travis's own felt betrayal and resentment. This the fare would appear to speak – again like a dream – directly into Travis's head.

Scorsese claims that he cast himself as the fare because of an injury to actor George Memmoli.[28] Even so, the casting has acute textual resonance. Scorsese's performance once more reflexively implies his extra-diegetic role as director. Not only does the character – with his nervous eyes and movements and intense, repetitive diction – virtually parody Scorsese's public image, but he explicitly 'directs' Travis's gaze, and that of the camera/spectator, to the window, where the woman's silhouette is 'like an image on a screen' (Rice 1976: 117). This potentially disrupts diegetic integration: it is as though Scorsese is 'authorizing' and calling attention to the scene's narrative import.

The reflexive connotations of Scorsese's presence are heightened by the scene's allusive intimations. In *Peeping Tom* Powell casts himself as the protagonist's psychologist father; a figure who, by prompting and filming the childhood fear of his son, Mark, is suggested to be responsible for the adult Mark (Carl Boehm)'s destructive association of desire, aggression and looking/filming. The association of the oppressive male gaze with that of the camera is also implied in *Psycho* when we share

Norman's point of view as he spies on Marion. In *Peeping Tom*, however, it is foregrounded by narrative context: Mark not only films his female victims as he kills them, but works as a focus-puller at a film studio. In both films the Look of their repressed protagonists leads to violence whose sexual reference is underlined by the characters' phallic weaponry: 'Mother''s knife, the bladed camera tripod. In *Taxi Driver* this is reflected by Travis's guns.

When Easy Andy and Travis enter an anonymous hotel room, Travis asks whether Andy has a .44 Magnum, the gun mentioned by the cuckolded fare. Not only is the pistol fetishized by a lingering tracking close-up, but Andy refers to his wares in distinctly sexual terms ('That's a beauty', 'Isn't that a little honey?'). The .44 Magnum is also the weapon associated with 'Dirty' Harry Callahan. Andy notes, racistly: 'I could sell those guns to some jungle bunny in Harlem .... But I just deal high quality goods to the right people.' Travis's first fatal victim is black, when he shoots a man (Nat Grant) holding up a supermarket. This consummates Travis's awareness of menacing black masculinity: we see youths throwing eggs and objects at his cab, Travis exchanging threatening looks with a young black outside the Belmore Cafeteria and his driving past an angry, raving man (Frank Adu). At the Belmore Cafeteria, the black cabbie, Charlie T (Norman Matlock), grinningly calls Travis 'Killer' and 'shoots' him with his forefinger. The combination of word and gesture both suggests that Charlie T somehow 'recognizes' Travis's latent threat and, in its further collapsing of race and phallic violence, implies another determining moment: all these incidents follow the scene at the greasy spoon.

The eventual suddenness of the supermarket shooting implies that Travis has acted almost despite himself. Confounded by the mess he has made, Travis is unsure whether he has killed or not. His .380 Walther lacks a permit: like Travis, it is not controlled. The implication is of a loss of conscious volition, of an unchecked, and deadly, return of long repressed impulses. When Travis's cab pulls up at the supermarket, the soundtrack replicates a three-note motif from the score of *Psycho* that is first heard when Norman reacts with sudden, psychotic intensity when Marion queries whether 'Mother' could not be put in an institution.[29] The motif's replication at this particular point in *Taxi Driver* would seem to aim to suggest that Travis and Norman are analogously 'disturbed'. Nevertheless, having relieved Travis of his gun and reassuringly ushered him out of the supermarket, the owner, Melio (Victor Argo), repeatedly and unsettlingly hits the dead black with an iron bar – violence that again contextually situates Travis's 'madness'. In such fashion, *Taxi Driver* renders critically apprehensible the racism that the urban western implicitly validates.[30]

The phallic connotations of Charlie T's gesture are underlined when Travis points his forefinger at the screen of a porno theatre. The gesture carries an intertextual charge: it is used, with similar phallic implication, not only by Charlie in *Mean Streets*, but by Ben, outside Alice's motel room, in *Alice Doesn't Live Here Anymore*. The gesture is further echoed when Travis aims the Magnum at his television and a black couple dancing on *American Bandstand*: a situation that again presents a condensation of sex, violence and racism. Soon after, Travis watches a soap opera while holding the Magnum at groin level and rocking the crate that supports the television with his foot. The rocking motion implies masturbation; the soap, in which a blonde woman (Brenda Dickson) tells a confused, desperate man (Beau Kayser) that their relationship is over, reflects Travis's relationship with Betsy. Finally Travis, in a metaphoric ejaculation, and another moment of destructive uncontrol, kicks over the television, which explodes.

Travis holds his head in his hands, and there is a dissolve to close-up. The intra-scene dissolve transmits reflected subjectivity, but also emphasizes Travis's despair: identification is enhanced both here and at the supermarket by the seeming inadvertency of his actions. This places Travis as the 'victim' of his situation and helps to keep him sympathetic. A similar affective function is performed by the scene in which Travis, with painful inarticulateness, asks Wizard for advice. With mythic cabbie verbosity, Wizard makes a speech that in effect declares the inevitability of social determination: 'a man takes a job ... and that job ... becomes what he is. ... You do a thing and that's what you are.' He concludes: 'you've got no choice anyway ... we're all fucked, more or less'. In terms of the text's allusiveness, Wizard's role here reflects that of the Curé de Torcy (Andre Guibert) in *Journal d'un curé de campagne*. Setting themselves up as sources of pragmatic wisdom, both characters give worthless advice that unintentionally speeds the protagonists' fates.

VIII

Having initially constructed Betsy as 'pure', Travis's final, angry words at Palantine headquarters recast her, no less inappropriately, as 'corrupt': 'You're in a hell. And you're gonna die in a hell like the rest.' Travis's terms of reference reflect the misogynistic dualism that, for example, both structures female representation in *film noir* and, as the madonna–whore dichotomy, has recurred somewhat problematically in Scorsese's previous films. It likewise informs Travis's subsequent, seemingly diametrical attempt to restore the whore Iris to innocence. This, however, is ironically paralleled with his relations with the 'pure' Betsy. As with Betsy, Travis meets Iris at work, seeks to 'save' her from an 'unworthy' setting, makes a date and, in a following scene, takes her to a coffee-shop. Betsy and Iris have similar hair colour and complexions, and when Iris joins Travis for 'breakfast' her hair, which when she works is curled, is straight and side-parted in a lank version of Betsy's. Just as Travis responds to his image of Betsy, not to her actuality, so he seems to regard Iris, whom he fallaciously constructs as 'imprisoned', as a youthful example of the romantic stereotype of the innately pure prostitute. Further, as Travis's monomania about Tom ('I don't like him ... I don't think he respects you') is replayed in relation to Sport ('He is the lowest kind of person in the world .... He's the scum of the earth'), so Betsy's defence of Tom ('he's very good at his job'), is mirrored by Iris's of Sport ('Sport never treated me bad ... he didn't beat me up or anything').[31]

As with Betsy, we are given a scene that occurs outside Travis's perception and undermines his vision of the female. Seeking to comfort Iris, Sport holds her in a close dance and speaks blandishments: 'When you're close to me like this, I feel so good. I only wish every man could know what it is like to be loved by you .... It's only you that keeps me together.' If, in themselves, Sport's words are as clichéd as Travis's to Betsy, they are spoken with an ambivalent tenderness as he gently strokes Iris's head. Moreover, as Iris hugs Sport tightly, and lays her head on his shoulder, eyes closed beatifically, she appears to obtain solace from the situation. As Wood notes, the scene would appear 'to call into question any easy assumption we might have that anything is preferable' for a teenage girl 'to prostitution' (1980: 30).

Schrader has referred to the scene between Iris and Sport as 'the "Scar" scene' (Corliss 1978: 46); that is, 'the equivalent of a "missing" (and arguably essential) scene in *The Searchers'* that would define the captured Debbie's relationship to her captor, Chief Scar, and to Comanche life (Wood 1980: 30). [32] Previously referenced in *Who's That Knocking at My Door?* and extracted in *Mean Streets* by Scorsese, *The Searchers* seems to be a similarly important film for Schrader – its influence informs many of his early projects.[33] The parallels between *The Searchers* and *Taxi Driver* – and, especially, between the protagonist of *The Searchers*, Ethan Edwards, and Travis – have been widely documented.[34] For instance, both characters are veterans of lost wars, both first appear in part of the uniforms of the losing sides and both are wanderers. Most substantively, Travis's desire to 'save' Iris reflects Ethan's desire to 'save' Debbie; Ethan is an inveterate racist, with an 'irrational' hatred of Native Americans; and Ethan's violence can, like that of Travis, be related to frustrated sexual desire. As with Ethan's hatred of Scar, Travis's animus toward Sport relates to the latter's embodiment of the protagonist's inadmissible self: like Scar with Ethan, Sport acts out Travis's id impulses. Sport's implicitly sexual relationship with Iris expresses what Travis can only repress: witness Travis's confusion when Iris makes her paid-for attentions in her room. This in addition clarifies Travis's shift of interest from Betsy to Iris, as well as his tacit linking of Sport and Tom, whom Travis earlier perceives as a sexual rival. When Sport dances with Iris, the phonograph plays 'Betsy's Theme', music elsewhere associated with Travis's desire.[35]

When Travis approaches Sport, their repetitive exchanges ('I'm hip'/'you don't look hip') recall those of Ethan and Scar when they finally meet:

> *Ethan*: You speak pretty good American, for a Comanch. Someone teach ya? ...
> *Scar*: You speak good Comanch. Someone teach you?[36]

Sport designates Travis 'a real cowboy': as for much of the film, Travis wears a check shirt, blue jeans, a large buckled belt and cowboy boots. His name is similarly 'western'. This further connects Travis with the urban western protagonists – apart from not looking 'hip', both Sport and Iris are unsure whether Travis is a cop. Sport's appearance, by contrast, evokes that of a Native American: he has long dark hair and wears a singlet and a necklace. He also speaks like a hipster and has painted the enlongated nail of his right little finger with red nail-varnish. This correspondingly reflects the urban western association of the counter-culture with criminality and depravity. Likewise Iris's room, with its beaded curtain, fringed lightshade, candles, posters and bright pink décor. Sport's immediate response upon seeing the clean-cut Travis is to hold out and slap his forearms and proclaim that he is 'clean'. Similarly, Iris notes that she does not remember getting into Travis's cab because she 'must have been stoned'. Travis's shocked response – 'they drug you?' – underlines his apartness from the counter-culture, as does his 'old-fashioned' approval of Iris's name: 'Well, what's wrong with that? That's a nice name.' In the following scene he advocates patriarchal familial norms: 'You should be at home now. You should be dressed up, you should be going out with boys, you should be going to school.' Iris queries whether Travis has heard of 'Women's Lib' and calls him 'square'. She also more pointedly notes: 'Why do you want me to go back to my parents? I mean, they hate me. Why do you think I split in the first place?'.

Yet Iris appears to be no happier about her prostitution. She becomes anxious in her room about Sport's reaction should she and Travis not 'make it' and at the coffee-shop both appears uneasy when Travis condemns her selling her 'little pussy for nothing' and laughs nervously when he claims that Sport called her 'a little piece of chicken'.[37] Seemingly touched by Travis's concern, she also tells Sport 'I don't like what I'm doing'. Her attempt to escape from Sport when stoned suggests the eruption of *her* repressed desire.

Iris's situation once more reflects critically upon the represented environment: she wearily says that when she is not stoned she has 'no place else to go'. Her statement that she would like to move to the alternative environment of 'one of them communes in Vermont' has, accordingly, a certain logic. Travis responds that he saw 'some pictures once' and it 'didn't look very clean'. This implicitly links the commune – and, again, the counter-culture – with Travis's vision of 'the excremental city'.[38] Travis nevertheless offers to give Iris the money to go.[39]

Travis's offer again figures his desire to supplant Sport; albeit in his psycho-sexual position as Iris's father-figure. This in turn relates to Travis's implied correlation of Sport and Palantine. (That for Travis Sport replaces both Tom and Palantine is another characteristically oneiric condensation.) When Palantine exits Travis's cab, Travis is given a large tip by his aide (Robert Shields). Cut to the next scene. Iris rushes into the cab's back seat. Sport pulls the struggling Iris from the cab and tosses a (typically 'unclean') crumpled bill on to the front seat. As both Palantine and Sport thus 'buy off' Travis, so they can be seen similarly to assert their patriarchal potency. (Travis subsequently separates Sport's bill from his other takings and eventually uses it to pay for his 'trick' with Iris – a repayment that correspondingly asserts his potency.)

Travis watches Palantine being interviewed on television. There is a cut from Travis's television's screen to his cab passing Palantine headquarters, and we are given a pair of shots, from Travis's point of view, of Palantine posters and Betsy's empty chair. Read through the narrative's associational logic, this suggests a connection between Palantine and Betsy's absence and, by extension, Travis's rejection. Cut to a black area, at night-time, and Travis dropping off a fare. As he drives away, Iris steps before his cab. 'Thrust' before Travis, Iris symbolically replaces Betsy; Travis immediately follows Iris and her colleague (Garth Avery) in his cab, an act that reflects his earlier spying on Betsy. As this makes Betsy uneasy – she gets Tom to ask Travis to move – so it does Iris and her companion (Iris's backward glances; 'guy keeps following'/'Don't look at him').The reactions mark the sexual oppressiveness of Travis's gaze. As Iris and her colleague walk along the sidewalk, they are passed by the raving black, who shouts: 'I'll blow her brains out. I'll kill her.' The girls greet Sport, who stands in his doorway. This restates Iris's relationship with Sport, that implies a structural parallel with that of Betsy with Palantine in both economic and psycho-sexual terms. In turn, the scene's relation of Travis's oppressive desire, the black's threat of phallic violence and the identification of a sexual/psycho-sexual rival implies the further (over-)determination of Travis's ideas: it is only after this scene that Travis's voice-over declares 'there is a change' and that he buys his guns.

The film's tacit association of Palantine with Travis's rejection by Betsy proffers a psycho-sexual rationale for his assassination attempt. This maintains the text's thematic–formal homology by implicitly re-enacting a *film-noir* scenario, what Frank Krutnik calls *noir*'s 'criminal-adventure'. Generally traced to the novels of James M. Cain, the scenario's seminal filmic embodiments are a pair of Cain adaptations, *Double Indemnity* (Billy Wilder, 1944) and *The Postman Always Rings Twice* (Tay Garnett, 1946). In both, a relatively young, virile male protagonist is driven by his desire for a sexually alluring woman/*femme fatale* of similar age to kill, with Oedipal suggestiveness, her older, materially comfortable husband.[40] Reflecting this, Travis is prompted by his frustrated desire for Betsy to try to kill Palantine, who is placed as his father-figure rival. Within this structure, Betsy – who both calls Palantine 'sexy' and, during the assassination scene, regards him from the platform with a coy, admiring glance – operates like a *femme fatale manquée*. Although Betsy's condemnation by Travis is manifestly unjust, her sexual refusal results in Travis's increasing physical and psychic immersion with the city's *noir*-ish world: like a classical *femme fatale* she effectively prompts his 'surrender to dangerous and disturbing passions' (Walker 1992: 13).[41]

While Travis's Oedipal revolt is psychoanalytically consistent with the return of his repressed desires, his almost successful transgression like-wise implies a failure of suger-ego dominance, suggesting that Palantine is a flawed authority figure. He is also, in another, implicating link with the urban western, identified as vaguely Left-liberal: Tom refers to his 'mandatory welfare program' and we hear him allude to Walt Whitman and complain about Vietnam.

It is in addition suggested that Palantine simply embodies the image of a populist politician. When he sits, tanned and groomed, in Travis's cab, he pithily talks in candidate-speak ('I have learned more about America from riding in taxi cabs than in all the limos in the country'). However, when he patronizingly asks 'What is the one thing about this country that bugs you the most?', Travis engages in a vehement diatribe: 'this city here is like an open sewer ... it's full of filth and scum ... the President should just clean up this whole mess here. He should just flush it right down the fuckin' toilet.' As Travis speaks, Palantine and his aide are shown sitting in uncomprehending unease. If Travis's language and intensity index disturbance, they also clearly lie outside Palantine's habitual frame of reference, and he can only respond impotently with further cliché: 'I think I know what you mean, Travis. But it's not going to be easy.' When Palantine speaks in the garment district, his head is never shown, as though he 'is merely a brainless puppet mechanically and incessantly mouthing platitudes' (Bliss 1985: 111). Similarly, during the assassination scene not only do his emphatic hand gestures tellingly replicate those he uses previously, but his repeated raising of his arms is ironically paralleled by the statue that stands behind him. No less ironic-ally, Travis's assassination attempt can be considered an acting out of Palantine's empty campaign slogan 'Let the people rule'.

Palantine's representation extends the film's concern with culturally determined identity: notably, he is seen as a reflection in Travis's rear-view mirror. So is Iris, whose large-brimmed hat, tight, stomach-reveal-ing top and white hotpants fix her as the epitome of a seventies teenage prostitute. Of like note is the comic encounter between Travis and a Secret Service agent (Richard Higgs), who – with his large stature, folded arms and dark glasses – 'inconspicuously' stands out. Once more, it is as though the agent is acting out an expected image; a con-notation drolly underscored by the way that *all* the film's Secret Service agents wear dark glasses. When Travis first stands beside the agent, he too adopts the image, identically folding his arms. It is also after this that Travis wears dark glasses and constructs a fantasy of working 'for the government'.

IX

During the preparation sequence, Travis, stripped to the waist, holds a tightly clenched fist over a flame on his gas stove.[42] Implying ritual purification, this also symbolically replaces retributive rain with apocalyptic fire. The figure recurs in the shorter preparation sequence that precedes his assassination attempt: Travis sets light to boot polish, then burns Betsy's dead returned flowers. This is complemented by Travis's intimations of martyrdom. First, he counts out five $100 bills on to a note to Iris that reads: 'This money should be enough for your trip. By the time you read this I will be dead.' Then, his voice-over states: 'Now I see it clearly. My whole life has pointed in one direction …. There never has been any choice for me.' Like a Bresson protagonist, Travis at this moment seems to be accepting a predetermined, self-sacrificial but implicitly redeeming fate.

Travis's voice-over is also the sound bridge to the assassination scene. When Palantine begins to speak, there is a cut to a shot of Travis's body leaving his cab followed, upon another shot of Palantine, by a low-angled tracking shot across the crowd. On reaching Travis, the camera stops and tilts first to show his combat-jacketed body, then, as he pops a pill, jarringly to reveal his shaven, 'Mohawked' head.[43] A calculated shock effect, the tilt shows Travis to be unequivocally deranged; a condition stressed by his manic grin and asynchronous applause. Robert B. Ray posits that Travis's revelation withdraws 'sympathy for Travis with a single shot' (1985: 357). Such a consequence, however, is mitigated by the suspense generated both by the assassination attempt, during which the scene cuts between Palantine and Travis, and by Travis's very appearance (what will he do …?). Hitchcock has stated that suspense is 'the most powerful means of holding on to the viewer's attention' (Truffaut 1978: 77). Here it tends to occlude, at least immediately, the scene's critical connotations.

Travis's switching of murderous intent from Palantine to Sport reflects his implicit relation of the characters. He nevertheless exchanges one generic mode of action for another. Instead of a *noir* Oedipal rebel, Travis becomes the hero of a captivity narrative, a structure that *Taxi Driver* reworks via *The Searchers*. Termed by Richard Slotkin 'the first coherent myth literature in America for American audiences' (1973: 95), the captivity narrative centres on the rescue of white women settlers captured by Native Americans by a white hero (or heroes). The rescue frequently becomes compromised, however, by the heroes' need to 'fight the enemy on his own terms and in his own manner, becoming in the process a reflection or double of his own dark opponent' (*ibid.*: 563). In *Taxi Driver* this is visually emphasized as the 'Mohawk' Travis confronts Sport who, with his long dark hair and 'hippy' headband, resembles an Apache.[44] This also highlights the return of Travis's repressed.

Once more, Travis and Sport's repetitive dialogue recalls Ethan and Scar's:

> *Sport*: Do I know you?
> *Travis*: No. Do I know you?

After goadingly taunting Sport, Travis pulls his .38 snub-nose and, saying 'Suck on this', shoots Sport in the stomach. Travis's words again flag sexual displacement. Given that Iris had earlier tried to fellate Travis, Michael Bliss reads this as turning that 'sexual trick against Sport' (1985: 108). However, as the shooting of Sport figures Travis's psychotic repression of his *alter ego* – even as ironically he has become his 'other self' – so the words imply a pathological denial of homosexual likeness. During their first scene, Travis naïvely takes out his wallet to pay Sport for Iris in the street. Sport responds: 'You wanna fuck me? You ain't gonna fuck me, you're gonna fuck her, you give her the money.' Then, when Travis moves to leave with Iris, Sport 'shoots' him from the hip with both forefingers. A mocking of Travis's 'cowboy' appearance, this might also be perceived, and is seemingly so by Travis, as a threatening phallic gesture, that Travis repays with interest. The structure of action here replays – in a darker register – the exchange of Sport's crumpled bill.

Travis enters Iris's block.[45] He shoots the fingers off the right hand of Iris's timekeeper with his Magnum. Travis is shot in the neck by Sport, who has staggered inside the block's doorway. Travis shoots Sport dead with his snub-nose, a job he 'completes' with two further shots. Travis shoots the timekeeper in his left arm, strikes him with the pistol's butt and ascends the block's staircase. The timekeeper crawls after him, repeating 'I'll kill you.' The mafioso leaves Iris's room and shoots Travis in his right arm. Travis drops the snub-nose, falls to the floor but ejects his .25 automatic from his gun-slide and shoots the mafioso repeatedly in the face and body. He topples back, dead, into the hysterical Iris's room. Travis rises to follow, but is grabbed from behind by the timekeeper, still repeating 'I'll kill you.' They fall on to the floor of Iris's room. Travis abandons his empty automatic, pulls his knife from his boot and stabs the timekeeper through his left hand. Travis picks up the mafioso's pistol and shoots the timekeeper in the head, spattering blood and brains on the wall behind.

With its shot and stabbed hands and arms, the massacre is suffused with Freudian castration imagery. Sport, as he lies dead, holds his pistol suggestively near to his groin; a detail emphasized by a close-up track along his body. Travis's actions imply another, and fatally destructive, metaphoric orgasm. To the end, violence is related to phallic displacement and psycho-sexual assertion: during the massacre, the combatants are implicitly fighting to control Iris's sexuality.

The scene is horrific; even more so when, following the massacre's reports and screams, we are left with a silence broken only by the unsettling sounds of dripping blood and Iris's sobs. Travis points the mafioso's (now empty) pistol beneath his chin and pulls the trigger five times. Retrieving his discarded automatic, he similarly 'shoots' the timekeeper three times in the head and clambers on to the sofa. A policeman enters the room, pistol first. Travis raises his bloodied left forefinger to his temple and 'shoots' himself three times. This both maintains the phallic implication of Travis's violence and – through the gestures of Charlie T and Sport – relates it to his suggested determination: it is no coincidence that during the narrative's initial night-time sequence Travis's cab is shown passing a marquee for *The Texas Chainsaw Massacre* (Tobe Hooper, 1974). Travis's attempts to 'shoot' himself also returns us to his fragmented subjectivity. As the massacre can be referred to the return of his repressed, so Travis has in effect become that which he first railed against – hence the analogous 'shooting' of himself and of the timekeeper. Considered thus, his violence enacts a (failed) desire for self-annihilation, for which his suicidal gestures stand as a metonym.

The film cuts to an 'objective' overhead shot of the room. The camera proceeds steadily to track and crane, via dissolves, out of the room, back down the staircase, through the hall and into a crowded street. Shots that reflect the reverse crane down a staircase from another scene of murder in *Frenzy* (Hitchcock, 1972), they present the massacre's consequences: the bodies of the timekeeper and the mafioso, blood-stained walls and floors, Travis's dropped firearms, Sport's body. After the unaccompanied and unsettling naturalistic noises of the massacre and its immediate aftermath, the shots are accompanied by a slower, menacing version of 'Betsy's Theme' that Herrmann, according to Michael Phillips, orchestrated to stress 'that this was where Travis' fantasies about women led him' (Amata 1976: 7).

The violence of the massacre has been criticized. Kolker calls it 'an excrescence, a moment of grotesque excess in an otherwise controlled work' (1988: 203). The violence and its aftermath are, however, anything but uncontrolled, being crucial to the film's dramatic and ideological effect. The massacre salutarily 'corrects' our identification with Travis. During *Psycho* our identification with and sympathy for Marion and Norman is punished respectively by the violence of the shower scene and the climactic revelation that Norman is 'Mother', a psychopathic killer. In a reflection of this, the massacre is, in the first place, a punitive culmination and release of the narrative's increasing violence and tension. Following the massacre's brutal scourging, the cut to the over-head shot constitutes a decisive distancing break in our identification with Travis, an effect compounded by the subsequent shots. These force us to contemplate the implications of our identification, the results of the phallic violence in which we have been complicit. This problematizes Travis's desires and actions and provokes reconsideration of the narrative and of Travis's point of view; a process that complements/is complemented by the text's reflexive elements. Having encouraged then undermined identification, the film prompts an aware-ness of our own subjective implication in destructive attitudes and myths. Through its evocation of the urban western, *Taxi Driver* in parti-cular challenges our ideological investment in violent, vengeful male heroes. At the very least, it unequivocally foregrounds the consequences of Right-wing vigilantism, that the film represents as the action of an explicitly disturbed individual. Travis's words to Iris at the coffee-shop, 'cops don't do nothing, you know that', echo Kersey's rationale for his vigilantism in *Death Wish*: 'If the police don't defend us, maybe we ought to do it ourselves.'

The violence similarly compromises the text's religious connotations. It exposes Travis's moral crusade to cleanse the city as destructive fanaticism. Like Travis's other 'justifications', the text's 'vindicating' religious implications are placed as more discredited misdirection. While Travis's attempts to 'shoot' himself further evoke his intimations of martyrdom, his putative bid for self-sacrificial redemption has only brought the death of others. This renders the parallels between *Taxi Driver* and *Journal d'un curé de campagne* mordantly ironic: in contrast to Travis, the Curé d'Ambricourt's ascetic, sacrificial self-denial calls forth, almost despite himself, a redeeming spirituality.[46]

X

The shot of the street cuts to the film's coda and a track across press-cuttings affixed to a wall of Travis's room. These reveal that Travis has become a media celebrity; precisely, 'the type of apparition that constructed him' (Sharrett 1993: 233). Following upon the preceding distanciation, the cuttings further invite us to consider the nature of media that champion a killer and a society that sanctions such representations. In this, the shot offers a comparison with the obsessive, but excruciatingly unreflective, representation of the media's charting of Kersey's killings and influence in *Death Wish*.

The track is accompanied by an old-ish male voice reading aloud a letter to Travis. Identified as that of Iris's father, the voice thanks Travis for returning Iris home, admits that she has found the transition 'very hard' but declares that steps have been taken 'to see she has never cause to run away again'. As the voice nears its conclusion the tracking shot reaches the letter itself taped to Travis's wall. Another 'doubling' of voice-over and writing, this correspondingly evokes the contingency of Iris's father's words. In particular, as he expresses a conventional and unspecific paternalism, his words renew the issue of Iris's familial oppression; a connotation augmented by his voice's deadening intonation. In effect, the voice-over clarifies why Iris left home and her reluctance to leave Sport.

Cut to outside the St Regis Hotel at night. Wizard tells Doughboy and Travis a tale about a guy whose wife was 'Miss New Jersey of 1957'. In contrast to his previous apartness, Travis seems openly to enjoy Wizard's talk and has apparently achieved a degree of social and personal integration. But at what cost? What does it mean to be integrated within the represented society? And has anything really changed? On joining the group, Charlie T once more calls Travis 'Killer'.

Travis is drawn away by a fare in his cab, who 'just happens' to be Betsy. The ensuing scene plays off that in *The Roaring Twenties* in which ex-gangster now taxi driver Eddie Bartlett (James Cagney) drives the object of his unrequited love, Jean Sherman (Priscilla Lane). As Travis drives, he notes that he has heard that Palantine has got the Presidential nomination, adding, with unconscious irony, 'I hope he wins.' Betsy ingratiatingly says: 'I read about you in the papers. How are you?' Travis dispels her concern off-handedly, 'it was nothing really ...'. The characters appear still to be acting out familiar roles: Travis that of stoic hero, Betsy that of admiring, inviting female. Both characters, moreover, are shown as reflected in the cab's rear-view mirror – during the ride, Betsy is only seen in the mirror. On exiting the cab, Betsy, with a sigh, tries both to pay Travis and to prolong their conversation. Travis stolidly refuses her money and, with a knowing smile, drives off. Continuing the part of the acclaimed, upright hero, Travis is here able to resist sexual temptation. However, his actions equally imply a vindictive punishment of Betsy, whose advances have 'ratified' Travis's earlier, misogynistic denunciation: when Travis drives off, Betsy is left on the sidewalk, a reversal of the characters' positions outside the porno cinema.

The camera pans across the vehicle's interior, resting in a position over Travis's shoulder that highlights his eyes as they are reflected in the rear-view mirror. Catching sight of his reflection, Travis, on a cut to reverse shot, touches the mirror and, accompanied by a jarring noise, quickly amends what it reflects. With the mirror connoting cultural determination, Travis's action implies that he has recognized something that – as before – he does not want to admit. The moment recalls Iris's response when Travis asserts that Sport is a 'killer' and a 'dope shooter': 'Didn't you ever try looking in your own eyeballs in the mirror?'.[47] The suggestion of Travis's continuing personal disjunction compounds the coda's implication that nothing has really changed. Typical of Scorsese's films, it is a suggestion underscored by the ending's formal cyclicity. As the end credits come up, Travis's cab is moving through the same night-time streets and the shots are accompanied by the same music as during the front credits.

The ending of *Taxi Driver* rounds off the text's reflexive allusiveness. Its effective denial of closure suggests that of *Psycho*, in which the police psychiatrist (Simon Oakland)'s glib explanation of Norman's condition is exploded when we see Norman in a cell but hear, in voice-over, 'Mother''s thoughts. Suggesting Norman's irredeemable subsumption by his psychosis, this effectively overwhelms the subsequent dissolve to the film's final, 'releasing' shot of Marion's car being pulled from the swamp. Foreshadowing *Taxi Driver*, the protagonist's threat remains.[48] The ending of *Taxi Driver* likewise reflects that of *The Searchers*, a film whose conclusion similarly mirrors its opening. *The Searchers* begins with a shot of a door opening, through which passes Ethan's sister-in-law, Martha (Dorothy Jordan), who – with her gathering family – watches Ethan approach from afar. It concludes with another family entering, along with Martin Pawley and the rescued Debbie, another door, that closes on Ethan as he walks away. Excluded from civilization by his savagery, Ethan must return – like Travis later – to wandering his own particular wilderness.

The soundtracks of *Psycho* and *Taxi Driver* both end with the repetition of the cited three-note motif. Associated with both films' protagonists' disturbance, the motif serves to heighten both films' lack of closure.

The final scenes of *Taxi Driver* also bring to a head the apparent tensions between Schrader's supposed intentions and Scorsese's realization of his script. Schrader would have preferred the 'decisive action' of the massacre to have had an abstract, ritual effect: 'The ending isn't meant to be realistic .... At that point, we're living out a psychopath's fantasy ... this dream of a glorious and meaningful death .... And it should be ... played out to the full extent of its fantasy glory. I would have loved to see sheets of blood, literally, flowing down the walls' (Corliss 1978: 46).[49] By contrast, Scorsese's representation of the massacre conveys a disquieting veracity: '[Schrader] saw it as a kind of Samurai "death with honour" .... What I wanted was a *Daily News* situation, the sort you read about every day' (Thompson and Christie 1996: 63). The script represents Travis after the massacre as more definitely 'cured' and concludes with Travis and Betsy reaching a tentative accord. Following his model of transcendental style, and crowning, not undermining, the narrative's religious connotations, Schrader's script implies the achievement of 'stasis', the attainment of a state of grace. That this was, at some level of intention, Schrader's aim is suggested by the evidence of his other work, but in particular *American Gigolo* and *Light Sleeper*. While both films recast Bressonian tropes and evoke transcendental style, *Light Sleeper* is in addition a self-conscious reworking of *Taxi Driver* and *American Gigolo*, replaying incidents, motifs, shots and even lines of dialogue. In both *American Gigolo* and *Light Sleeper* 'statis' is achieved, albeit again at the cost of other peoples' lives. The victims of gigolo Julian Kay (Richard Gere) and drug-dealer John LeTour (Willem Dafoe) are, like Travis's, social 'undesirables' – a gay black pimp (Leon/Bill Duke) in *American Gigolo*, a rich, murderous junkie (Tis/Victor Garber) and his gun-toting associates (Brian Judge and Vinny Capone) in *Light Sleeper*. However, these deaths are not critically reflected upon. Instead, the killings are largely – and problematically – dismissed and justified as necessary for the protagonists' redemption.

XI

Taxi Driver once more reflects upon the posited formal and ideological limitations of New Hollywood Cinema. As the film encourages and then critiques our identification with Travis and, through this, to paraphrase Roland Barthes, the ideological abuse hidden therein, it takes a position in relation to mainstream Hollywood filmmaking comparable to that of post-structuralist critiques of the classic realist text.[50]

The suggestion is complemented by the text's 'correcting' integration of critically reflexive, 'Brechtian' techniques – the allusions to Godard's filmmaking in addition imply a nod to an exemplary influence. The film's reflexive address nevertheless and – given its means of production – necessarily remains embedded within what is fundamentally a realist text. It consequently proffers one *possible* reading. Ray is doubtless accurate in asserting that for 'the proponents of "counter cinema"' *Taxi Driver* would be 'too situated within Hollywood's traditional paradigms to produce an effective critique of the ideology those paradigms sustain' (1985: 362). However, Ray also claims that 'because *Taxi Driver* draws on both Hollywood's thematic and formal paradigms, only to criticize them' it presents 'a model for a "radical" American movie' (*ibid.*: 363). This overstates the case. At most, *Taxi Driver* marks some of the radical parameters for a film financed and distributed by a major studio in the mid-seventies.

With regard to this, *Taxi Driver* presents a trenchant vision of a culture that could produce a Travis Bickle. In terms of Scorsese's authorial discourse, the film's critique of misogynistic precepts has a surety lacking in his earlier work. Following *Alice Doesn't Live Here Anymore*, this might be attributed to his moving away from the closely biographical and his direction of others' scripts enabling a more consistent critical distance. Nevertheless, the representation of American society in *Taxi Driver* is depressive. Individual action is demonized. Politics, in the shape of Palantine, is 'exposed' as a sham. The ending suggests an unchanged, and seemingly unchangeable, situation. The one alternative mentioned in the film, the commune in Vermont, is 'given no concrete realisation' (Wood 1980: 28). Despite Travis's money, Iris is returned to her parents. This would appear to bear out Kolker's contention that although New Hollywood Cinema at times carries on 'an ideological debate with the culture', it never confronts 'that culture with another ideology, with other ways of seeing itself' (1988: 10). The films hence 'speak to a continual impotence in the world, an inability to change and to create change' (*ibid.*). This, however, is once more a function of a broader lack of available or acceptable ideological alternatives within American culture. Indeed, *Taxi Driver* has been seen to hold an intimate mirror to its historical moment. Made during the period of national uncertainty and impotence that affected the USA following, *inter alia*, Watergate, defeat in Vietnam and 'the failure and collapse of the New Left and counter-culture' (Quart and Auster 1984: 103), the film powerfully conveys what Kolker himself describes as the time's 'mixture of anger, guilt, and frustrated aggressiveness' (1988: 240). Schrader admits: '*Taxi Driver* was as much a product of luck and timing as everything else .... Marty was fully ready to make the film; De Niro was ready to make it. And the nation was ready to see it' (Kelly 1992: 90).

Hitting its February release date, *Taxi Driver* took $12.5 million in rentals to become the twelfth highest earner at the American box-office in 1976. It was a success matched critically. Winner of the Palme d'Or at Cannes, the film was voted among the year's ten best films by the National Society of Film Critics and nominated, unsuccessfully, for four Oscars: Best Picture, Best Actor (De Niro), Best Supporting Actress (Foster) and Best Original Score (Herrmann). De Niro, however, won the Best Actor award from the New York Society of Film Critics and Foster a Golden Globe.

8
(Failed) Blockbuster Cinema:
New York, New York

I

New York, New York was instigated by producer Irwin Winkler, who commissioned a script from Earl MacRauch. Scorsese read about the script in *The Hollywood Reporter*. Scorsese thought of shooting the film as 'a two-million-dollar, straight low budget picture', 'strictly a love story' (Dugas 1977: 11). He envisaged Robert De Niro as the film's male protagonist, Jimmy Doyle, and sought 'an actress rather than a singer' (*ibid.*) as the female lead, Francine Evans. This was exploded when Winkler sent the script to Liza Minnelli. Following her Best Actress Oscar for *Cabaret* (Bob Fosse, 1972), Minnelli was, in 1974, among Hollywood's most bankable female stars.[1] Minnelli's casting as Francine instantly increased the scale of the project and made the package of herself, De Niro and Scorsese eminently attractive to United Artists. Her singing ability led to greater emphasis being placed on the project's musical elements. United Artists hired the musical supervisor of *Cabaret*, Ralph Burns, and engaged the film's songwriting team, John Kander and Fred Ebb, to write four new songs. Evidently, the studio saw *New York, New York* as a chance to repeat Minnelli's previous success.

New York, New York was slated for a 1975 start, but this was postponed to May 1976. Like the hiatus that preceded *Taxi Driver*, this was largely beneficial to the status of those involved in the project. The box-office success of the Oscar-winning *Rocky* (John G. Avildsen, 1976) gave producers Winkler and Robert Chartoff increased clout with United Artists. Before *Rocky*, they had had years of only limited success.[2] Scorsese, following *Alice Doesn't Live Here Anymore* and *Taxi Driver*, seemed to offer an irresistible combination of artistry and profit; not least when working with De Niro, whose reputation *Taxi Driver* had likewise enhanced. By contrast, Minnelli had in the interim suffered a pair of critical and commercial failures: *Lucky Lady* (Stanley Donen, 1975) and *A Matter of Time* (directed by her father, Vincente Minnelli, 1976). She nevertheless retained top billing.

New York, New York was initially budgeted at $7.2 million. This not only greatly exceeded the budgets of any of Scorsese's previous films, but was considerably higher than the 1976 Hollywood average of $5.4 million. While Scorsese's other films had been mainly location-based, *New York, New York* was conceived, from an early stage, as studio-bound. Scorsese's idea was to make 'the picture in the old style, which is ... sound stages and back lots. A movie called *New York, New York* shot entirely in Los Angeles' (Kaplan 1977: 41). A good deal of the film's below-the-line cost was consumed by set construction. During the time of the studio system, studio shooting had kept down budgets. With the system's break-up it had become almost prohibitively expensive. To create a look analogous to that of the classical musical most of the sets for *New York, New York* had to be built from scratch on MGM's sound stages. The main exception was the New York set of *Hello, Dolly!* (Gene Kelly, 1969), that still stood on the Fox lot.

The production designer for *New York, New York* was industry veteran Boris Leven, who was employed both for his experience of studio production and for his work's recurrent stylization.[3] Costumes were another big expense. Apart from the period fashions required for supporting actors and the film's many extras, Minnelli had about 50 costume changes, De Niro about 30. Costume design was by Theadora Van Runkle, who had costumed, among others, *Bonnie and Clyde, The Godfather* (Francis Ford Coppola, 1972) and *Cabaret*.

With its sizeable budget, high production values, twin stars and 'name' director *New York, New York* was clearly conceived by United Artists as a blockbuster: a spectacular 'event' movie upon which large monies are expended in the hope of garnering large returns. Although Hollywood has produced blockbusters in various guises throughout its history, the seventies saw the majors' increasing investment in and dependence on blockbuster filmmaking. In the sixties, the majors' attempts to follow up the success of *The Sound of Music* (Robert Wise, 1965) with further blockbusters were disastrous.[4] In the seventies, it was demonstrated that blockbusters, when supported by forceful distribution and sophisticated marketing, that could cost more than a third of a film's budget, had the potential to reap huge profits. It became industry wisdom that blockbusters, that could generate massive hype and pre-sales, were less risky than smaller, possibly more idiosyncratic and 'uncommercial' (that is, less marketable) films.

A key determinant in the majors' shift towards a blockbuster strategy was the success of *Jaws* (Steven Spielberg, 1975). With a negative cost estimated to be between $8 and 10 million dollars – over twice its initial budget ($3.5–4 million) – *Jaws* was extensively promoted nationwide before being one of the first major Hollywood features to benefit from the (exploitation cinema) technique of blanket distribution, opening on 20 June on 464 screens. The film's promotion costs were $1.8 million, of which $700 000 was spent on intensive prime-time television advertising on 18–20 June. *Jaws* took $14.3 million in its first week on release, and eventually grossed $129.5 million, making it at the time the most successful film ever.

The blockbuster syndrome can once more be related to conglomeration. Not only do the resources of the corporate body underwrite the cost of the films' production and extensive marketing, but its conglomerated interests in, say, publishing, music and merchandising multiply opportunities for promotion and exploitation. The downside of blockbusters is that, costing so much to produce and market, they require massive returns to make a worthwhile profit. As the example of *American Graffiti* (George Lucas, 1973) demonstrates, smaller budgeted films can be proportionately more profitable.[5] Following corporate logic, however, the majors would have appeared to have been more interested in stable profits than in taking the chance of making more, and possibly more risky, films. For all its historical reputation for artistic independence, United Artists was in 1976 still a subsidiary of Transamerica Corporation, a conglomerate whose chief interests were in the more controlled, and controllable, realm of financial services.[6] Moreover, as the seventies progressed the majors were perceived to be concentrating their resources on fewer, bigger-budgeted films. This increased the majors' market control. Lessening competition between themselves, it also strengthened their position with product-light exhibitors, from whom they could – at least for blockbusters – demand preferred playdates, minimum runs, guaranteed returns and beneficial box-office splits, with up to 90 per cent of the gross reverting to the distributing studio. Scarcity of product similarly aided the films' box-office potential – 'increasingly we are all going to see the same ten movies' (Monaco 1984: 393).

During the seventies, many of Hollywood's most commercially successful films denied their fraught present before a nostalgic, if symptomatic, re-creation of and return to a more comforting, mythic past.

Note, for example, *Summer of '42, Paper Moon* (Peter Bogdanovich, 1973), *American Graffiti* or *The Sting*. *New York, New York* might appear to propose like nostalgic pleasures. Set in the immediate post-war years, the film reworks the classical Hollywood musical and stars the daughter of Vincente Minnelli and Judy Garland: one of Hollywood's biggest mid-seventies successes was *That's Entertainment!* (1974), a compilation of clips from MGM musicals. *That's Entertainment!* was in addition directed by Jack Haley Jr who, at the time of *New York, New York*, was Liza Minnelli's husband.

The nostalgic and commercial potential of *New York, New York* would have seemed to have been further assured by its similarities to another box-office success, *The Way We Were* (Sydney Pollack, 1973). Both films present paired stars (Barbra Streisand/Robert Redford; Minnelli/ De Niro) in an 'impossible' romance during war-time/post-war USA. Not only was Streisand at one point interested in playing Francine (with Ryan O'Neal as Jimmy), but MacRauch has admitted that he used *The Way We Were* as a model for *New York, New York*, replacing the former's political context with that of the music business. Yet while the political context of *The Way We Were* encompasses the Spanish Civil War, World War II and HUAC, they are significantly – and 'nostalgically' – relegated before the film's romantic elements.[7] *New York, New York* underscores its relation to *The Way We Were* through likenesses of narrative situation and structure. Both films would also have appeared to contain a hit title song; an important consideration in conglomerated Hollywood.[8] However, equally telling are the films' differences. As *Taxi Driver* 'corrects' *Death Wish*, so *New York, New York* 'amends' *The Way We Were* and the nostalgic imperative that it typifies.

This can be attributed to Scorsese's increasing involvement in the project. Although MacRauch worked on the script for two years, Scorsese declared himself dissatisfied with the result, feeling it was too conventional and too literary. To rectify matters, Scorsese asked his wife, writer Julia Cameron, to work with MacRauch. When MacRauch left the film about a month before shooting, Scorsese brought in Mardik Martin. Scorsese had begun extensive, initially recuperative, improvisations with De Niro and Minnelli. While writing 'some scenes, some key dialogue' (Kaplan 1977: 42), Martin's chief task was, with Cameron, to write-up and structure these improvisations. This continued throughout shooting, with Martin writing scenes 'the night before' they were filmed in an attempt 'to save the picture' (Kelly 1992: 104).

The emphasis on improvisation had textual and extra-textual consequences. With Scorsese and Cameron's marriage, despite their collaboration and Cameron's pregnancy, near breakdown, the narrative – that centres upon the difficulties of Jimmy and Francine's relationship, that are exacerbated by Francine's pregnancy – became increasingly informed by Scorsese and Cameron's situation. Add the pregnancy of De Niro's wife, Diahnne Abbott, and an affair between Scorsese and Minnelli, and *New York, New York*, that began as a producer-led, major studio blockbuster, became one of Scorsese's most 'personal' projects: 'I wanted to capture a relationship between two people who were doing creative work and trying to live together ....The film was very autobiographical – it was about my second marriage' (Scorsese 1981: 139).[9]

The use of improvisation was a factor in the film taking 22 rather than the scheduled 14 weeks to shoot. With sets being constructed in advance, Scorsese and his actors had to find ways to improvising in and out of scenes and sets: 'once you start improvising in one set you soon improvise your way out of that set into another situation. In the meantime, they're building a different set because it's in the script! So you have to go back and shoot some more to get yourself back in line to use that second set' (Thompson and Christie 1996: 72). This helps to account for the length both of some scenes and of the film itself – Scorsese's first cut was 269 minutes long. The film's final negative cost was $9.7 million, $2.5 million over budget.

With his first cut commercially unreleaseable, Scorsese faced an intensive period of editing. The production wrapped in early October, and United Artists demanded a June 1977 release. Scorsese worsened the situation by becoming involved, during the last week of shooting, with *The Last Waltz* (1978), that had to be filmed at The Band's farewell concert on Thanksgiving Day, and by setting up the documentary *American Boy: A Profile of Steven Prince* (1978); commitments that evoke parallels with the destructive rock'n' roll lifestyle that the films themselves describe. As with the pressurized editing of *Taxi Driver*, Scorsese cut *New York, New York* with a team of editors, including Irving Lerner, director of *Murder by Contract*, and Marcia Lucas.[10]

New York, New York premiered in New York on 21 June 1977 in a cut running 153 minutes. It opened to mixed reviews and poor box-office. For the film's general American and European release another 17 minutes were cut. The cuts were decided by Scorsese, to whom Chartoff and Winkler had granted right of final cut. Scorsese denies (overt) studio pressure: '[United Artists President] Eric Pleskow said to me, "Look, we haven't been doing very well with it ... if you can cut another twelve minutes out of it on the general release, we'll be able to make some

money." Because we had gone way over budget, I felt a responsibility'
(Kelly 1992: 111). However, the film still lost money, finally returning
just $6 million.

Given Scorsese's 'contrite' re-editing of the film, it might seem
reasonable to ascribe its failure, as some critics have, to directorial
indulgence. This has in turn been used to indict a lack of studio and/or
producer control, to highlight the folly of allowing young(-ish), 'over-
praised' directors their head and to reveal, by extension, the fallacy of
auteurism. It is an argument added force by the similar big-budget
failures of other filmmakers who had been successful with more
'controlled' films; for example, Bogdanovich with *At Long Last Love*
(1975) or William Friedkin with *Sorcerer* (1977). Scorsese is not innocent of the charge of indulgence. He has admitted that having received
the Palme d'Or and extensive praise for *Taxi Driver* he felt that he
could eschew his previous extensive storyboarding and improvise the
whole film. Criticism has also been made regarding Scorsese's affair
with Minnelli, his much-publicized drug problems and his 'irresponsible' involvement in *The Last Waltz* and *American Boy: A Profile of Steven
Prince*. *New York, New York*, however, is hardly an indulgent *text*. The
performances of De Niro and Minnelli are detailed and focused, and
powerfully trace complex emotions. Improvisations were carefully
structured, being videotaped, written up by Cameron and Martin and
further refined before being 'set'.

Further, when *New York, New York* was re-released in 1981 in a cut
running 163 minutes it was in general praised.[11] The extra footage
comprised the 'Happy Endings' sequence. Having cost $35 000 and
taken ten days to shoot, the sequence had been cut, but for a few
images, two weeks before the film's premiere *because* Scorsese did not
want to be considered indulgent.[12] However, in its fullest available
version *New York, New York* is marked by a cogent narrative and formal
rigour. It is, moreover, precisely the film's artistic success that helps to
explain its commercial failure.

II

The success and failure of *New York, New York* connects with its status as a
revisionist musical. This informs its denial of the nostalgic. Where
nostalgia films provide a comforting release from contemporary tensions
through a return to a mythic past, revisionism's critical demystifications
deny such comfort by revealing the ideologically dissimulative terms of
that release. An accepted ideological function of the musical is its

provision of a model for heterosexual relationships: 'Indeed, we will not be far off the mark if we consider that the musical fashions a myth out of the American courtship ritual' (Altman 1989: 27). In *New York, New York* this myth is progressively, if sadly, dismantled. Instead of an ameliorative return to the predominantly upbeat world of the studio musical, the film affords an unremitting representation of heterosexual tensions. This within a narrative that plays off and consistently frustrates generic expectation. Not that *New York, New York* lacks any nostalgic appeal. Part of the pleasure of the film derives from the stylized scale and glamour of its sets and costumes that, on one level, embody an extended *hommage* to Hollywood studio style. Of like celebratory effect are the cameo of Jack Haley, the Tin Man in *The Wizard of Oz*, and Minnelli's father-in-law, in the 'Happy Endings' sequence and the casting of Hollywood veteran Lionel Stander as Francine's agent, Tony Harwell. Notwithstanding, critical revisionism remains central: Stander's casting evokes not only Hollywood's 'golden age', but, as a blacklisted and exiled victim of HUAC, its tarnished past.[13]

Like the New Hollywood Cinema with which it is frequently linked, revisionist filmmaking enjoyed inconstant commercial success. Robert B. Ray divides the seventies American audience into 'ironic' filmgoers, who 'favored art films and revisionist reworkings of Classic Hollywood formulas', and 'naïve' filmgoers, the majority group, who preferred 'unselfconscious forms' and retained 'affection for traditional genre pictures straightforwardly told' (1985: 327). When revisionist films did become box-office hits, this was often attributable to ancillary elements. *Cabaret* is a revisionist musical that powerfully charts the rise of Nazism. It is also set within a seductively decadent past and interspersed with camp, impressively staged numbers. Similarly, while *The Godfather* revises the gangster film, its success has been related to its 'nostalgic' evocation of family values.[14] *The Godfather, Part II* downplays its nostalgic elements before its attack on American capitalism and was markedly less profitable than its forerunner. The revisionist *film noir Chinatown* (Roman Polanski, 1974), despite its stars, lush production values, critical praise and 11 Oscar nominations, failed to recoup its cost. For Ray such failures 'reconfirmed the audience's fundamental conservatism, its persisting reluctance to part with the mythological categories that [the] films challenged' (1985: 328). It is these very 'mythological categories' that the nostalgia films tend to uphold. That by the late seventies revisionist filmmaking had largely disappeared within Hollywood underlines how closely the films were tied to a specific historical context. Most that were commercially successful pre-date the mid-seventies.

The revisionism of *New York, New York* can be approached through the 'Happy Endings' sequence. Diegetically, 'Happy Endings' is a Hollywood musical in which Francine stars. Comprising an extended musical number, the sequence functions formally as a *mise-en-abyme*: a textual passage that summarizes and reflects upon the whole. In 'Happy Endings' Francine plays Peggy Smith, a cinema usherette who is picked up by Broadway producer Donald Langley (Larry Kert). Peggy reveals her singing talent, and Donald promotes her career, but, when Peggy becomes a star, Donald leaves her, claiming an inability to live in the shadow of her fame. Peggy's rise continues, and she is reunited with Donald at a testimonial dinner. At this, Peggy's success is revealed to be a daydream, only for her meeting with Donald to be 'actually' repeated and 'Happy Endings' to end with celebratory song and dance. The sequence is intentionally parodic; this whether one considers its boy-meets-girl–loses-girl–gets-girl storyline, its overtly factitious stylization and pantomimic acting or its purposely un-synched vocals and reflexive, mind-numbing lyrics ('Lovely lady, gallant fellow/Meet one evening, hear that cello …'). Briefly, the sequence – that refers explicitly to Peggy's story as 'a legend, a myth' – foregrounds and mocks some of the musical's more easily burlesqued conventions and clichés.

The narrative sketched in 'Happy Endings' presents a counterpoint to that of *New York, New York*, underlining how the latter relates to and deviates from generic norms. *New York, New York* begins on VJ Day with newly demobbed jazz saxophonist Jimmy meeting singer Francine at New York's Moonlit Terrace. A whirlwind, if initially touchy, romance follows, but is interrupted when Francine leaves to tour with Frankie Harte (Georgie Auld)'s big-band. Jimmy follows, joins the band and he and Francine marry. Jimmy takes over the band, whose success becomes increasingly dependent upon Francine. Francine returns, pregnant, to New York, and Jimmy signs over the rapidly declining band to pianist Paul Wilson (Barry Primus). In New York, Jimmy plays be-bop at the Harlem Club. This heightens tensions within his and Francine's marriage that explode in a violent confrontation in their car. During this Jimmy expresses a masculine insecurity that, with Francine having been offered a record deal, offers comparison with that expressed by Donald in 'Happy Endings'. The clash precipitates the birth of their child, but Jimmy leaves Francine without seeing the baby. The film nevertheless sets up Jimmy and Francine's possible reconciliation, a few years later, at the Starlight Terrace. However, unlike Peggy and Donald's 'fantasy' reunion, reconciliation does not occur.

'Happy Endings' also reflects but contrasts with the analogous *mise-en-abyme* sequences that became a virtual constant of the Arthur Freed-produced, integrated MGM musicals of the forties and fifties, but especially of those starring Gene Kelly.[15] Compare, for instance, sequences like 'A Day in New York' in *On the Town* (Kelly and Donen, 1949), 'The *American in Paris* Ballet' in *An American in Paris* (Vincente Minnelli, 1951) or 'The Broadway Ballet' in *Singin' in the Rain* (Kelly and Donen, 1952). The relation of 'Happy Endings' to the latter in particular is underpinned by the sequences' mutually minimalist sets, the oversaturated red decor and rhythmic choreography of their respective nightclub and café scenes and their reflective final shots: 'The Broadway Ballet' ends with Kelly's figure being enlarged and removed from its backdrop, a trope repeated with Liza Minnelli at the close of 'Happy Endings'. In each case, the sequences in the Kelly films offer a stylized summary of the enclosing narrative. Unlike 'Happy Endings', however, the sequences are invariably the most overtly 'artistic' segments of the films, featuring balletic dancing, complexly orchestrated and largely instrumental music and, in 'The *American in Paris* Ballet', sets based on the work of nineteenth- and early twentieth-century painters. This bears out the claim that one of the musical's chief concerns is aesthetic self-justification: the aim of the sequences would seem to be a validation of the musical (and Hollywood)'s artistic status, a self-conscious denial of the genre (and institution)'s perceived limitations.[16] It is, by contrast, such limitations that 'Happy Endings' seeks to highlight. Kelly's star image, moreover, forms the foundation of Jimmy's characterization.

Another reference point for 'Happy Endings' is the 'Born in a Trunk' sequence in *A Star is Born* (George Cukor, 1954).[17] 'Born in a Trunk' is similarly a film-within-a-film that presents a 'fictionalized' account of the rise to fame of its female protagonist, Esther Blodgett (Garland).[18] Like 'The Broadway Ballet', 'Born in a Trunk' too evinces minimalist set design and the use of primary colours. These links are unsurprising. *A Star Is Born* is not only a narrative template for *New York, New York*, in which Minnelli in part 'plays' her mother, but implies a riposte to *Singin' in the Rain*. Both *Singin' in the Rain* and *A Star Is Born* open with a big Hollywood bash; both deal with the rise, with the help of an established male star, of a younger female performer; both foreground and parody Hollywood practices; and both problematize the dominance of the male protagonist.[19] But whereas *Singin' in the Rain* is optimistically comic, *A Star Is Born* is keenly melodramatic. Most significantly, *A Star Is Born*, in a move repeated by *New York, New York*, proceeds beyond the point of closure of most Hollywood musicals – heterosexual union – to represent what most musicals occlude: the tensions of patriarchal marriage, especially when both partners are performers and the success of the woman outstrips that of the man. Rick Altman characterizes *A Star Is Born* as being itself a revision of the musical.[20] *New York, New York* compounds this revision.

Early in *New York, New York*, Jimmy stops and watches, from the steps of the El, a white-clad sailor and woman dancing silently, balletically and incongruously within a dimly lit, abstractly barren space. An allusion to the 'A Day in New York' sequence in *On the Town*, the dance ends with the pair disappearing into the surrounding darkness. Despite it being, diegetically, 1945, the suggestion is that both the musical as typified by *On the Town* and the romantic mythology that it upholds are out of time.[21] The scene's low-key lighting and the barred shadows cast by the El and by the simulations of passing trains evoke *film noir*: after its protagonists' wedding *New York, New York* becomes – tonally and stylistically – increasingly *noir*-ish. This implies the admitted influence of the post-war, *noir*- inflected musical *The Man I Love* (Raoul Walsh, 1946). The film also informs Francine and Jimmy's representation. The protagonists of *The Man I Love* are Petey (Ida Lupino), a singer, and Sam (Bruce Bennett), a jazz musician.

In general, *New York, New York* lacks the musical's distinctive audio and visual dissolves; the means by which the films, during numbers, achieve a seamless transition from their diegetic worlds to an alternative spatio-temporal realm where non-diegetic music directly orchestrates action.[22] The only time that such transitions happen in *New York, New York* is as mimicked during 'Happy Endings'. Apart from this sequence, numbers in *New York, New York* occur as diegetic performance. This reflects *The Man I Love*, in which it helps to maintain the film's downbeat, *noir*-ish mood, as well as *Cabaret*, where it connects with the film's updating of the musical, its making it 'realistic'. In *New York, New York* the diegetic integration of numbers complements, and is complemented by, the film's particular, generically untypical dramatic texture. For while performance and incident are mannered and highly worked, the extensive use of improvisation effects an edgy naturalism.

The film's narrative is nevertheless played out within a stylized artificial *mise-en-scène*, a world of sets, painted backdrops and back projection. With the entire film shot on sound stages and back lots, this affords a hermetic sense of heightened reality – everything is just a little too big, too clean, too perfect. In this, *New York, New York* self-consciously recalls the 'New York' of the studio films: 'in MGM and

Warner Brothers musicals, New York kerbs were always shown as very high and very clean. When I was a child, I realized this wasn't right, but was part of a whole mythical city that they had created' (Thompson and Christie 1996: 69). *New York, New York* adheres more closely to the conventions of continuity editing than any of Scorsese's previous films. It also has a more considered cutting rhythm, features extensive montage sequences and resuscitates the wipe. Shot selection is dominated by 'classically' framed medium, two- and close shots – 'they never came in really tight, except for love scenes or their equivalent' (Pye and Myles 1979: 216). Scorsese even wanted to replicate, through film stock or masking, the period's Academy ratio, but was informed that this was commercially impracticable.[23]

As this stylization contrasts with the film's naturalistic dramaturgy, so there occurs a constant and occasionally endistancing disjunction between narrative action and the generic expectations raised by the *découpage* and *mise-en-scène*. As this in turn reflects back upon how these (ideologically informed) expectations are determined and transmitted by conventions of form and style, so *New York, New York* implies Bertolt Brecht's notion of the 'radical separation of elements'. Instead of its elements combining to create a 'seamless', 'organic' whole, the film reflexively invites consideration of the way in which these elements actively contribute to the creation of meaning. Following Brecht, the intention would seem to be to encourage a comparatively more 'intellectual' and critical consideration of the meanings generated.[24]

This complements the film's generic revision: it parallels stylistically the deconstructive juxtaposition of the main narrative and 'Happy Endings' (within which performance and incident are a stylized whole). In short, *New York, New York* reflexively highlights and unpacks the fusion of realism and fantasy that is central to the musical's romantic-cum-ideological mystification, but especially in the integrated musical that the film specifically revises.[25] Complicating this, the musical is the most reflexive of the major genres. However, the musical, with further self-vindication, tends to admit its constructedness the better to sustain it, using 'reflexivity to perpetuate rather than to deconstruct the codes of the genre' (Feuer 1981: 173). While this is typified by the overall narrative trajectories of, among others, *The Barkleys of Broadway* (Charles Walters, 1949), *Singin' in the Rain* and *The Band Wagon* (Vincente Minnelli, 1953),[26] it can be exemplified in microcosm by the 'You Were Meant for Me' scene in *Singin' in the Rain*. This opens with Don Lockwood (Kelly) taking Kathy Selden (Debbie Reynolds) on to a sound stage where he reflexively constructs a 'proper setting' for his wooing: he illuminates a sunset backdrop, switches on lights and a wind-machine and places Kathy, in a parody of Juliet's balcony, on a metal ladder. Yet upon the non-diegetic accompaniment to Kelly's singing appearing, unremarked, and in a model audio dissolve, on the soundtrack, the setting's reflexivity is subsumed by Don's expression of desire and the reciprocal grace of the characters' dancing and the scene's crane shots. Consequently, the setting, and its reflexive construction, are diegetically recuperated as crucial to the expression of 'true love', thereby validating, through its admission, the necessity of the musical's factitiousness.[27] *New York, New York* denies such recuperation by maintaining its contrast of naturalism and stylization throughout.

The reciprocal narrative and stylistic deconstruction of *New York, New York* is reflected in the strategies of certain other revisionist films. With respect to this, the films invite a parallel with Brechtian counter-cinema, that seeks to complement 'different' subject matter with a form that challenges and/or refuses the conventions of classical narrative.[28] *Little Big Man* (Arthur Penn, 1970) augments its demystifying inversion of western conventions by employing an unreliable, mythopoeic narrator, while *The Godfather, Part II* supports its ideological critique by eschewing a unified narrative for an extended, analytical juxtaposition of nineteen-hundreds and nineteen-fifties USA. Similarly, as Robert Altman's seventies films almost systematically revise many of the major genres, they characteristically present a combination of dense, fragmented sound-tracks, a frequently cluttered, anamorphically flattened widescreen space and a recurring probing use of the zoom to create a distinctive and relatively decentred narrative realm.[29]

The stylistic singularity of *New York, New York* further militated against its potential profitability.[30] James Monaco states that for a blockbuster to be successful 'the structure of the film must be designed to appeal to the broadest possible mass audience, to offend the smallest number of people' (1984: 21).This is the case with nostalgia films. Consider *The Way We Were*. Although its narrative covers a number of years and is fairly episodic, it is smoothly transitive with strongly marked transitions.[31] Shot on a combination of studio sets and locations in New York and Hollywood, the film similarly embodies a 'tastefully' seamless stylization that, as it creates a detailed and well-turned vision of the past, underpins the film's comforting nostalgic evocation.

III

The stylized *mise-en-scène* of *New York, New York* is introduced by its brief, early Times Square scene, the set for which combines massive, neon-lit, unblemished fronts with a shiny 'rain-slicked' street. Within this, a mass of extras present a complex of individuated celebration, with the whole being filmed in a sweeping crane shot. Like the camera-work, the scene's scale and detail are imposingly impressive but also broadcast an artificiality that is reflexively underscored by a cinema marquee bearing the words 'New York, New York' and a red neon arrow that swings in screen right to point out Jimmy as he moves through the crowd.

There follows a 16-minute scene at the Moonlit Terrace, a large white ballroom set complete with more revelling extras and a painted New York skyline through its windows. Jimmy tries to pick up Francine. Generically, the situation is familiar: the energetic, importunate 'boy' attempts to force himself upon the stand-offish 'girl'. Whereas Jimmy moves, jigging to the music, through the crowd, Francine sits clicking her fingers; whereas Jimmy is gum-chewing and garrulous, Francine talks calmly and, at first, monosyllabically; whereas Jimmy is active, Francine, with gendered typicality, is passive. That Francine is still wearing her USO uniform whereas Jimmy wears a garish outfit of blue-patterned Hawaiian shirt, white trousers and two-tone shoes that he has won in a card game further marks them, with similar generic and gendered typicality, as respectively conforming and non-conforming figures.

Rick Altman writes of Kelly: 'his adolescent energy and ego never disappear. Like a child, Kelly seems always to be looking out for himself' (1989: 57). Nevertheless: 'No matter how childish Kelly's behaviour sometimes appears, it is always joyous and somehow appealing in spite of its egotism' (*ibid.*). Although at the Moonlit Terrace Jimmy is plainly out for his own (adolescently sexual) ends, his energy and clothes make him engagingly *outré*: even his repeated, obvious chat-up lines are, through their dynamic transparency, rendered (at least superficially) comic. When, despite Francine's protests, he presses his attentions, not only is his insistence expressed mainly through a combination of verbal play and physical clowning, but the characters' initial exchange becomes a comedy routine as Jimmy's loquaciousness is met by Francine's variations on the word 'No'.

Jimmy's insinuating garrulity reprises that of both Harry Palmer (Kelly) toward Jo Hayden (Garland) in *For Me and My Gal* (Busby Berkeley, 1942) and Serafin (Kelly) toward Mañuela (Garland) in *The Pirate* (Vincente Minnelli, 1948). Similarly insistent are the initial advances of Jerry (Kelly) toward Lise (Leslie Caron) in *An American in Paris*. After bumping into Lise in a café, Jerry, much to Lise's shocked politeness, falsely claims acquaintance (compare Jimmy's repeated 'I know you from someplace...') and, removing her from her friends, impels her to dance. Moreover, like Jerry with Lise, and Serafin with Mañuela, Jimmy's sexualized insistence follows his fixing Francine with his gaze. We first see Francine from Jimmy's point of view, a trope that is repeated throughout the scene. This presents a contrasting gendered perspective to that of *The Way We Were*, in which, during a matching early ballroom scene, that likewise features forties décor and a jazz orchestra, Katie (Streisand) fixes Hubbell (Redford) with her Look. Not only does this imply Streisand's greater star status, but it relates to *The Way We Were* being, generically, an updated woman's film. By contrast, while Francine is given some point-of-view shots during the Moonlit Terrace scene, they are – despite Liza Minnelli's top billing – numerically and rhetorically subordinated to those afforded Jimmy. This reflects upon Scorsese's authorial discourse. For all Scorsese's claimed desire 'to make a film with two central characters' (Pye and Myles 1979: 215), *New York, New York* again affirms his authorial investment in masculine identity. Indicatively, it is De Niro, not Minnelli, who is given a star entrance: a tilt up from his two-tone shoes, via his colourful attire, to the sight of him putting some gum in his mouth.[32]

Despite Jimmy's likenesses to characters played by Kelly, his sexual intent is broadcast much more overtly. He openly says to his army buddy, Eddie (Frank Sivera): 'It's VJ Day.... I wanna get laid'. While this sexual openness is attributable to a changed censorship regime, it in addition connects with the film's revisionism. When Jimmy, despite his previous failures, prompts Eddie to introduce him to Francine, he stresses, with contradictory insistence, and after saying that he wants 'to really screw her', that Eddie impresses that he is 'sensitive'. It is usually upon the revelation of their 'sensitivity' that the characters played by Kelly mitigate their sexual assertiveness and prove themselves worthy of the love of their objects of desire. Hence, say, Don's romancing of Kathy in the 'You Were Meant for Me' scene, or Gabey (Kelly)'s sudden romantic obsession with Ivy Smith (Vera-Ellen) in *On the Town* or Harry's contrite admission to Jo that he has tried to trick her into becoming his stage partner in *For Me and My Gal*. Jimmy, however, quickly decides that a sensitive masquerade is beneath his masculine pride. The incident typifies the film's deconstructive approach. On one hand, it is a denial of (here strategically unconvincing) dissimulation that naturalistically jars against and plays off the connotations carried by situation and décor. On the other, as it highlights and undermines the means by which Kelly's sexual aggressiveness is masked and rendered acceptable, it lays bare what is latent and repressed in Kelly's star image.

Nevertheless, Jimmy is 'unaccountably' attracted to the 'impossible' Francine. In classical musicals this is 'explained' – via the myth of love at first sight – as the protagonist's innate recognition of his or her complement. Francine is likewise, despite herself, implied to be interested in Jimmy. In line with the film's revisionism, these romantic connotations, while offered, are naturalistically tempered. Jimmy's admiring 'how cocky she is' suggests that he feels that in Francine he has finally found a woman worthy of his swaggering bravado. Francine's attraction is afforded a reciprocal sexual motivation. Apart from Jimmy's energy broadcasting sexual potency, he is placed as the most attractive man in the room. Having spoken to the nerdy Arnold (David Nichols) and waved across the dancefloor to Paul Wilson, who embarrassingly dances some forced steps and blows a kiss, Francine turns to be faced by Jimmy as he repeats Arnold's adoring praise: 'Don't ever change, Francine, you're beautiful.' Francine's discomfiture hints at her unacknowledged desire, a suggestion underscored by the way that she subsequently scans the room – half-nervously, half-desirously – for Jimmy. Further, when Arnold first catches Francine's attention, she immediately turns her head to look at Jimmy's retreating figure. We are given a shot from her point of view of the back of Jimmy's shirt that – with phallic implication – is dominated by illustrations of the Empire State Building and the legend 'World's Tallest Building'. Even so, reflecting the scene's – and the film's – gendered emphasis, this point-of-view shot is situationally reactive: Jimmy's point-of-view shots are intimately related to his instigation of the scene's action.

The suggestion of Francine's desire for Jimmy is sustained when she turns up the next morning at his hotel. 'Justified' by Francine seeking her friend Ellen (Kathi McGinnis), who has spent the night with Eddie, this compounds the subtextual connotation of her handbag getting caught on Jimmy's arm as she gets up to leave him at the Moonlit Terrace. The device again finds precedent in *The Pirate*: as Mañuela walks away from Serafin, she is halted by her hat blowing into a puddle. While Francine hardly helps Jimmy in his dispute with the desk clerk (Dimitri Logothetis) by falsely recognizing Jimmy's fake signature, she is prevailed upon by Jimmy to fetch his saxophone from his room and is shown smiling indulgently at his clowning.[33] After easily satisfying her concern about Ellen, Francine finds herself with Jimmy in a mock-up of a taxi.[34] She ends the scene both accompanying him to an audition and sitting with his hand on her knee.

As Francine's implied desire complicates her seeming aloofness, so the related connotation of confused chasteness implies the star image of Garland. Francine's uncertainty about Jimmy recalls that of Esther when approached by Norman Maine (James Mason) in *A Star Is Born*, as well as that of a number of characters played by Garland when confronted by others played by Kelly; be it Mañuela when confronted by Serafin in *The Pirate*, Jane Falbury when confronted by Joe Ross in *Summer Stock* or Jo when confronted by Harry in *For Me and My Gal*. Jo ends *For Me and My Gal* wearing the uniform of the YWCA, the World War I equivalent of the USO. Minnelli's natural resemblance to Garland is in *New York, New York* accentuated by her period costumes, heavy make-up and styled hair.[35]

IV

The sexual aggressiveness that underpins Jimmy's pestering advances is briefly laid bare when, sitting exasperated and uninvited opposite Francine, he mockingly mouths a kiss before leaning forward intimidatingly and saying: 'Let's get down to business. It's getting a little tiring here. Give me your 'phone number.' This introduces a pattern of progressively clarifying and critical repetition that constitutes the narrative's chief structuring factor. The structure reflects that of *Mean Streets*; the narrative of *New York, New York* is similarly episodic, elliptical and tends to privilege narrative moment before narrative flow. While the latter might be attributed – at least to a degree – to the narrative's improvisatory development, the structural relation of *New York, New York* to *Mean Streets* might no less suggest the influence of Mardik Martin.

At the audition at the Palm Club Jimmy plays be-bop. The club's owner (Dick Miller) complains. Francine – who has been admiring Jimmy's playing – suggests that he plays something 'smoother, like a ballad'; counsel that Jimmy brusquely refuses. The club-owner suggests that he play 'Chevalier'. Jimmy's response to this unhip advice is predictably negative, but his altercation with the club-owner is abbreviated when Francine – revealing herself as a performer – begins to sing a Chevalier standard, 'You Brought a New Kind of Love to Me', and gets Jimmy to join her in accompaniment. Their performance gets them booked as a 'boy–girl act'. The central couple, and the values that they embody, thus come together in a number; generically, the privileged site of narrative and thematic reconciliation. Not only does Francine's choice of song state her desire, but her intervention, and her and Jimmy's subsequent performance, that is swinging but not too hip, balances the club-owner's desire for 'Chevalier' and Jimmy's be-bop.

The scene confirms Jimmy as aggressively, 'masculinely' noncon-
formist and Francine as his appeasing, 'feminine' opposite. But it is
Francine's intervention that gets them the gig.

The scene's pattern of action is reflected when Jimmy catches up
with Francine on tour at The Meadows nightclub. Jimmy announces
his arrival with prolonged, disrupting applause. As at the Palm Club,
Francine seeks to conciliate. She prevents Frankie Harte from confronting Jimmy, then attempts to mediate Jimmy's desire that she talk
to him and Frankie's desire that she return to the stage, only to be
pulled away by Jimmy.[36] Outside, Jimmy's insistence on having the
last word, 'you don't say goodbye to me, I say goodbye to you', repeats
that toward the club-owner ('that's what I said'; 'No, that's what I
said'). Likewise, when Francine tells Jimmy that Frankie will let him
audition, Jimmy's response recalls his earlier intransigence: 'I'll play for
him. I won't audition.'

Jimmy's refusal to conform carries Oedipal connotations. His
excessive hotel bill and aggression toward the desk clerk, who calls the
hotel manager, can be read metaphorically as a denial of patriarchal
authority, of symbolic castration. It is a psycho-sexual implication
inversely underscored when Jimmy pretends that his writing arm is
useless and that he has a wooden leg: afflictions symbolic of a
castration directly at odds with Jimmy's energy. Noteworthy is the
type of music that Jimmy plays. Following Freud's correlation of
sexual and creative energy, Jimmy's intense jazz can be seen as an
expression of untrammelled male libido.[37] The saxophone itself has
phallic connotations – these in addition inform Francine's regard of
Jimmy's playing.[38] His rejection of the suggestions of the owner of the
Palm Club, who is structurally positioned as a father-figure, correspondingly implies continued denial of symbolic castration. Implicitly
a transgression of the patriarchal Law, it threatens social exclusion –
Jimmy is not going to get the gig. He is also thrown out of the
hotel.

That in both cases Francine intervenes on behalf of patriarchal
authority is consistent with her implied conformity. Moreover, it is only
by accepting the Law that Jimmy, with further Oedipal suggestion, can
'obtain' Francine: witness the sanctioning of their relationship by their
employment by the Palm Club owner and by Frankie's hiring of Jimmy –
another gig that Jimmy gets through Francine's intercession and, in a
mitigation of both his transgressive disruptiveness and his refusal to
audition, his playing for and accommodation of Frankie, who stands as
another father-figure.

These Oedipal connotations culminate with Jimmy's marriage to Francine and his taking over the band, and hence the role of symbolic father. This first occurs temporarily when Frankie has to bail out a band member who, in an extension of Jimmy's phallic transgressiveness, has been found in his room with a 13-year-old girl, grabbed the hotel detective's gun and 'started shooting out all the lights'. Frankie only leaves Jimmy in charge after refusing (repressing?) Jimmy's request to try out some of his own arrangements. Jimmy's accession to band leader proper follows a scene on the band's 'bus between Frankie and Francine during which, as Frankie talks about past tours and possibly handing over the band, the characters seem like father and daughter (note their similar names). Before speaking to Frankie, Francine covers the sleeping Jimmy with a coat; a 'motherly' act that reciprocates Jimmy's replacement of her 'father'. Yet while Francine once more intercedes with Frankie, with patriarchal authority, on Jimmy's behalf, her intervention again furthers his normative psychosexual integration.[39]

Jimmy's acceptance of the Law is nevertheless insecure. When Francine fails to show at the Palm Club, he reverts to playing be-bop before walking out as the owner, in a futile gesture of patriarchal assertion, threatens to fire him. Jimmy's transgressive energy similarly bursts from its repression when, after joining Frankie's band, he is unable, in one scene, to restrain himself/accept his symbolic castration and, breaking ranks, blows an energetic, spontaneous solo.

The film cuts from Frankie and Francine talking about the band's future to a shot of Jimmy completing a 'hot' solo. Now the band's leader, Jimmy's recourse to 'less repressed' jazz underlines the contingency of his Oedipal determination. The scene, however, proceeds to re-enact the pattern erected. Jimmy's solo and the band's more aggressive jazz brings a (now predictable) frostiness from the ballroom's owner, Horace Morris (Murray Moston). Morris asks to hear Francine. After calling Morris by his correct name – Jimmy discourteously calls him 'Mr Horace' – Francine sings what Morris wants to hear, a big-band standard. Morris accepts Francine and, implicitly, as she sings 'The Man I Love', her partnership with Jimmy. Even so, in her interventions Francine can, to quote Susan Morrison: 'be seen to be ... supplanting [Jimmy's] authority/artistic presence.... On the one hand, he gets the jobs and keeps the band together, but on the other, he loses his uniqueness, his originality' (1986b: 21).

What is psycho-sexually at stake for Jimmy is underscored by the marriage sequence. When Jimmy knocks on a glass pane of the Justice of the Peace (Bernie Kuby)'s front door, it shatters and he cuts his hand.[40] An incident that, in Freudian terms, can be read as symbolizing castration, it suggests Jimmy's unconscious fear regarding his masculine autonomy, that is tacitly threatened by his proposed nuptials. A complementary suggestion is afforded when Jimmy lies behind the taxi that has transported him and Francine and tells the driver to reverse over his body. Although Jimmy does this to 'force' Francine to marry him, it can be read as a displaced expression of castration anxiety. Throughout the sequence, Jimmy's actions transmit a conflation of romantic desire and reactive masculine aggression. He hustles Francine to the Justice's without telling her why, then responds fractiously when she hesitates when she works out what Jimmy is doing. His voice rises, he hits a clenched fist against the Justice's porch and grabs Francine forcefully by her upper arms. This is a reiterated gesture. First used at the hotel when he impresses upon Francine to retrieve his saxophone, it is repeated outside The Meadows, where it is more complexly combined with his declaration of love. However, on blurting out 'I love you', Jimmy hastily corrects himself, ' I dig you.... I like you a lot'. While this ironizes Jimmy's machismo, it also suggests a gendered fear of admitting emotional dependence, of losing masculine control. Jimmy's rationale for wanting to marry Francine similarly implies as much a desire for possessive sexual dominance as for romantic fulfilment: 'I love you.... I don't want anybody else to be with you.'

Jimmy's volatile, conflicted condition places him as another characteristically alienated Scorsese male protagonist. As the marriage sequence suggests, it is an alienation that, likewise characteristically, is related to and reflects upon contradictory cultural and psycho-sexual demands. Fusing, with generic appropriateness, the interpersonal and the creative, the text's Oedipal connotations resonantly underpin Jimmy's inability to reconcile his desire for 'transgressive' masculine and musical autonomy and that for Francine and professional success.[41] If the force of the former is implied by his intense aggressive and musical outbursts, the lure of the latter is succinctly figured by his self-delight and exchange of prideful glances with Francine when he temporarily fronts the band. Significantly, similar explanation is denied Francine's subjectivity. The terms of her conforming stability are not explored but largely accepted as a cultural given. Nevertheless, whereas Scorsese's analyses of masculine alienation have previously focused mainly upon single men living on the social margins, *New York, New York* proceeds to examine the same within the context of patriarchal marriage. In terms of Scorsese's *oeuvre*, the film can be read as a male-centred companion-piece to *Alice Doesn't Live Here Anymore*; not least as Jimmy, in a mirror to Alice's partners, is represented as increasingly 'threatened' by Francine's domestic assertiveness and professional acclaim.

V

The centrality of Francine to the band's success is reflected by a pair of posters for Morris's ballroom on which, within three weeks, she moves from supporting to top billing. The tensions that this creates within her and Jimmy's personal and professional relationship are fore-grounded by the scene in which they rehearse the band. The band loses the beat. Blocking Francine's intervention, Jimmy complains vehemently first to a trombonist (Phil Gray) and then to the band's drummer, Nicky (George Memmoli). Francine typically suggests a more sympathetic approach, at which Jimmy affirms his masculine and musical dominance, again while holding Francine by her upper arms: 'You're not the band leader... don't tell me how to do it.' Francine responds by reminding Jimmy that they have only 15 more minutes in the room and that she has to fix her hair and nails, press Jimmy's shirt and call her agent: a list that – as it combines professional concerns with wifely chores and intimations of sexual objectification – implies a more generalized gendered oppression. Indicatively, Francine's com-plaints dwindle before Jimmy's prolonged, threatening gaze. Nevertheless, that Jimmy is contested by Francine's unprompted expression of *her* problems is an important narrative development. Previously, her resistance to Jimmy's demands has been cursory or, at best, retortive.

Continuing through repetition, the second half of the scene develops these connotations. The rehearsal restarts, only for Nicky to lose the beat. Nicky claims that Francine is 'slowing it down', a tacit assault on Jimmy's marital control. Jimmy counters – again blocking Francine's intervention – by attacking Nicky's musicianship. Nicky begins to pack up his kit, Jimmy throws some tables over: masculine posturing that is once more followed by Francine's conciliatoriness, 'if we get this thing right we'll blow the roof off this place'. She joins Jimmy in counting-in the band. Jimmy responds aggressively. He orders Francine to 'come here', grabs her roughly by the arm and 'reproaches' her in terms that mirror and intensify his response to her earlier suggestions: 'You do not kick-off the band.... Don't ever do it again. Ever again.' The incident pointedly reflects previous scenes. Jimmy's 'come here' repeats his identical commands to Francine both at the Palm Club and outside The Meadows, while at the Palm Club he also grabs her arm and reacts to her advice by stating: 'Don't do that [that is, "challenge" his masculine dominance] in front of anybody.' In the previous scenes Jimmy's demeaning misogyny is assuaged by his and Francine's coming together as a couple. In the rehearsal scene this extenuation is denied. Jimmy turns Francine around and slaps her backside. A petulant reaction, this caps Jimmy's uptight aggression throughout the scene to confirm his seeming inability to deal with Francine's increasing public and personal agency. As in the first half of the scene, Francine reacts assertively. She finishes the song they are rehearsing – 'Taking a Chance on Love' – and defiantly knocks over her microphone.

The scene serves a similar structural function to that of the shooting in the bar in *Mean Streets*: it reflects back upon and critically clarifies what has been previously implied but dramatically underplayed. This in addition lends the scene a summary quality, releasing the narrative to work through the implications of the established situation.

Jimmy wants the pregnant Francine to stay with the band. Her leaving for New York maintains her new assertiveness. When Francine asks 'Do you want this baby?', Jimmy can only give hesitant and grudging assent. The situation suggests a trans-generic constant of American cinema: the opposition of wandering male and domesticating female. When Francine departs, Jimmy continues the tour with another singer, Bernice Bennett (Mary Kay Place), with whom Jimmy, confirming his wandering maleness, is implied to have an affair. A montage charting the band's decline cuts to Tony Harwell praising Francine to Decca record producer Artie Kirks (Lenny Gaines) as she makes some demos: regulated, commercial work that Jimmy dislikes but that accords with Francine's status as a 'domesticated' mother-to-be. By contrast, Jimmy's relinquishing of the band marks his abandonment of the musical mainstream.

After Jimmy returns to New York, Francine wakes to the sound of his playing the piano. With Jimmy sitting in his braces, the situation implies a clichéd 'composer working at night' scenario. But instead of such scenes' usual representation of achieved harmony, the scene marks the protagonists' ongoing dissonance. Jimmy, who has gone missing for three days since parting with the band, refuses to talk about the situation. He closes down discussion by insisting that Francine agrees that she understands that she does not understand his need to be alone – a bleak statement of gendered non-communication.

Francine's desire to relate with and to domesticate Jimmy reflects Petey's desire regarding Sam in *The Man I Love*. Similarly, just as Sam, when threatened by domesticity, flees to the 'low' jazz environment of the Bamboo Club, so Jimmy absconds to the Harlem Club. Jimmy meets Francine with a car outside a recording studio after another demo session. It is revealed that Jimmy has again gone missing – he has spent the previous night at the Harlem Club without letting Francine know. Francine's irritation is interrupted by a row with another couple who want Jimmy's parking space and whom Francine, in an expression of marital solidarity, vehemently warns off. Just as Jimmy is implied to desire both autonomy and acceptance, so Francine's estrangement from Jimmy is complicated and rendered poignant by the reciprocal connotation of her sustained love and need: witness both her relieved delight when Jimmy returns home and her upset bafflement when Jimmy insists that she does not understand. Nevertheless, after seeing off the couple, Francine resumes her complaints, pointing out that now that she is pregnant Jimmy has got to be more attentive, for instance ensuring that she can get into the car. Jimmy's response moves from immature self-pity ('I just lost a band ...') to censurable selfishness as he claims that as he did not stop Francine from returning to New York she cannot stop him playing saxophone at night. The gendered cultural split between female domesticity and conformity and male wandering and autonomy seems unbridgeable – Jimmy notes that the 'other guys are married too'. Exasperated, Jimmy gets out of the car, gets his saxophone from the boot and, in an expression of castration anxiety, asks whether Francine wants him to smash it against the wall, because 'that's what you're telling me to do'.

The castrating threat of domesticity is reiterated when, having created a disturbance at the Up Club, Jimmy meets Francine outside a hospital with a car full of flowers. This time Jimmy ensures that Francine gets into the car comfortably, but traps his hand in its door as he closes it, a moment that recalls his cutting of his hand during the wedding sequence.

VI

The sequence at the Up Club forms a pairing with another at the Harlem Club that, in its systematic parallels and contrasts, serves to imply the irrevocability of Jimmy and Francine's separation. The pairing no less confirms the text's discursive privileging of Jimmy's perspective. For although both sequences invite further criticism of Jimmy, they also mark the text's complicity with him.

Jimmy and Francine go to the Up Club to see what is now the Paul Wilson Orchestra. The place is a site of much that 'threatens' Jimmy.

Its representation is, however, loaded. Its red neon décor is garishly unpleasant, and in itself virtually justifies Jimmy's animus toward the cultural mainstream to which the club belongs. Jimmy is hesitant about even entering. He tells Francine that he will park the car, then reappears late and slightly drunk, joining Francine at a table with Ellen and Artie Kirks. Kirks, who represents the commercial music industry, is wizened and glib. His forced assertiveness toward a waiter, whom he calls, with false gruffness, 'dear', only implies his own masculine lack. A like 'castration' is suggested by Paul having added to the band, in a crass, commercial move, a 'softening' string section. This is clearly meant to be contrasted negatively with the hard, 'masculine' be-bop that we have seen Jimmy playing at the Harlem Club. Casting is in addition significant. Trumpeter Cecil Powell, whose combo Jimmy joins at the Harlem Club, is played by Clarence Clemons, then saxophonist with Bruce Springsteen's E Street Band. This affords a connotation of hipness and achieved musicianship against which Kirks and Paul, whom Frankie tells 'should be glad to be working for anybody', cannot compete.

Jimmy reacts against his situation irascibly. He bluntly refuses Kirks's (admittedly patronizing) offer of a 'sloe gin fizz', leaving Francine to maintain her conciliatoriness by accepting it instead. Jimmy gets at Francine via Ellen: his vindictive questioning about the apparently long-forgotten Eddie suggests that he sees himself – pathetically – as similarly 'abandoned' by his wife.

Jimmy states his discontent openly, grabs Francine by her wrist and tells her that they are leaving. Francine complains that Jimmy is hurting her and, in another assertion of self, declares that she is staying. Jimmy moves to a side bar, where he gets more drunk. While this spatially figures Jimmy's alienation, it likewise underlines its relation – as Jimmy does not leave the club – to his inability to resolve his competing desires. Jimmy's masculine authority is further challenged when Paul sits in 'his' seat at the table and talks to Francine. Recalling the existing relation suggested between Francine and Paul at the Moonlit Terrace, this stokes Jimmy's possessiveness. Unlike Jimmy, moreover, Paul has made the band a success.

When Paul speaks to Jimmy in the side bar, Jimmy's disparagingly ironic 'praise' for Paul's musicianship, 'I think you're so good that I can't even top you', is met by Paul's equally ironic and disparaging 'praise' for Jimmy: 'Everybody feels you're great, even your wife.' Paul returns to the stage, Jimmy to the table, from where he sees Paul talking intimately with Bernice. The suggestion is that Paul has replaced him sexually with Bernice. It is apparently the final straw for Jimmy's embattled masculinity: he moves on the stage and attacks Paul. Jimmy's rationale – 'Wife is out' – coextensively implies his threatened male dominance and compensatory masculine assertion. Jimmy is ejected from the club by its bouncers.

Jimmy's assault crowns the resentment that he displays toward Paul. Apart from Jimmy's implied sexual jealousy, Paul – as his changes to the band suggest – typifies the mutual musical and psycho-sexual repression that Jimmy seeks to deny. When Jimmy pulls Francine outside at The Meadows he in addition overrides Paul's intervention on Frankie's behalf, and when Jimmy breaks ranks when playing with the band he does so to interrupt a solo by Paul. That Paul, despite his limited musicianship, can yet become a success not only further indicts mainstream culture, but makes Jimmy's resentful aggression, if not admirable, then somewhat understandable. Throughout the film, moreover, Jimmy's music and musical opinions are privileged as exemplary norms against which other music and musical opinions are tacitly judged and, largely, found wanting.

Jimmy's drunkenness at the Up Club recalls that of Norman in *A Star Is Born*. Norman's drunkenness is related explicitly to his felt failure of professional and masculine potency. When the out-of-contract actor signs for a parcel and the mailman calls him 'Mr Lester' – that is, by Esther's screen name – he promptly hits the bottle. The moment is cited in 'Happy Endings' when Donald fears that he will be known as 'Mr Peggy Smith'. Jimmy's assault on Paul in turn replays Norman's drunken interruption of Esther's on-stage acceptance of her Best Actress Oscar; during which he accidentally, but in a possible expression of unconscious resentment, slaps Esther in the face.[42] Like Jimmy, moreover, Norman can be seen to have an apparent animus toward the commercial mainstream. Twice he is shown drunkenly disrupting functions associated with the Hollywood institution: the opening benefit show at the Shrine Auditorium and the Oscar ceremony. Norman's nemesis is reciprocally the head of studio publicity, Matt Libby (Jack Carson), while his contract is paid off at the behest of the New York front office.[43] Further, latent throughout *A Star Is Born* is the suggestion that Norman has been 'unmanned' by Hollywood.

The Harlem Club sequence begins with Cecil Powell interrupting Jimmy as he shares some dope in a toilet to tell him that Francine has turned up with 'two cats'.[44] Whereas the Up Club is vulgarly modish, the Harlem Club is shabby, smoky and, in line with blacks' post-war status, and the presence of drugs, seemingly marginalized. It is also a site of unrestrained musical (and masculine) expression. Accordingly, whereas the Up Club, with its affluent, all-white clientèle, is marked by a polite (repressed) quietness, the Harlem Club, that is frequented by an historically suggestive combination of blacks and some slumming white socialites, upholds the conventional (racist?) association of blacks and sexuality by presenting a more lively and untrammelled setting – the club's décor features murals of jungle and wild animals. The first shot of the sequence is a close-up of the toilet's yellow door from which the camera tracks back to show Francine in a bright red jacket that stands out incongruously against the club's drabness. It also recalls the décor of the Up Club. Further, when Jimmy and the heavily pregnant Francine talk before the club's bar, two reddish big cats can be seen looming from amid a jungle mural. Reflecting Powell's comment, this compounds the implication that Francine 'threatens' Jimmy.

The 'two cats' with Francine are Kirks and Tony Harwell. Kirks wants Francine to sign the record deal. Jimmy queries, with a certain hypocrisy, the fate of the baby should Francine have to tour. Kirks's response that he will get Francine 'the best nurse', a car and 'treat the kid like it's my own kid' reflects Jimmy's earlier offer to buy a car and to make things comfortable to enable Francine to continue touring when pregnant. That, unlike before, Francine seems to accept the proposal in effect abrogates Jimmy's masculine authority regarding his wife and child. This is implicitly linked with a reaffirmation of the patriarchal Law. Kirks's offer places him as a surrogate father-figure; a position analogously filled by Tony who, on Francine's return to New York, has 'paternally' found her session work.

There occurs an almost diagrammatic exemplification of Jimmy's situation. Jimmy leaves the table and makes a 'phone call in a corridor half-way between the table and the stage. The camera zip-pans from Jimmy to show Kirks and Tony kissing Francine before leaving. The shot cuts to the stage, where a female singer performs 'Honeysuckle Rose'. The camera tracks in to a long-held close shot of Jimmy. As Lez Cooke notes, this encourages us 'to empathise' with the character's 'dilemma' (1986: 104). Placed between Francine and the stage, between 'represssing' conformity and domesticity – and now seeming redundancy – and 'free' musical and masculine release, Jimmy is positioned between the poles of his alienating situation. Casting is again notable. The singer is played by Diahnne Abbott, then De Niro's wife, a connotation that helps to balance the emotional weight of table and stage. When she passes Jimmy/De Niro on the way to the stage, the singer/Abbott also says, suggestively: 'Family night?'. Diegetically, not only does this refer to Francine's presence, but the familiarity implied both by the comment and by Jimmy's attempt to grab the singer's arm suggests an illicit, 'wandering' relationship. Extra-diegetically, the comment invites recognition of the players' marital status.

As Jimmy has moved from an uneasy encounter at a table to a side space, the sequence reflects that at the Up Club. As it has focused, for all the talk of Francine's career, on Jimmy's predicament and reactions, it has similarly upheld his textual centrality. Like Jimmy at the Up Club, Francine gets drunk. Jimmy joins the band on stage. He begins to play a be-bop version of 'Just You, Just Me', a song previously performed with shared joyousness by Jimmy and Francine. Again like Jimmy at the Up Club, Francine approaches the stage, but when she begins to ascend it to join the band, Jimmy changes the tune, ups the tempo, the band smilingly follow, and he drives Francine from the stage with a furious, antagonistic solo. A violent expression of male sexual energy, it underscores Jimmy's choice of stage over table by figuring a vengeful rejection of Francine's presence. Bowing with embarrassment, Francine leaves the stage before dancing and leaving the club with another man. This further challenges Jimmy's masculinity and prompts him, on finishing his solo, to unhook his saxophone and to jump from the stage in possessive pursuit.

The forceful rejection of Francine parallels the forceful ejection of Jimmy at the Up Club to complete the sequences' pairing. It is a parallel that decisively marks the characters' gendered division: they are not only respectively uncomfortable and incongruous within but violently expelled from spaces redolent of the other.

VII

When Jimmy drives from the Harlem Club, Francine announces her presence in the car's back seat by putting her hands, in a drunken prank, over Jimmy's eyes. Francine's action figures castration, and causes Jimmy to drive the car on to the kerb – an analogous halting of his 'wandering'. The ensuing scene reflects and critically brings to a head tensions dramatized in the previous car scenes. The characters' argument quickly moves from Jimmy attacking Francine's prank and her behaviour at the Harlem Club to the nub of the matter: the threat posed by Francine's pregnancy. With a vehemence that betrays his fear of domesticity, Jimmy shouts: 'Did I tell you to have that baby? ... You have it, now keep it.' A misogynistic denial of responsibility, this causes the upset Francine to hit him frantically. There follows a revealing statement of Jimmy's jealous insecurity: 'What are you scared about? You've got everything, man. I'm the one that's scared... . 'Cos you got it easy. I got nothing.' For all Jimmy's apparent rejection of mainstream success and, in turn, his relationship with Francine, the implication is of a lingering, alienating investment in both. Francine responds by again indicting Jimmy's selfishness: 'You care about your clubs, and your friends, and your music.' Stung by what, in essence, is an attack on his masculine identity, Jimmy starts hitting Francine, who hits back. The fight caps the intensity of the preceding exchanges to render the scene a graphic and disturbing representation of marital violence.[45] Yet the fight also makes Francine go into labour, the characters regain their togetherness and Jimmy speeds Francine to a hospital.

This raises hopes just to dash them. The subsequent hospital scene reflects in narrative placement and situation a similar scene in *The Way We Were*. The scenes, however, have contrasting emphases. Both open with the arrival of the male protagonist, but whereas Hubbell brings Katie some reading-matter and has seen their child, Jimmy turns up empty-handed, has not seen his child and does not even know its sex. Jimmy's refusal to see the child sustains his rejection of domesticity. This is affirmed when Francine tells him that she has named the baby 'Jimmy'. Jimmy sees this not only as an appropriation of his paternal right, but as a bid to induce guilt, to impel him to accept his paternal role. He also notes, in an assertion of fragile machismo: 'I don't wanna see the kid, because if I see the kid I'm gonna break up.' Even so, on saying that he is 'going away', Jimmy does 'break up' and begins to cry. On one hand, this implies the anguish of his continuing inability to reconcile his contradictory impulses. On the other, it once more intimates a childish immaturity; a suggestion both complemented by Francine 'maternally' holding Jimmy to her breast as he sobs and that again evokes, albeit with more critical implication, the text's Oedipal connotations. With further conflict, Jimmy says 'There's no way ... I love you', kisses Francine, walks out of shot, returns to the bed and embraces her before removing her hands from her face and leaving her to cry alone.

The scene's denial of the conventional unifying function of childbirth again reflects *The Way We Were*, in which the birth of Katie and Hubbell's child fails to heal the couple's split. However, although Hubbell and Katie decide to part before their baby's birth, Hubbell agrees to stay until the child is born to help Katie through. Jimmy's sudden declaration that he is leaving is much more jarring and brings into painful relief the complex of tensions and emotions that has made their relationship both unavoidable and unworkable.

VIII

That both *The Way We Were* and *New York, New York* reach climactic points with their central couples not united but separated marks the films' 'modernness'. By the seventies, it was accepted that men and women could live fulfilled lives outside the traditional home and family. With the greater part of *New York, New York* having examined the problems raised by the formation of the couple, the film's coda would appear to bear this out; at least with regard to those involved in 'creative work'.

The coda opens with a scene in a recording studio, during which Francine/Minnelli gives an impassioned, one-take performance of 'But the World Goes Round'. The scene cuts to a montage that charts her success and takes us to 'Happy Endings'. This cuts to Jimmy in a cinema watching the film. There follows another montage that maps Jimmy's success. A shot of a newspaper headline – 'Celebs Turn Out for Jimmy Doyle's New Jazz Nite Spot' – dissolves to an establishing shot of the club: 'Jimmy Doyle's Major Chord'. This revives a motif. During the ride to the Palm Club audition, Jimmy defines his notion of the 'major chord' as the moment when everything 'works out perfectly': 'You have the woman you want, you have the music you want and you have enough money to live comfortably'.

As Robert Phillip Kolker points out, Francine and Jimmy's mutual success presents a contrast to *A Star Is Born* 'where the husband fails as the wife triumphs' (1988: 227).[46] It does, however, mirror the apparent continued success of Katie and Hubbell presented by the coda of *The Way We Were*. When they meet unexpectedly in New York, Katie is still campaigning politically, this time against the bomb, while Hubbell is in the city writing a television show. Even so, from Katie's – and the film's – point of view, this sustains the suggestion that Hubbell has 'sold out'. Having started as a novelist, Hubbell's closing status, reached via a spell as a Hollywood scriptwriter, is represented as exemplifying cultural decline.

For much of *New York, New York* this point of view finds a parallel in the film's privileging of Jimmy's music and musical opinion. The coda, however, seemingly validates both protagonists' art. 'But the World Goes Round' is arguably the most impressively performed number in the film.[47] Moreover, in the period elided since the main narrative Jimmy would have appeared to have moved toward the mainstream. His hit record, that accompanies his montage, is mellower than the be-bop that he played at the Harlem Club. The Major Chord has modish black and white décor, design-coordinated fittings and a well-dressed, predominantly white clientèle. The older Jimmy also appears to be calmer. Nevertheless, his refusal of a customer's questionable credit implies that the club is hardly full mainstream, as does the on-stage presence of Cecil Powell. Jimmy's approach to a pair of young women at the club's bar suggests that he is still 'wandering'.[48]

This also suggests that while Jimmy might have the music he wants and enough money to live comfortably, he lacks a woman. He 'phones for 'one' ticket for Francine's concert at the Starlight Terrace: outside The Meadows Jimmy tells Francine that he meant 'major chord', 'about you'. Cut to Jimmy entering the Starlight Terrace as Francine finishes 'But the World Goes Round'. With the protagonists returned to a site visually identical to that of their first meeting, and Jimmy's 'changed' self, the scene seems to be set for their reconciliation. Intimations remain, however, that this is inadvisable.

As at The Meadows, Jimmy responds to Francine's performance with prolonged applause. But this is not now disruptive, being of a piece with the audience's rapturous response. Similarly, instead of his brash attire of the film's opening, Jimmy now wears a dark suit. Nevertheless, when Francine receives an on-stage kiss from Paul, who is playing piano, Jimmy shoots him a hostile, sidelong glower. By contrast, when Jimmy watches Francine sing 'Theme from New York, New York' – that she dedicates, with a glance, to Jimmy, 'a great believer in major chords' – his face, framed in close shot, is suffused with love. This reflects a shot of Hubbell near the end of *The Way We Were* when he watches a home movie of Katie. Both obtain effect by happening after the characters have 'lost' their wives.

Francine/Minnelli's rendition of 'Theme from New York, New York' matches in power that of 'But the World Goes Round'. Of additional import is Francine's representation. With her cropped hair, loose top and tight pants, her appearance recalls a look associated with Minnelli's mother. Yet while Garland is similarly evoked by Francine's hesitant, 'sincere' thanks to her audience, and the character's energy and studied, practised gestures as she sings 'Theme from New York, New York' reflect Garland's concert style, the latter also imply Minnelli as Minnelli. In a quasi-Brechtian interplay of character and actor, the suggestion is of Francine/Minnelli finally expressing herself; something that, in a parallel to Jimmy's expression throughout, and in acute revision of the musical's correlation of romantic and professional success, is implicitly related to personal and creative autonomy. Complementing this, the first diegetic intimation of the 'real' Francine/Minnelli occurs when she sings 'There Goes the Ball Game' at the session during which Tony 'sells' her to Kirks. 'There Goes the Ball Game' is, like 'But the World Goes Round' and 'Theme from New York, New York', a Kander and Ebb composition, with all three songs embodying the lushly melodramatic musical style that is associated with Minnelli.[49] Further, at the Starlight Terrace we only hear Francine/Minnelli sing Kander and Ebb compositions; there is no intimation of the standards that the character sings when with the band.

Jimmy joins a party in Francine's dressing-room. Francine is surrounded by mirrors. As in previous Scorsese films, in *New York, New York* mirrors imply a figure of cultural determination. When Jimmy returns to New York and enters his and Francine's apartment, his reflection is caught in a mirror that Francine and Ellen are hanging; a frame-within-frame image that evokes – symbolically and spatially – Francine's repeated attempts to affix Jimmy's Oedipal positioning. Francine is later shown staring wistfully into the same mirror. Long-held, the shot not only suggests Francine's conformist determination but, problematizing this, poignantly implies her 'impossible' desire for Jimmy: the incident occurs between her putting of photographs of herself, Jimmy and the band in an album and the Harlem Club sequence. Even so, when Cecil Powell tells Jimmy that Francine has turned up at the Harlem Club, Jimmy passes a mirror in the toilet with barely a glance; the significance of which is marked by the camera tracking slightly left and holding the mirror in shot after Jimmy leaves the frame.[50]

Not only is Jimmy once more uneasy within 'Francine's' space, but their exchanges restate their gendered artistic differences. Of Francine's version of 'Theme from New York, New York', for which, diegetically, Jimmy has written the music, Francine the words, Jimmy gives only qualified praise. When Francine says that their son – whom Jimmy has sent a (domestically disrupting) drum kit – has talent, Jimmy interjects that he gets it from his father just before Francine can say that he gets it from his mother. Jimmy also notes that he has seen 'Sappy Endings'. However, Francine's sassy response, 'you seen one you seen 'em all, huh?', clearly attracts Jimmy. If this recalls Jimmy's attraction to Francine's 'cockiness' during the opening sequence, throughout the scene a mutual desire is implied by the characters' suggestive hesitations and silences, as though they cannot say what they feel.

Jimmy's discomfort within Francine's environment is underlined when he has to ask her the way out. He nevertheless acts upon their implied desire and, once more taking an assertive male role, 'phones Francine in her dressing-room and asks her to join him for 'Chinese food'. Francine agrees to meet him at the stage door. Significantly, Jimmy seeks to remove Francine from 'her' space. Shots of Jimmy outside the Starlight Terrace and his point of view of the stage door cut to shots of Francine walking toward the stage door from inside, her point of view of the door and her turning back. There follows cross-cutting between Jimmy waiting, Francine calling a lift, Jimmy moving away and the lift doors closing over Francine's face. Implying a mutual decision to let things lie, the shots mark the characters' final separation. The final shot of Jimmy cranes down his body to show his shoes on a rain-slicked studio sidewalk before they walk out of frame. A parallel and reversal of the shot that introduces Jimmy, this both rounds off his textual centrality and ends the film on an authorially familiar cyclical note. Despite the difference implied by Jimmy now wearing brogues instead of two-tones, he ends the film as he began it, alone. The further implication is that, had he and Francine been reconciled, they would only have replayed their past.

The ending's critical potential is enhanced by its denial of the expectations raised during the coda. This also enhances its dramatic effect. The final shot of *New York, New York*, up which the end credits roll, is of a rain-drenched, empty studio street. The shot is evocative of tears. It is not ironic. Although the ending of *New York, New York* suggests that the continued separation of Jimmy and Francine is necessary, it is a necessity that the film regrets. The coda's suggestion of the characters' ongoing attraction and desire implies that they are still each other's complement. Just as the characters are caught, throughout, in a irreconcilable situation, so *New York, New York* ultimately upholds the desirability of romantic love while suggesting its virtual impossibility.[51]

The ending of *New York, New York* presents another parallel with *The Way We Were*. On unexpectedly meeting Hubbell, Katie invites him to her home for drinks, only for Hubbell to note, pragmatically, that he 'can't'. That the scene lacks the edge of its counterpart in *New York, New York* again relates to notable differences of emphasis. Unlike Jimmy and Francine, Katie and Hubbell are not 'available' : Katie has remarried and Hubbell is with his new partner. (True, we do see Paul with Francine both on-stage and in the newsreel that proclaims her return to New York, but he is absent from the scene in the dressing-room.) Moreover, both Katie and Hubbell's replacement relationships would seem to be eminently workable – Katie notes that her husband is a good father to Hubbell's child. Finally, where the ending of *New York, New York* refuses expectations, that of *The Way We Were* fulfils them: Katie's acceptance of Hubbell's decision completes the film's relation to the woman's film, with Katie putting activist duty, and her second marriage, before her love. The melodramatic release offered by the film's conclusion, while not 'happy', is both conventional and conventionally comforting.

Comforting melodramatic release is similarly sought by the ending of *A Star Is Born*. Foreshadowing *New York, New York*, the film ends as it began, at a benefit show at the Shrine Auditorium, the site of Esther and Norman's first meeting. However, that Esther should, following Norman's suicide, introduce herself as neither Esther Blodgett nor Vicki Lester but 'Mrs Norman Maine' not only commemorates her husband, but elides both her individual and creative self, and the untenability of her relationship with Norman, before a sanctifying of patriarchal marriage. Norman, moreover, sacrifices himself to enable Esther's continued professional success. Indeed, the closing melodramatic occlusions of *A Star Is Born* imply – despite, or maybe because of, the film's revisionism – a certain ideological hysteria. In the words of Jane Feuer: 'The final shot of *A Star Is Born* in which a heavenly choir accompanies the camera craning further and further back from the triumphant "Mrs Norman Maine" is perhaps the most mystifying shot in the entire history of the genre' (1993: 120).

IX

As the ending of *New York, New York* follows through the logic of the text, it can be read as the corrected inverse of the forced climax of *Alice Doesn't Live Here Anymore*. The latter film nevertheless presages *New York, New York* in its dichotomy of the creative and the domestic. Whether Alice's marriage or relationships are interfering with her singing, or her singing is interfering with her relationship with Tommy, family and art seem irreconcilably opposed. Given Scorsese's evident difficulty in balancing relationships and his career, his return to this problematic in the 'biographical' *New York, New York* is maybe unsurprising. Even so, art, fame and their difficult relation to everyday expectations is a constant, if variously foregrounded, concern throughout his early films. In his student shorts it is traceable in the films' subtextual unease about cinematic obsession, that in *Who's That Knocking at My Door?* is implicitly related to J.R.'s involvement with the girl. In *Boxcar Bertha*, the film's protagonists become problematically enraptured by their criminal success, while Scorsese has described *Mean Streets* as initially being 'like an allegory for what was happening to me trying to make movies... . I drew from personal experience about a guy trying to make it' (1975: 17). Finally, as Travis's violence brings him fame in *Taxi Driver*, so the very value and nature of media acclaim is brought into question; a connotation that finds displaced reflection in the representation of the cultural mainstream as embodied by Artie Kirks and the Paul Wilson Orchestra in *New York, New York*.

The coda of *New York, New York* yet carries intimations of aesthetic self-validation. While Jimmy's professional situation during the final scenes marks the reconciliation of his implied desire for both artistic expression and professional success, his representation as a cutting-edge artist who had moved toward the mainstream and made his art more accessible and profitable without 'selling out' implies a self-referential allusion to Scorsese's own position in making *New York, New York*. Hence, perhaps, the coda's seeming – and seemingly unacknowledged – shift in the film's evaluation of success from that of personal fulfilment and artistic innovation to public acclaim and commercial recognition. The neatness of these claims falters at a crucial point: *New York, New York* proved neither accessible nor profitable.

Conclusion: 'That's the worst part. That's the whole thing. Going on …'[1]

Four weeks before the premiere of *New York, New York*, on 25 May 1977, *Star Wars* (George Lucas) opened. The film replaced *Jaws* as the most commercially successful film then produced. Costing $11.5 million, *Star Wars* grossed $193.5 million domestically and over $500 million worldwide. This paled before the take from associated merchandise. By the early eighties 'sales of *Star Wars* goods were estimated to be worth $1.5 billion a year' (Maltby and Craven 1995: 75).[2] It was a success that had significant institutional resonance, heralding, in Scorsese's words, 'a whole new period of filmmaking' (Hodenfield 1989: 51).

If *Bonnie and Clyde* provides a convenient starting-point for the institutional phase of New Hollywood Cinema, the coeval success and failure of *Star Wars* and *New York, New York* conveniently signals its end. Formally, *Star Wars* replaces the layered characterization and integrated stylistic complexity of *New York, New York* with a collection of superficial character types and a weak narrative that primarily serves as a framework for a series of spectacular but quasi-discrete set-pieces. This marks a shift from the modernist to the postmodernist that is complemented by the films' generic reference. While *Star Wars* is generically self-conscious, it replaces revisionism with pastiche. To quote Fredric Jameson: 'Pastiche is, like parody, the imitation of a peculiar mask, speech in a dead language: but it is a neutral practice of such mimicry, without any of parody's ulterior motives, amputated of the satiric impulse' (1984: 65).

Star Wars looks forward to and provides a model for much successful big-budget filmmaking in the eighties and nineties. In doing so, it is formally and ideologically a culmination of certain trends within seventies cinema. Andrew Britton relates *Star Wars* with the disaster movie cycle and with *Rocky*.[3] It can also be considered as a nostalgia film. Despite its futuristic setting, *Star Wars*, that opens with the title 'A long time ago in a galaxy far, far away ...', similarly seeks to place the spectator within a comforting, mythic realm.[4] Robin Wood notes of *Rocky*, *Star Wars* and their eighties progeny that ideologically 'Reassurance is the keynote' (1986: 162). Moreover, it is a reassurance that, in contradistinction to much New Hollywood Cinema, Wood sees as founded upon the *'Restoration of the Father'*: 'The Father must here be understood in all senses, symbolic, literal, potential: patriarchal authority (the Law), which assigns all other elements to their correct, subordinate, allotted roles' (*ibid.* : 172).

Similar impulses are implied politically by the election of Ronald Reagan, 'a candidate untouched by a sense of complexity and ambiguity, who could successfully package a simple belief in American might, power and opportunity to right the ills of the nation' (Quart and Auster 1984: 104). Reagan's election ushered in one of the most politically and socially reactionary periods in American history. This was reciprocated by a matching reactionariness within Hollywood cinema. The same month as Reagan's election, November 1980, United Artists released *Heaven's Gate* (Michael Cimino). Originally budgeted at $12 million, this epic revisionist western eventually cost $36 million, and its disastrous box-office performance ($1.5 million) contributed substantially to the end of the tenure of United Artists as a separate Hollywood financer-distributor. The film's failure enacted an unhappy coda to the majors' indulgence of New Hollywood Cinema. It confirmed – seemingly conclusively – the folly of staking large budgets on the personal visions of putative *auteurs*: if nothing else, Cimino's structurally unconventional and ideologically critical representation of a nascent American socialism crushed by a state-supported capitalist elite was decidedly out of time.

In the aftermath of *Heaven's Gate*, Transamerica sold United Artists to MGM, creating MGM/UA.[5] Since then the company has struggled, seemingly lurching from one crisis to another.[6] During the same period the other majors have, by contrast, largely enjoyed sustained growth. This has been founded upon the consolidation of the changes in structure and practice introduced in the seventies. Notable has been the majors' increasing facility in exploiting their product; whether this be through secondary distribution systems (especially pay-television and video) or through its translation into other media forms (publications, toys, CDs, computer software, theme-park rides and so on). Speeding this facility was the *laissez-faire* attitude of the Reagan administrations toward cross-media ownership. The same deregulatory emphasis saw the Justice Department declare in July 1986: 'The 1948 consent decrees are outdated.' Although some of the majors had already reacquired theatres, this nevertheless validated the tacit re-establishment of vertical integration.[7] Significantly, for all the monies attained through ancillary media forms, and the fact that since 1986 revenue from pay-television and video has exceeded the (itself increasing) revenue from the box-office, domestic theatrical success is still the 'engine' that powers success in other markets. Moreover, formally 'films with minimal character complexity or development and by-the-numbers plotting' remain 'the most readily reformulated and thus the most likely to be parlayed into a full-blown franchise' (Schatz 1993: 29). Correspondingly, the seventies blockbuster has been seen to have transmuted into the high concept film; a major strain of Hollywood production that, foregrounding the relation of the economic and the aesthetic, centrally combines an 'emphasis on style', 'marketing hooks' and 'reduced narratives' (Wyatt 1994: 29, 22).[8]

The developments within the Hollywood institution both illuminate and are further illuminated by Scorsese's career since *New York, New York*. *Raging Bull* again brought together Scorsese and Robert De Niro. Unflinching in its representation of violent masculinity, the film was a critical success, and won Oscars for De Niro and editor Thelma Schoonmaker, but failed to recoup its $17 million cost. *The King of Comedy* (1983) has been discussed as both (and simultaneously) a biting critique of the media and 'one of the most radical' Hollywood films 'about the structures of the patriarchal family' (Wood 1986: 260). The film was a box-office disaster, returning just $1.2 million. Scorsese's institutional obsolescence was seemingly confirmed by his abortive attempt later in 1983 to realize a longstanding desire to make *The Last Temptation of Christ*.[9] After nine months of pre-production, Paramount halted the project four weeks before shooting. This was in part because of rising costs. The project had further attracted protests from the Christian Right. Ultimately, the film would appeared to have presented too many parallels with *Heaven's Gate* – it was likewise a size-ably budgeted, ideologically contentious 'personal' project that had the potential to spiral out of control. Paramount was also, during the eighties, the studio most associated with the development of high concept filmmaking.

Symptomatically, Scorsese repaired to New York. The low-budget pick-up *After Hours* (1985) enabled him 'to re-think and re-learn' (Andrew 1994:21). *After Hours* was completed for $4.5 million in 42 days. Similar discipline informed *The Color of Money* (1986). Characterized by Scorsese as an attempt 'to do a real Hollywood picture' (DeCurtis 1990: 108), the film features twin stars, Paul Newman and Tom Cruise, and adhered to contemporary Hollywood practice by being a (long-delayed) sequel to *The Hustler* (Robert Rossen, 1961). For Jim Hillier, sequels have become 'almost emblematic of the industry' (1993: 17). On one hand, sequels have a clear commercial logic: they are presold by their forerunners. On the other hand, sequels, along with remakes, 'only point to timidity, the reluctance to take risks that is so prevalent in the industry' (*ibid.* : 30). Scorsese's uncertain status within mid-eighties Hollywood was nevertheless underlined by both he and Newman having, in order to make *The Color of Money*, to put up one-third of their salaries against the film's on-budget completion. In the event, the film was completed under budget and a day early. Made for Touchstone, Disney's adult arm, it gave Newman a long-awaited Oscar and Scorsese his first considerable box-office success since *Taxi Driver*.[10]

The influence of agents within Hollywood has continued. When promoting *The Color of Money* Scorsese began talks with agent Michael Ovitz. Then head of Creative Artists Agency (CAA), Ovitz is widely considered to have been the most influential player in Hollywood during the past two decades.[11] Scorsese became a CAA client on 1 January 1987. Almost immediately *The Last Temptation of Christ* became revived as a project, with a deal being offered by Universal. Even so, the film's final cost was only $6.7 million.

After the 'Life Lessons' section of *New York Stories* (Scorsese, Francis Coppola and Woody Allen, 1989), Scorsese made *GoodFellas* (1990) for Warner Bros: 'That was the best of both worlds: $26 million to make a personal movie' (DeCurtis 1990: 108). The film's critical and commercial success almost at a stroke appeared to confirm Scorsese's institutional recuperation.[12] In particular, it led in April 1991 to a six-year deal with Universal. However, the first result of the deal was *Cape Fear* (1991), a remake of the 1962 thriller: 'Sometimes it's a trade-off. You have to do a certain kind of film in order to get maybe two others of your own that you want' (*ibid.*). *Cape Fear* was Scorsese's most commercially successful film to date, taking over $78 million at the box-office. Nevertheless, while Universal financed and distributed *Casino* (1995), it passed on Scorsese's adaptation of Edith Wharton's novel *The Age of Innocence* (1993). Twentieth Century-Fox also pulled out. The film was financed and distributed by Columbia.

That Scorsese experienced some difficulty in finding a studio to back *The Age of Innocence* in spite of his seeming bankability implies the limitations of Hollywood's commercial appropriation of authorship –

plainly, a nineteenth-century costume drama did not fit Scorsese's marketable star image. Read in relation to Scorsese's authorial discourse, however, *The Age of Innocence* is significantly 'authored'. Stylistically, the film is informed by an expressionism that variously inflects camerawork, editing, colour and, at one point, incident: the remarkable moment when Newland Archer (Daniel Day-Lewis) is 'embraced' by Ellen Olenska (Michelle Pfeiffer). This is combined with an almost obsessively detailed, 'documentary' reconstruction of the time's physical and ideological space, of its customs, codes and rituals as well as its décor, dress and objects. Through this the film represents a culture that is no less repressive and, finally, ruthless than that of, say, the Little Italy of *Mean Streets*. Moreover, as its determining influence impacts upon Newland's transgressive desire for Ellen, so the character enters Scorsese's gallery of alienated male protagonists, where he joins such apparently contradictory figures as the Jake La Motta (De Niro) of *Raging Bull* and the Christ (Willem Dafoe) of *The Last Temptation of Christ*. Indeed, post-*New York, New York* Scorsese's features have continued to privilege a male point of view and to centre thematically upon a dissection of tensions within masculine heterosexual identity.

Raging Bull and 'Life Lessons' reflect *New York, New York* in positing a disjunction between successful heterosexual coupling and achieved professional or artistic expression. This connects with a self-referential emphasis within Scorsese's later features upon the nature and cost of fame. *The King of Comedy* structurally replays *Taxi Driver*, but shifts the issue of celebrity from the margins of the text to the centre. The film invites parallels between Rupert Pupkin (De Niro), the driven wannabe, and Jerry Langford (Jerry Lewis), the established but isolated star, and Scorsese's 'past' and 'present' selves. Scorsese's 'comeback' film, *The Color of Money*, revises the pattern. As the innocent Vincent Lauria (Cruise) becomes corrupted by success, so the cynical Eddie Felson (Newman) is rejuvenated as he once more becomes – literally – a player. In *Raging Bull* Jake's world championship is tainted by his humiliating (Oedipal) concessions to the mob, while in *Casino* the hubristic vitiation of 'Ace' Rothstein (De Niro)'s success is marked by his hosting of his own television show.

Replicating casting, structure, and incident, *Casino* reworks *GoodFellas* on a broader canvas. In its representation of everyday Mafia life, *GoodFellas* in turn recalls *Mean Streets*. Like *Mean Streets* it, too, implies an ambivalent complicity with what it critiques, conveying a nostalgic sadness for the 'old ways' whose passing the film charts. Based on actual events, *GoodFellas* and *Casino* highlight the documentary impulse of

Scorsese's authorial discourse. Likewise, their elliptical narratives continue to pronounce a formal and stylistic debt to the *nouvelle vague*. The extensive use of voice-over at the beginning of *GoodFellas* explicitly plays off that which opens *Jules et Jim*, returning us to Scorsese's very first film, *What's a Nice Girl Like You Doing in a Place Like This?*.

The similarities between *GoodFellas* and *Casino* implies the input of Nicholas Pileggi. Not only did Pileggi co-write both scripts with Scorsese, but he wrote the book, *Wiseguy*, on which *GoodFellas* is based. However, the comparative foregroundedness of Scorsese's authorial discourse in the features that he has directed since *New York, New York* reflects the way that, despite his fluctuating institutional position, he has maintained a comparatively greater autonomy over his filmmaking than earlier in his career. This is conversely attributable to his largely working within either a low- or a high-budget context: the largish budgets that his features have enjoyed at both the beginning and the end of the period in question have been predicated upon his status as an *auteur*. The exception to this scenario of low- or high-budget autonomy is *The Color of Money*. Of medium budget, and a demonstration of Scorsese's commercial 'responsibility', the film is marked by an 'impersonal' flatness of narrative and style, within which the explosions of virtuoso camerawork and editing during the pool-playing scenes transmit a rather forced assertion of authorial signature. After Scorsese's initial problems in obtaining finance for *The Age of Innocence*, the film was made for $34 million. He was also permitted ten months to edit the film.

Similarly consider *Kundun* (1987). Costing $28 million, and financed jointly by Touchstone and French major UGC, the film presents an account of the early life of the Dalai Lama, was shot mainly on location in Morocco with a non-professional cast and becomes, formally, increasingly an associative play of images.[13]

Authorial connotations notwithstanding, Scorsese's later features are inescapably informed by and reflect upon their broader cinematic and historical contexts. For example, *After Hours* is part of the 'yuppie nightmare' cycle; a group of films that, produced during the period of Right-wing triumphalism that followed Reagan's re-election, articulate repressions and tensions existing beneath the public façade of mid-eighties USA.[14] *GoodFellas* sits within the noteworthy gangster film cycle of the early nineties, and uses the genre to mount an acerbic critique of the excesses of the Reagan–Bush years. A similar attack on eighties materialism is essayed in *The Color of Money*. *Casino* ambitiously ups the ideological stakes. Using Las Vegas as a national metaphor, it presents a complex thesis on the structure of power, ending with a voice-over that tacitly collapses the mob and the financial institutions. In turn, *Kundun* was one of at least three features variously supportive of Tibet and/or critical of Beijing released in the USA in1997.[15]

This returns us finally to our point of departure. In each of his films, Scorsese's authorial discourse functions in a complex, shifting and reciprocally inflecting relation with the text's other constituting elements. While unpacking this relation points up the frequent complications involved in ascribing individual authorship, it places authorial analysis within a theoretically cogent explanatory framework that respects both the complexity of textual determination and the plurality of meanings offered by any text. Yet if this validates authorial criticism, analysis of Scorsese's *oeuvre* no less validates *auteur* cinema. As noted, much is frequently made of Scorsese's personal investment in his material. Granted, this is often a selling device. Such investment is nevertheless the mainspring of Scorsese's best work, fuelling an intensity of expression and an engaged willingness to confront and unpack the implications of the films' subject matter with a frequently unsettling but unyielding honesty. That this combines with and is tempered by a highly developed stylistic and formal intelligence renders this work, for this writer, cumulatively the finest body of films of any contemporary American director. As, with respect to this study, *Mean Streets*, *Taxi Driver* and *New York, New York* demonstrate, Scorsese's most achieved work is 'personal' not just in the sense of its possible biographical reference, but in terms of a salutary integrity and intransigence. If this has tended to militate against his films enjoying the massive success of those of some of his peers, it also asserts that the 'death of the author' has been greatly exaggerated.

Notes

1 Introduction: Martin Scorsese, Authorship, Context

1. Scorsese's comment was made in an edition of Cinemax's 1993 television series, *Favorite Films*.

   Astruc outlines his concept of the *caméra-stylo* thus: 'the cinema is quite simply becoming ... a form in which and by which an artist can express his thoughts, however abstract they may be, or translate his obsessions exactly as he does in the contemporary essay or novel. This is why I would like to call this new age of cinema the age of *caméra-stylo* (camera-pen)' (1948: 17–18).
2. See Barthes (1968).
3. See, for example, Medhurst (1991), Powell (1994) and Holmlund (1996).
4. See, on one hand, Livingston (1997) and Gaut (1997) and, on the other, Maher (1998).
5. The following account of auteurism and the debates surrounding film authorship broadly parallels those offered, with contrasting emphases, by Lapsley and Westlake (1988: 105–28), Stoddart (1995) and Crofts (1998). Like so much recent work on authorship, this orthodoxy finds its provenance in Caughie (1981a).
6. While auteurism is afforded a convenient starting-date by François Truffaut's polemical article, 'Une certaine tendance du cinéma français' (Truffaut 1954), auteurism hardly occurred in a vacuum. Apart from the influence of Astruc, auteurist analyses *avant la lettre* are apparent, for example, in the predecessor of *Cahiers*, *La Revue du cinéma*, and in Lindsay Anderson's writing for the British magazine *Sequence*. However, *la politique des auteurs* took the issue of authorship further than any previous formulation.
7. See, for example, Althusser (1964).
8. For a critique of the theoretical limitations of *auteur*-structuralism, see Henderson (1973).
9. See Crofts (1998: 319–22).
10. In a footnote to the translation of the Editors of *Cahiers du cinéma*'s 'John Ford's *Young Mr Lincoln*', the *Screen* editors relate the notion of inscription to Jacques Derrida:

    > This usage of inscription (*l'inscription*) refers to work done by Jacques Derrida on the concept of *écriture* in *Theories d'ensemble* (Collection Tel Quel, 1968).... . Cahiers' point here is that all individual texts are part of and inscribe themselves into one historically determined 'text' (*l'histoire textuelle*) within which they are produced; a reading of the individual text therefore requires examining both in its dynamic relationship with this general text and the relationship between the general text and specific historical events (1970: 44).

    Without wishing to appear too instumentalist, when considering authorship a parallel is offered between Derrida's 'individual' and 'general' texts and the single 'authored' film and the 'general text' of his or her *oeuvre*, that, no less than Derrida's 'general text', has a 'dynamic relationship' with its historical context.

2   New York, NYU, and the European Influence: *What's a Nice Girl Like You Doing in a Place Like This?; It's Not Just You, Murray!; The Big Shave*

1. An amusing account of one of these attempts, *Vesuvius VII*, is given by childhood friend Dominic Lo Faro in Kelly (1980: 38–9).
2. Scorsese: 'I never went to the Village until I enrolled at New York University in 1960.... From 1950 to 1960, for ten years, I never ventured past Broadway and Houston Street. I remember a friend of mine – I was about nine years old – his mother took us to the Village to see the little houses and flowers. It was like a wonderland. It was a very different culture' (DeCurtis 1990: 64).
3. According to Michel Ciment, the Left Bank group, that included Alain Resnais, Agnès Varda and Chris Marker, was thus termed 'because their approach was more intellectual and sophisticated, but also because their politics were definitely left-wing' (1984: 39).
4. Following common practice, films throughout this study are dated according to their release. In terms of production, *Le Beau Serge* was shot December 1957–February 1958, *Les Quatre Cent Coups* November 1958–January 1959 and *A bout de souffle* August–September 1959.
   Where there is an accepted English version of a non-English film title, it is given in the Filmography.
5. The term *nouvelle vague*, moreover, 'was coined by the journalist Françoise Giraud, who was conscious of the birth of "youth culture" at the end of the 1950s and who wrote a series of portraits of young people and their aspirations for the magazine *L'Express*' (Forbes 1998: 463).
   Not that all the filmmakers who directed their first features were young. The emergence of the *nouvelle vague* similarly 'opened the door to older directors, professionally trained, famous for their short films... . Georges Franju and Alain Resnais were thus able to direct their first features' (Ciment 1984: 39).
6. Although the NYU film school may, in the early sixties, have encouraged 'personal' filmmaking, it hardly followed auteurism's critical emphasis on Hollywood, upholding instead the then largely pro-art cinema orthodoxy. Scorsese notes: '*Movie* magazine appeared from Britain with its list of great directors, and there were Hawks and Hitchcock at the top. The professors were totally against these critical views' (Thompson and Christie 1996: 18).
7. In 1962, Scorsese co-directed and photographed a short with fellow student Robert Siegel. Titled *Inesita*, the film represents a flamenco dancer. Manoogian dismisses it thus: 'It was very, very traditional in terms of its camera work and very ordinary, and what they had done primarily was to present Inesita as the dancer. She was very good. The film was just another one of those films' (Kelly 1980: 60).

8. According to Allan Arkush, the situation at NYU had hardly improved by the late sixties:

> The higly respected 'N.Y.U. Film School' consisted of four small rooms on the eighth floor of a building a block and a half from Washington Square Park. We had four movieolas that ate student films at an alarming rate and only one camera capable of sound.... Haig Manoogian coped as best as he could but all he could offer was enthusiasm and a Bell & Howell Filmo. The Filmos were virtually indestructable cast-iron cameras that had to be wound up with a door knob because all the keys had disappeared years ago (1983: 57).

9. See Kelly (1980: 12).
10. Godard's oft-quoted maxim is, 'cinema is not the reflection of reality, but the reality of that reflection'. See, for example, MacCabe (1980: 110).
11. The tension between the documentary and the reflexive extends to Scorsese's documentaries *Italianamerican* (1974), *The Last Waltz* (1978) and *American Boy: A Profile of Steven Prince* (1978). Reflecting the opening sequence of *It's Not Just You, Murray!*, the films contain numerous elements that problematize documentary 'objectivity' by reflexively foregrounding their constructedness and, further, Scorsese's 'subjective' control of the projects: the crew are seen and/or heard; interviews are 'revealingly' stopped and restarted; Scorsese sets up interviews, prompts subjects from a script, directs the camera and so on.
12. Mary Pat Kelly makes a similar point: 'As Murray drives ... he holds up the picture.... There is little Joe. But then the photograph moves. The little boy goes running down the walk in the jerky, all-at-once style of the early film. Appropriately, Joe's beginning steps are linked with the start of the movies' (1980: 155).
13. See Ciment and Henry (1975: 9).

3   Entering the Marketplace, Developing a Style: *Who's That Knocking at My Door?*

1. In discussing his use of mirrors, Scorsese (unsurprisingly) offers a biographical rather than a Lacanian/psychoanalytic provenance. It is, however, a biographical reference that suggestively evokes a desired identification with and internalization of a succession of ego ideals: 'My training in handling actors came from watching a lot of movies and being thrilled by them. That's how a lot of mirror scenes in my movies came about. I used to fantasize in front of the mirror, playing all my heroes' (Thompson and Christie 1996: 42).
2. In Lacanian psychoanalysis, this sexual inequality is related to the role of the phallus as 'the privileged signifier in the child's entry into the Symbolic' (Johnston 1976: 321). Given the 'phallocentrism of patriarchal culture is founded on the paradigm of male sexuality – the penis' (*ibid.* : 322), the female suffers 'negative entry into the Symbolic' and a consequent secondary cultural definition 'as *that which is not male*' (*ibid.*: 321, 322).
3. Scorsese: 'J.R., c'était moi!' (Ciment and Henry 1975: 10).

4. Films made by Engel, Rogosin and Clarke include *Lovers and Lollipops* (Engel, 1955), *On the Bowery* (Rogosin, 1956), *Come Back Africa* (Rogosin, 1959), *The Connection* (Clarke, 1961) and *The Cool World* (Clarke, 1963).
5. Although shot in 16 mm, *Shadows* was blown up into 35mm for commercial distribution and exhibition.
6. Acknowledging this, the credit sequence of *Shadows* includes the title, 'Presented By Jean Shepherd's Night People'. Cassavetes's 'use' of *Edge of the City* to finance *Shadows* looks forward to the way in which in future he was to use the money that he earned as an actor to help to finance the films that he made as a director.
7. Cassavetes amended the original version of *Shadows*, which premiered in late 1958, because he thought it too stylized. Abandoning over half the footage of the original version, Cassavetes shot eight new scenes, and, after three months of re-editing, premiered the extant version of *Shadows* on 11 November 1959. For a more detailed discussion of Cassavetes's filmmaking style, see Margulies (1998).
8. For further consideration of the relation of Comolli's position on direct cinema to Cassavetes's filmmaking, see Kouvaros (1998: 253–6).
9. Scorsese has admitted that his ambition had been fired by the success of *Prima della rivoluzione* (Bernardo Bertolucci, 1964) at the 1964 New York Film Festival – Bertolucci was just two years older than himself. See, for example, Scorsese (1981: 134) and (1997c: 94–5).
10. For a version of Scorsese's treatment for *Jerusalem, Jerusalem*, see Kelly (1980: 42–56).
11. The exact duration of *Bring on the Dancing Girls* appears to be a matter of some uncertainty. Haig Manoogian has described the film as running 'about fifty-eight minutes' (Kelly 1980: 63), while Scorsese has also stated that it was 'an hour and ten minutes long' (Taylor 1981: 308).
12. In another (coincidental?) link with the *nouvelle vague*, one of the women was Anne Colette, who appears in two of Jean-Luc Godard's short films, *Tous les garçons s'appellent Patrick* (1957) and *Charlotte et son Jules* (1958).
13. Scorsese: 'It was supposed to be a full life-size statue of Jesus which he kisses on the feet. And then when he comes up, there was supposed to be blood coming out of his mouth or just blood from the feet. And we never had it … . There was a stupid little plastic thing on the wall and the blood didn't come out of the mouth right. It was a mess.' (Morrison 1986a: 11).
14. For more on acting in Cassavetes's films, see, again, Margulies (1998) and, in particular, on the complex commutations of character and actor, Kouvaros (1998).
15. This despite Scorsese's claim: 'I don't know what the method is or any of that stuff' (1975: 19).
16. Another acknowledged influence on Scorsese's investment in Method-based actors are the films of Elia Kazan: 'I saw *On the Waterfront* [Kazan, 1954] and *East of Eden* [Kazan, 1955] and those two boys, Marlon Brando and James Dean, changed my life completely' (Thompson and Christie 1996: 42).
17. Scorsese decided to use rock and pop songs after viewing *Scorpio Rising* (Kenneth Anger, 1962). See Thompson and Christie (1996: 21).
18. Three volumes of Chion's work on film sound remain at the time of writing untranslated into English: *La Voix au cinéma* (1982), *Le Son au cinéma* (1985)

and *La Toile trouée* (1988). *Audio-Vision* (1994) in part summarizes some of the ideas developed in these volumes.

19. The shot during the scene of J.R. and the girl's first meeting implies an elaboration of the similarly mobile take that films the conversation between Nana (Anna Karina) and the journalist (Paul Pavel) in *Vivre sa vie* (Godard, 1962).

20. In the name of precision, the credits of *Who's That Knocking at My Door?* are actually intercut with the second pre-credit scene.

21. The situation has in addition biographical overtones – 'in the neighbourhood where we lived there were fights all the time, many of them with the Puerto Ricans who were moving into the area' (Scorsese 1981: 133).

22. Sigmund Freud: 'The female genitals are symbolically represented by all such objects as share their characteristic of enclosing a hollow space which can take something into itself: by *pits*, *cavities* and *hollows*, for instance, by *vessels* and *bottles*, by *receptacles*, *boxes*, *trunks*, *cases*, *chests*, *pockets*, and so on' (1917: 189).

23. Les Keyser identifies the figure carrying the eyes as 'Santa Lucia', whom he terms, 'Sicily's most important female saint': 'Italians idolized her for gouging out her eyes rather than marrying' (1992: 26).

24. *Who's That Knocking at My Door?* also contains a montage of stills from another Wayne western, *Rio Bravo* (Howard Hawks, 1959), a film that J.R. takes the girl to see.

4 Exploitation Cinema and the Youth Market: *Boxcar Bertha*

1. Direction of *The Honeymoon Killers* was assumed by its writer, Leonard Kastle. The film was released in 1970. Perhaps ironically, given Scorsese's dismissal, the finished film, that combines a 'direct cinema' ambience reminiscent of *Who's That Knocking at My Door?* with a tendency towards camp, melodramatic overstatement, is marked by long takes.

2. Among the films that Scorsese screened were *Force of Evil* (Abraham Polonsky, 1948), *The Band Wagon* (Vincente Minnelli, 1953), *Johnny Guitar* (Nicholas Ray, 1954), *The Searchers*, *The Nutty Professor* (Jerry Lewis, 1963) and *El Dorado* (Howard Hawks, 1967). See Taylor (1981: 314).

3. James Monaco explains that 'the group took its name from the short didactic newsreels produced anonymously in France two years earlier during the aborted rising of May–June 1968' (1984: 153).

4. Scorsese: '[Warner Bros vice-president] Freddie Weintraub needed somebody to salvage *Medicine Ball Caravan* because they had a nine-hour cut – it was in three gauges – 35 mm Techniscope, 16 mm and 8 mm ... nobody knew what was happening. It had no continuity, nothing' (1975: 8).

5. Scorsese: 'It had been retitled because the manager didn't like the original and preferred to use the main character's name!' (Thompson and Christie 1996: 30).

6. For fuller discussion of the difficulties facing fifties Hollywood, see, for example, Pye and Myles (1979: 15–37) and Schatz (1983: 169–87).

7. For numerous (apocryphal?) stories about Corman's filmmaking, see Naha (1982) and Corman with Jerome (1990).

8. See, for example, Will and Willemen (1970) and Dixon (1976).

9. A transition in *The Oklahoma Woman* also suggestively anticipates *Who's That Knocking at My Door?*. The film dissolves from 'good' woman Susan (Cathy Downs) to 'bad' woman Marie as she fixes her hair before a mirror: a shot that, in terms of scale and set-up, context and connotation, invites parallels with that of the 'broad' brushing her hair in Gaga's flashback.

10. After making *Von Richthofen and Brown* (1971), Corman effectively retired from directing. He has directed just one film since, *Roger Corman's Frankenstein Unbound* (1990).

11. New World's nurse cycle comprises *The Student Nurses* (Stephanie Rothman, 1970), *Private Duty Nurses* (George Armitage, 1972), *Night Call Nurses* (Jonathan Kaplan, 1972), *The Young Nurses* (Clinton Kimbrough, 1973) and *Candy Stripe Nurses* (Allan Holleb,1974), while its women-in-prison films include *The Big Doll House* (Jack Hill, 1971), *The Hot Box* (Joe Viola, 1972), *The Big Bird Cage* (Hill, 1972), *Caged Heat* (Jonathan Demme, 1974) and *Jackson County Jail* (Michael Miller, 1976). The company's biker films are *Angels Die Hard!* (Richard Compton, 1970), *Angels Hard as They Come* (Viola, 1971) and *Bury Me an Angel* (Barbara Peeters, 1971).

    For more on New World Pictures, see Hillier and Lipstadt (1986).

12. Roger Corman interviewed by author, Leeds 27 October 1988.

13. Apart from directors, Corman has given opportunities to numerous actors, scriptwriters, craftspersons and executives; including, for example, Jack Nicholson, Bruce Dern, Robert Towne, Laszlo Kovacs and Gale Anne Hurd. For a fairly detailed account of a number of the people granted breaks by Corman, see Newman (1985a) and (1985b).

14. The editing of *Boxcar Bertha* is credited to Buzz Feitshans. According to Scorsese: 'He was down on location with us but he never even saw the cut' (1975: 8). A reason why Scorsese could not receive the credit was that in directing *Boxcar Bertha* he became a member of the Directors Guild of America.

15. See Ciment and Henry (1975: 14). Corman contends that the discontent with Scorsese was also 'a function of internal politics at AIP': '[James H.] Nicholson had died, and there was a big executive production staff trying to make points and advance their careers' (Corman with Jerome 1990: 186).

16. See Ciment and Henry (1975: 14).

17. For a discussion of the outlaw-couple films, see Krutnik (1991: 213–26).

18. To be fair, for Kolker the outlaw-couple films essentially comprise 'the minor country thieves variation of the gangster film'. Accepting that the term 'outlaw-couple' has become the customary critical designation for the earlier grouping of films, this study will keep the appellation 'country thieves' for the post-*Bonnie and Clyde* cycle; not least because the films do not necessarily centre upon the couple – witness, in particular, *Bloody Mama* and *Dillinger*.

19. John Belton breaks the figures down further: 'By 1970–1971, over 43 percent of all viewers were between the ages of 12 and 20... . An additional 30 percent of the total audience were between the ages of 21 and 29, making almost 75 percent of the film audience under age 30' (1994: 303–4).

20. The seminal, much-anthologized statement on the erotic objectification of the female in filmic representation is Mulvey (1975).

21. Laura Mulvey: 'Traditionally, the woman displayed has functioned on two levels: as erotic object for the characters within the screen story, and as erotic object for the spectator within the auditorium, with a shifting tension between the looks on either side of the screen' (1975: 11–12).

22. With respect to this, Cook somewhat coyly writes of Corman's 'sexual role-reversal films' casting 'women as mirror images of men, without questioning those images too much' (1985: 369).

23. In Freudian dream symbolism: '*Shoes* and *slippers* are female genitals' (Freud 1917: 191).

24. We might further ponder how Scorsese's diegetic appearance relates to, or even plays off, the similarly reflexive but expressly misogynistic moment when Bertha mistakenly opens a bedroom door at the brothel and, in an incident that alludes to *Vivre sa vie*, finds cinematographers John Stephens and Gayne Rescher examining a naked woman.

25. Specifically, Matthew 6: 19–20. Scorsese has stated that the use of the passage was his idea. See Ciment and Henry (1975: 14).

26. The crucifixion was in the original script; Scorsese 'had nothing to do' with it (Thompson and Christie 1996: 36). However, Scorsese has admitted to using the scene as directed as a template for the crucifixion scene in *The Last Temptation of Christ* (1988): the shots of a spike being driven into Bill's hand and of Bill's agony before dying are replicated almost exactly.

27. Studies of genre informed by this position include Cawelti (1971), Wright (1975), Schatz (1981) and (1983) and Altman (1989). For Lévi-Strauss's model of myth, see Lévi-Strauss (1958: 206–31).

5   New Hollywood Cinema: *Mean Streets*

1. Scorsese: 'One of my old professors at NYU told me, "Hey, nobody wants to see films about Italian-Americans anyway so forget about it." This was about a year before *The Godfather* was written as a book' (1975: 8). The professor in question was Haig Manoogian.

2. *I Escaped from Devil's Island* was eventually directed by William Witney and *The Arena* by Steve Carver. Both were released in 1973.

3. See Bliss (1985: 82).

4. See Scorsese (1975: 10).

5. Scorsese: 'Sid came in and ... made an initial cut into the last section... . The rest of it I cut. Brian De Palma came in and helped and Sandy Weintraub helped me' (1975: 8).

6. See Scorsese (1975: 12–13).

7. The reasons for and consequences of Hollywood's post-war difficulties have been much rehearsed. See, for example, Pye and Myles (1979: 15–47), Hugo (1980) and Schatz (1983: 169–87). For further and fuller discussion of the divergent applications of the term 'New Hollywood', see Kramer (1998: 295–305).

8. For more on this particular episode, see Pye and Myles (1979: 85–9).

9. Ned Tanen: 'Ours ... weren't "youth films" as such. They were Milos Forman's *Taking Off* [1971], Dennis Hopper's [*The*] *Last Movie* [1971] ...

Douglas Trumbull's *Silent Running* [1971], Peter Fonda's [*The*] *Hired Hand* [1971], John Cassavetes' *Minnie and Moskowitz* [1971], *Diary of a Mad Housewife* [Frank Perry, 1970], *Play It As It Lays* [Perry, 1972], *Two-Lane Blacktop* [Monte Hellman, 1971], *Ulzana's Raid* [Robert Aldrich, 1972]. They were all made for about one million dollars... . The only one of those pictures that made any money was *Diary*' (Bygrave 1981: 75–7).

10. Strictly speaking, *Easy Rider* was made by Raybert Productions, a company formed by Bob Rafelson and Bert Schneider. The company became BBS when Rafelson and Schneider were joined by Steve Blauner. Following the success of *Easy Rider*, Columbia made a deal to finance and distribute unseen any BBS production that cost less than $1 million. The films produced under the deal were *Five Easy Pieces* (Rafelson, 1970), *A Safe Place* (Henry Jaglom, 1971), *The Last Picture Show* (Peter Bogdanovich, 1971), *Drive, He Said* (Jack Nicholson, 1972), *The King of Marvin Gardens* (Rafelson, 1972) and *Hearts and Minds* (Peter Davis, 1974). Of these, only *Five Easy Pieces* and *The Last Picture Show* turned a profit. For more on BBS, see Grimes (1986).

11. For Barthes's definition of the codes, see the section 'The Five Codes' (1970: 18–20).

12. Bordwell and Staiger's investment in this position veers toward the overt when they compare *The China Syndrome* (James Bridges, 1979) unfavourably to the expressly Brechtian *Tout va bien* (Jean-Luc Godard and Jean-Pierre Gorin, 1972). See Bordwell and Staiger (1985: 372).

13. Barthes uses the term 'readerly' to describe (rather monolithically) the way that classical narratives position the reader/spectator as a 'passive' textual consumer: '[The] reader is ... plunged into a kind of idleness ... instead of functioning himself, instead of gaining access to the magic of the signifier, to the pleasure of writing, he is left with no more than the poor freedom either to accept or reject the text' (Barthes 1970: 4).

   For MacCabe's fullest exposition of his concept of the classic realist text, see MacCabe (1974).

14. On the formation of their production company The Archers in 1942, Powell and Pressburger shared the idiosyncratic credit 'Written, Produced and Directed by', although it is accepted that Pressburger was primarily responsible for the films' scripting and Powell for their direction. Previous to *Mean Streets*, intimations of the influence of Powell and Pressburger's films on Scorsese are supplied by Murray's smashing of his mirrored reflection, that recalls the similar act of Lermontov (Anton Walbrook) in *The Red Shoes* (Powell and Pressburger, 1948), and by the naming of a pair of secondary characters in *Boxcar Bertha* 'Michael Powell' and 'Emeric Pressburger'.

   In a parallel to Scorsese's relationship with Cassavetes, Powell moved from being an admired filmmaker to become a personal friend of and adviser to Scorsese.

15. See, in particular, the chapter 'The map of misprison' (Bloom 1980: 83–105).

16. Jeffrey Sconce makes a similar claim in relation to 'trash' cinema, for which he coins the term 'paracinema'. Alluding to Peter Wollen's opposition of the 'seven cardinal virtues' of Godardian counter-cinema to the 'seven deadly sins' of mainstream film (1972: 7), Sconce observes: 'One cannot

help but be struck by how certain paracinematic titles, especially genre hybrids like *Glen or Glenda* [Edward D. Wood, 1953], match Wollen's criteria point by point' (1995: 392 n56).

17. Scorsese: 'When we tried to get the film off the ground in Hollywood, the studio critiques were that it had a very bare story line and it was filled with digressions' (Delson 1973: 29).

18. Scorsese: '*Mean Streets* has no establishing shots, practically ... we just didn't have time' (1975: 5); 'I think *Mean Streets* is a very sloppy film, only because we had to shoot it in twenty-seven days. I'm not giving excuses. That's reality' (Macklin 1975: 24).

19. Scorsese: 'I was Charlie ... but there were other elements of a friend of mine because I never had enough money – I couldn't sign for those loans.... . The conflicts within Charlie were within me, my own feelings' (1975: 17).

    A similar biographical reference is afforded by the credit sequence, in which the represented piece of leader, that bears the words 'Scorsese baptism', and the actual shots of a baptism derive from footage shot by Scorsese's father of the baptism of one of his godchildren in 1965. See Ciment and Henry (1975: 18–19).

20. The cut from church to bar implies an allusion to *The Red Shoes*. Near the end of 'The Red Shoes' ballet, the ballet's protagonist (danced by Victoria Page/Moira Shearer) is pulled by her magical shoes away from the steps of a church and the embrace of a priest to an infernal, red-lit space inhabited by the ballet's demonic shoemaker (Ljubov/Leonid Massine).

21. The passage is John: 18. 33–6.

22. Scorsese: '[There is] an old heretical sect that felt they were not worthy of anything. They would go to confession but would not go to communion because they felt they were not worthy' (1975: 5).

23. Lee Lourdeaux writes that the relation of epilepsy to 'mental illness' is 'an old Italian superstition' (1990: 242).

24. See Ciment and Henry (1975: 14).

25. Apart from being the original title of *Mean Streets*, 'Season of the Witch' is the title of a song by Donovan.

26. Scorsese has noted of the Mafia: 'In my neighborhood you dealt with the "organization" – I don't like to call it anything else' (Taylor 1981: 304).

27. Despite its outlandishness, the scene is, according to Scorsese, based on an actual incident. See Ciment and Henry (1975: 9).

28. Charlie's setting light to the glass of spirits repeats the identical act of Rake in the church scene in *Boxcar Bertha*. Intertextually, this lends the fire imagery in *Boxcar Bertha* a specific religious/symbolic resonance that, on textual evidence alone, it somewhat lacks.

29. Scorsese originally wanted to use a clip from *Donovan's Reef* (John Ford, 1963) in which Donovan (John Wayne) fights with Gilhooley (Lee Marvin). This had to be changed when Wayne objected to 'appearing' in a R-rated film. Notwithstanding, the scene from *The Searchers*, as it represents *Martin* fighting *Charlie*, invites reflexive/biographical interpretation – at one point Charlie even exclaims 'Marty, that ain't fair.'

    The fight at the pool hall implies a similar scene in *Coogan's Bluff* (Don Siegel, 1968), not least as in both a character (Coogan/Clint Eastwood and Johnny) stands atop a pool table, wielding a (respectively unbroken and broken) pool cue and kicking out, before being beaten upon the floor by a number of his assailants.

30. While coherent, the killing's homoerotic connotations were born out of production exigency. Scorsese recalls: 'the kid who did the scene was in another picture and he couldn't cut his hair. Now, I knew that we had to write that in the script, and figure out a way that would work in terms of the whole picture ... something sexual's gonna happen, and ... bam!' (Goldstein and Jacobson 1976: 31).

31. The character's naming and the film's Catholic reference have led to parallels being drawn between Teresa and Teresa of Ávila, a figure often discussed in relation to the confusion of religious and sexual ecstasy. See, for example, Hosney, Wollman and Engdahl (1993: 182).

32. The shots are near-replicas of like shots in Joey's car in *Who's That Knocking at My Door?*.

33. The incident on the landing evokes the scene in *Ladri di biciclette* (Vittorio De Sica, 1948) in which Antonio (Lamberto Maggiorani) confronts the youth (Vittorio Antonucci) whom he claims has stolen his bicycle. The youth suffers an epileptic fit, and is comforted by his plump, middle-aged mother.

34. Neale's reference to the musicality of the classical text suggests the influence of *S/Z*. See the section 'The Full Score' (Barthes 1970: 28–30).

35. 'Rendering' is another concept coined in relation to film sound by Michel Chion: 'The use of sounds to convey the feelings or effects associated with the situation on screen – often in opposition to faithful *reproduction*... . Rendering frequently translates an agglomerate of sensations' (1994: 224).

36. Lawrence S. Friedman, however, pointedly notes that in wounding Charlie 'superficially', Scorsese 'confers upon him(self) the punishment he craves without the destruction he fears' (1997: 38).

37. Scorsese has explicitly referred to Charlie's wound as 'stigmata' (Macklin 1975: 26).

38. Even in late drafts of the script for *Mean Streets* Jerry's party was a costume party, with Charlie attending dressed as Christ. The implied association between Charlie and Christ recalls the similar parallels suggested between J.R. and Christ in *Who's That Knocking at My Door?* and between Bill Shelley and Christ in *Boxcar Bertha*.

39. Writing contemporaneously Elsaesser noted that Hollywood cinema: 'remains an audience-orientated cinema that permits no explicitly intellectual narrative construction. Consequently, the innovatory line in the American cinema can be seen to progress not via conceptual abstraction but by shifting and modifying traditional genres and themes, while never quite shedding their support' (1975: 18).

40. Mardik Martin: 'At the time [of writing *Season of the Witch*], *The Godfather* was a book. To us [Martin and Scorsese], it was bullshit. It didn't seem to be about the gangsters we knew, the petty ones you see around. We wanted to tell the story about real gangsters' (Kelly 1992: 72).

41. This definition of melodramatic and tragic protagonists derives from Heilman (1968). For an intelligent précis and discussion of Heilman's work, see Walker (1982).

42. See, for example, those of *Five Easy Pieces* and *Two-Lane Blacktop*.

6   Into the Mainstream: *Alice Doesn't Live Here Anymore*

1. Burstyn further recalls: 'We met in John Calley's office... . I asked, "What do you know about women?" And [Scorsese] said, "Nothing. But I'd like to learn." I thought that was a wonderful answer' (Kelly 1992: 83).
2. Scorsese: 'the sooner we got Alice moving, the more favorable were the preview audiences' responses' (Carducci 1975: 14).
3. Apart from Warner Bros, in 1974 Paramount was part of Gulf + Western, United Artists was part of Transamerica, Universal was part of Music Corporation of America (MCA), while MGM had been bought by Las Vegas financier Kirk Kerkorian. For more on conglomeration, see, for example, Monaco (1984: 29–35) and Wyatt (1994: 69–81).
4. Hence John Beckett, Chairman of Transamerica, on the acquisition of United Artists – 'the reason we bought the darn company in the first place was we hoped it would have some effect on the Transamerica stock' (Bach 1985: 25).
5. Former President of United Artists and Paramount, David Picker, notes of conglomerates: 'They felt that manpower could be replaced by manpower, that no executive was a unique asset' (Laskos 1981: 27). Mike Medavoy, ex-West Coast production chief of United Artists, similarly notes of James Harvey, former Transamerica executive vice-president: 'He felt, as most conglomerate executives do, that anybody can do the job I do' (*ibid.*: 28).
6. Karyn Kay and Gerald Peary note that Scorsese 'set a new directorial record ... in talking of *Alice* to four film periodicals in one month: *Filmmakers Newsletter*, *Film Comment*, *Film Heritage*, and *AFI Report* (1975: 5).

   Star image is a concept developed by Richard Dyer in relation to film stars, although it can be usefully adduced in relation to other filmmaking personnel: 'A star image is made out of media texts that can be grouped together as *promotion*, *publicity*, *films* and *commentaries/criticism*... . Promotion is probably the most straightforward of all the texts which construct a star image, in that it is the most deliberate, direct, intentioned and self-conscious' (Dyer 1979: 68).
7. Scorsese: '[*Alice Doesn't Live Here Anymore*] isn't breaking away from the autobiographical because the setting changes and the people change a little. The feelings, the emotions, and the situations are pretty similar to things I am going through or have gone through or hope never to go through again... . *Alice* is from my own life; it's just not blatant' (Howard 1975: 22–3); '*Alice* to me was not fun... . It was a very draining process because of the personal involvement in it' (Macklin 1975: 24).
8. 'Ostensiveness' is a term used by James Naremore to characterize that which marks performance as performance: 'At its simplest level, the activity of any performer can be described in terms of a mode of address and a degree of ostensiveness' (1988: 34).
9. Burstyn's playing of Alice presents a number of suggestive parallels with her playing of Chris McNeil in *The Exorcist*, both in terms of character and of performance. Diegetically another, if more successful, performer (a Hollywood star), Chris is also, like Alice for most of *Alice Doesn't Live Here Anymore*, a single parent with a precocious child in its teens – a daughter

Regan (Linda Blair) – with whom Chris enjoys a close, 'modern' parent–child relationship. With regard to performance, that of Burstyn as Chris foreshadows that of Burstyn as Alice not only in its like ostensiveness but in its allowing the actress to demonstrate her prowess as she expresses a comparable range of states and emotions – from professional nervousness to maternal affection to strident righteousness to weary, tearful, almost inarticulate despair.

10. 'Implied film maker' is a translation of the literary concept of the 'implied author'. See, in particular, the chapter 'General Rules, II: "All Authors Should Be Objective"' in Booth (1961: 67–86).

11. Within American cinema, many of the conventions of the road movie can be traced to the numerous westerns that centrally contain a journey or a quest. *Easy Rider* acknowledges the debt through its self-conscious western allusions.

12. The narrative of *Coney Island* is underpinned by Eddie's exploitation of female sexuality. After running a *risqué* kooch show he becomes a successful stage-manager and remodels Kate into an image of his ideal woman. For this he is rewarded with Kate's gratitude and, eventually, love.

13. Extending the parallels between the performances of Burstyn in *The Exorcist* and *Alice Doesn't Live Here Anymore*, the scene in which Tommy quizzes Alice about her relationship with Donald recalls a similar, and similarly bedtime, scene in which Regan, with analogous Oedipal implication, asks Chris whether she is going to marry film director Burke Dennings (Jack MacGowran), prompting Chris to assert that she 'loved' Regan's father/her ex-husband. The scene in which Alice kisses the sleeping Tommy mirrors that in *The Exorcist* in which Chris pulls the bedclothes over and kisses a sleeping Regan.

14. Mirrors abound in *Alice Doesn't Live Here Anymore*, especially during the scenes in motel rooms. However, we must needs be wary of assigning all examples of mirrors symbolic pertinence. Many would appear to be used to create visual and dramatic variety in the staging of scenes within cramped and unprepossessing settings. The instances that invite symbolic reading are those during which characters explicitly contemplate their reflections. For example, upon arriving in Phoenix, Alice looks at herself in a mirror and says: 'I got to get a new hair-do tomorrow and buy myself something sexy to wear.' Here the mirror also suggestively reflects the room's television set. When David cancels the fishing trip, Alice studies her reflection in a bathroom mirror and speaks, with clear self-reference, 'to' Tommy: 'Cheer up. Tomorrow you're twelve years old, you're fully grown, and you can do whatever you want. Go fishing or ... get married.' The shot cuts to that of Tommy's reflection.

15. Sigmund Freud proceeds to list some possible examples of such compulsion, including 'the lover each of whose love affairs with a woman passes through the same phases and reaches the same conclusion' (1920: 292).

16. Faye's rendition of 'You'll Never Know' is from *Hello Frisco, Hello* (H. Bruce Humberstone, 1943).

17. Scorsese: 'we had the set dresser from *Citizen Kane* [Orson Welles, 1941], and it was interesting to see how much pride these guys were taking in doing the set' (Howard 1975: 26).

18. Scorsese himself refers to the moment as 'that kind of crazy Brechtian nonsense that I try to do' (Macklin 1975: 26).
19. Scorsese: 'At one point John Calley called me into his office to talk about the film. He said, "I gotta tell you one thing. My boss, Ted Ashley, said he wants a happy ending. That's it"' (Ehrenstein 1992: 42).
20. For more on the different endings proposed for *Alice Doesn't Live Here Anymore*, see Thompson (1976b: 141–2) and Keyser (1992: 56–7).
21. Scorsese claims that the presence of the sign was a fortuitous accident: 'The cameraman said ... "You won't believe it. Look through the lens." And I lined up on the sign, Monterey. Monterey Village... . It was an area in Tucson where everybody goes shopping, and he said ... "Want to knock it out?" I said, "No, no, if it came into the frame that way, it must be a sign. Leave it"' (Macklin 1975: 21–2).

7   An Italo-Judeo Production: *Taxi Driver*

1. In addition to its box-office success, *The Sting* dominated the 1973 Academy Awards, winning Oscars for Best Picture, Director, Original Screenplay (David S. Ward), Editing (William Reynolds), Adapted Score (Marvin Hamlisch), Art Direction (Henry Bumstead) and Costume Design (Edith Head).
2. Scorsese claims that he withdrew because he and Brando could not 'map out a script' (1981: 138). Julia Phillips claims that Scorsese withdrew because some Native Americans got drunk and tried to rape Sandra Weintraub (1991: 241–2).
3. In 1977, Begelman was revealed to have embezzled monies amounting to $61 000, including the forging of cheques to actor Cliff Robertson, director Martin Ritt and Los Angeles *maître d'hôtel*. Pierre Groleau. Despite petitioning, successfully, for Begelman's resignation, Hirschfield was fired as President in July 1978. For a detailed account of the Begelman Affair, see McClintick (1982).
4. Julia Phillips: '[Begelman] hates the script. He has hated it for years... . Begelman detests it ... he has told us so' (1991: 241).
5. See Phillips (1991: 240).
6. To avoid legal problems, Schrader ensured that the script 'was registered before the diary came out, and that nothing was changed after the diary's publication' (Thompson 1976a: 11). For some of the similarities between Bremer and Travis, see Rice (1976: 111–12).
7. This discussion of the urban western cycle is indebted to the characterization of 'Left' and 'Right' cycles of late sixties and early seventies filmmaking in Ray (1985: 296–325).
8. That is, *Per un pugno di dollari* (Leone, 1964), *Per qualche dollaro in più* (Leone, 1965) and *Il buono, il brutto, il cattivo* (Leone, 1966).
9. Schrader: 'About six weeks before shooting, I went [to New York] and we went through everything again; I rewrote the script at that time, sitting in a hotel room with the people involved in the film' (Thompson 1976a: 13).
10. At the time of writing, a fourth Scorsese–Schrader collaboration, an adaptation of Joseph Connelly's novel *Bringing Out the Dead*, is in post-production.

11. For more on Schrader's upbringing and early career, see Thompson (1976a: 6–9) and Jackson (1990: 1–15).
12. For his first, unproduced script, *Pipeliner*, Schrader claims that he 'created a complete structure which tried to adhere to the transcendental style I had just written the book about' (Thompson 1976a: 8).
13. See Thompson (1976a: 8). Further: 'The book I reread just before sitting down to write the script was Sartre's *Nausea*, and if anything is the model for *Taxi Driver*, that would be it' (Jackson 1990: 116).
14. Scorsese has also noted that at the time that he read the script for *Taxi Driver* he wanted Schrader 'to write a version of Dostoyevsky's *The Gambler*' for which Schrader had 'written an outline' (Scorsese 1981: 138). Scorsese was eventually to make a version of *The Gambler* in his 'Life Lessons' segment of *New York Stories* (Scorsese, Coppola and Woody Allen, 1989).
15. For more on the coffee-shop scene incident, see Hodenfield (1989: 48) and Ehrenstein (1992: 115–16).
16. Scorsese: 'to really stop Columbia from redoing things, I suggested the idea of draining the color out of that scene ... it was also a way of making it appear that I was doing something to tone things down in the scene itself. So I toned down the color, and we got the R rating, but I didn't tone down the scene. When I finally saw the scene with Julia, we started laughing – the toning down of the color made it look even *worse!*' (Ehrenstein 1992: 116).
17. Herrmann was also the consultant for the electronic soundtrack of *The Birds* (Hitchcock, 1963) and arranged the theme and wrote the music for a number of episodes of Hitchcock's TV programme, *The Alfred Hitchcock Hour*.
18. For a detailed musical analysis of Herrmann's Hitchcock scores, see Brown (1982).
19. Schrader has categorized *Obsession* as one of the films he 'felt strongly about, but which now have little or no connection to me' (Thompson 1976a: 14): 'The film that got made had to be done quite cheaply, and my script was heavily cut so I dropped out of it' (Jackson 1990: 115).
20. See Schatz (1983: 261–69).
    In a bleak coda to the commitment of those involved in *Taxi Driver*, Herrmann died in Hollywood on Christmas Eve 1975, just hours after finishing recording the score. Although Herrmann had been ill for some time, it is believed that his return from London to the USA – where, as a major studio film, *Taxi Driver* had to be scored – speeded his death. *Taxi Driver* is dedicated to Herrmann: 'Our Gratitude and Respect to Bernard Herrmann, June 29, 1911–December 24, 1975'.
21. See Kolker (1988: 187).
22. Scorsese: 'many of [De Niro's] close-ups aren't at the usual 24 frames per second. They're at 36, which makes them a little slower, more deliberate and off-kilter' (Amata 1976: 6–7). Scorsese has referred this use of slow-motion to the films of Powell – 'when we were doing the close-ups of De Niro's eyes for *Taxi Driver*, I shot those at 36 or 48 frames per second to reproduce the same effect that I'd seen in the Venetian episode of *The Tales of Hoffmann*, when Robert Helpmann is watching the duel on a gondola' (Thompson and Christie 1996: 6). Lesley Stern describes the close-ups as producing 'a sense of disturbing concentration' (1995: 234).

23. Another possible influence on the scenes of Travis's night-time driving is the similarly Herrmann-scored *On Dangerous Ground* (Nicholas Ray, 1951). The film's credit sequence comprises a night-time shot of a rain-slicked, neon-lit city street filmed through the windscreen of a moving car, while the sequence in which Jim Wilson (Robert Ryan) drives from city to country foreshadows Marion's journey in *Psycho*, minus subjective voice-over.

24. See Sontag (1964: 179–85).

25. Amy Taubin writes that even Travis's status as a Vietnam veteran 'may not be true since we have only Travis' word for it' (1999: 17).

26. Schrader: '[Bresson's] sound track consists primarily of natural sounds: wheels creaking, birds chirping, wind howling. These minute sounds can create a sense of everyday life that the camera cannot ... they establish a great concern for the minutiae of life' (1972b: 69).

27. Talking of his youthful 'fantasizing' before the mirror, Scorsese notes that he remembers 'trying to do Alan Ladd in *Shane*' (Thompson and Christie 1996: 42). The scene, moreover, was largely an improvisation between Scorsese and De Niro: 'We improvised the mirror scene... . It was in the script that he was doing this thing with the guns and looking at himself, and I told Bob he's got to say something. He's got to talk to himself. We didn't know what. We started playing with it, and that's what came out' (DeCurtis 1990: 108).

Also worthy of note is the exchange between Ellen Graham (Veronica Lake) and Philip Raven (Ladd) as they travel by train from San Francisco to Los Angeles in *This Gun for Hire* (Frank Tuttle, 1942):

> *Ellen*: ... you're not asleep.
> *Raven*: You talking to me? What do you want?

28. See (Morrison 1986a: 11).

29. Royal S. Brown: 'First heard during the cue labeled "The Madhouse" ... this slow-tempo motive is formed of a rising minor seventh and a falling minor ninth, the latter an especially dissonant interval to the Western ear' (1982: 42).

30. The hitting of the dead body was another incident that troubled the MPAA.

31. Cynthia J. Fuchs points out some further parallels:

> Both women remark [Travis's] unusual intensity: Betsy is intrigued by its strangeness ('I don't believe I've ever met anyone quite like you'), and Iris identifies with it ('I don't know who's weirder, you or me'). And both encounters are filmed as a series of alternating single shots (the one of the woman is over Travis's shoulder), with opening, middle, and closing two-shots (1991: 53).

32. Wood adds the pertinent qualification that 'to equate life with the Comanches to life in a brothel may strike one as dubious on several counts' (1980: 30).

33. Apart from its significance for Scorsese and Schrader, *The Searchers* has been recognized as a key film for seventies Hollywood in general, with its influence being cited in relation to such diverse films as *Ulzana's Raid*, *The Wind and the Lion* (John Milius, 1975), *Star Wars* (George Lucas, 1977) and *Close Encounters of the Third Kind* (Steven Spielberg, 1977). See Byron (1979).

34. See, for example, Boyd (1976), Wood (1980), Kolker (1988), Stern (1995) and Friedman (1997).

35. With regard to Schrader's *oeuvre*, Ethan's quest also affords the narrative model for Harry (Robert Mitchum)'s mission to retrieve his friend's daughter in *The Yakuza*, Jake (George C. Scott)'s hunt for his daughter in *Hardcore* (Schrader, 1979) and Charlie (William Devane)'s revenge in *Rolling Thunder* (John Flynn, 1977).

   Sport was initially written by Schrader as a black character: 'in the draft of the script that I sold, at the end all the people [Travis] kills are black. Marty and the Phillipses and everyone said, no, we just can't do this, it's an incitement to riot; but it was true to the character' (Jackson 1990: 117).

36. The scene is that recounted by J.R. to the girl in *Who's That Knocking at My Door?*.

37. We never actually hear Sport say this. Is this a continuity error? Was Sport's statement edited out? Or are we to take it that Travis is making this up?

38. See Wood (1980: 28–30).

39. In another parallel with his relations with Betsy, Travis's comment to Iris 'I don't have anything better to do with my money' recalls his 'What else am I gonna do with my money?' when he hands Betsy a present of a Kris Kristofferson record.

40. For more on the 'criminal-adventure' scenario and its relation to the novels of James M. Cain, see Krutnik (1991: 136–63) and Walker (1992: 12–14).

41. In discussions of the relation of *Taxi Driver* to *film noir*, the film has been referred repeatedly to Schrader's description of what he terms the 'third and final phase of *film noir*' – a 'period of psychotic action and suicidal impulse' during which the psychotic killer 'became the active protagonist' (1972a: 12). See, for example, Kolker (1988: 186–7) and Fuchs (1991: 41).

42. Although the incident recalls Charlie's placing of his finger over flames in *Mean Streets*, Scorsese notes that it 'came directly from Schrader's script': 'You see, that's why I said it's almost as if I'd written it' (Morrison 1986a: 11).

43. The Mohawk carries specific connotations of the Vietnam War: 'in Saigon, if you saw a guy with his head shaved – like a little mohawk – that usually meant those people were ready to go into a certain Special Forces situation. You didn't even go near them. They were ready to kill. They were in a psychological and emotional mode to go' (1997b: 42).

44. The point is discussed by Wood (1980: 31).

45. The ill-lit narrow hall of Iris's block, with its dingy yellow walls and bare staircase, reflects that entered by Mark and the prostitute (Brenda Bruce) at the start of *Peeping Tom*. Heightening the link, both of Travis's entries are filmed with a forward tracking shot, as is the entry of Mark and the prostitute.

46. During the course of *Journal d'un curé de campagne*, the Curé d'Ambricourt spreads, despite initial, guilty hostility, a widespread holiness. He breaks through the Countess (Marie-Monique Arkell)'s bitter despair, allowing her to accept God's grace, and oversees the transformation of her daughter, Chantal (Nicole Ladmiral), from selfish vindictiveness to almost submissive awe. Under his influence, Séraphita (Martine Lemaire), one of his confirmation class, moves from coquettish insolence to saving the Curé

when he collapses; while the robust Curé de Torcy, who has severe doubts about the Curé d'Ambricourt's weakness, comes to recognize his goodness and begs his blessings. Finally, the Curé redeems his friend, Olivier (Jean Danet), a lapsed seminarian, by asking for, and accepting, absolution at his hands.

47. See also Kolker (1988: 203).

48. A similar comparison between *Psycho* and *Taxi Driver* is made by Kolker (1988: 206–8).

49. In accord with Schrader's description of the 'decisive moment' as 'a totally bold call for emotion which dismisses any pretense of everyday reality' and which thus 'breaks the everyday stylization' (1972b: 46), his script for *Taxi Driver* contains, regarding the massacre, this 'Screenwriter's note': 'The screenplay has been moving at a reasonably realistic level until this prolonged slaughter. The slaughter itself is a gory extension of violence, more surreal than real.'

50. In *Mythologies*, Barthes states his purpose to be 'to track down, in the decorative display of *what-goes-without-saying*, the ideological abuse which, in my view, is hidden there' (1957: 11).

9   (Failed) Blockbuster Cinema: *New York, New York*

1. Minnelli's bankability was further underpinned by her recording and concert success, her Best Actress Tony, as a 19-year-old, for *Flora, The Red Menace* and her Emmy for her TV special *Liza With a Z*.

2. Chartoff and Winkler had been partners since 1965. Their varied projects had included *Double Trouble* (Norman Taurog, 1967), *Point Blank, The Split* (Gordon Flemyng, 1968), *They Shoot Horses, Don't They?* (Sydney Pollack, 1969), *Leo the Last* (John Boorman, 1970), *The Strawberry Statement* (Stuart Hagmann, 1970), *The Gang That Couldn't Shoot Straight* (James Goldstone, 1971), *Believe in Me* (Hagmann, 1971), *Up the Sandbox* (Irvin Kershner, 1972), *The New Centurions* (Richard Fleischer, 1972), *The Mechanic* (Michael Winner, 1972), *The Gambler* (Karel Reisz, 1974), *Busting* (Peter Hyams, 1974), *SPYS* (Kershner, 1974), *Breakout* (Tom Gries, 1975) and *Nickelodeon* (Peter Bogdanovich, 1976).

   Rocky won Oscars for Best Picture, Director and Editing (Richard Halsey and Scott Conrad).

3. Leven's credits included *The Shanghai Gesture* (Josef von Sternberg, 1941), *Invaders from Mars* (William Cameron Menzies, 1953), *The Silver Chalice* (Victor Saville, 1954), *Giant* (George Stevens, 1956), *West Side Story* (Robert Wise, 1961), *The Sound of Music* (Wise, 1965) and *The Andromeda Strain* (Wise, 1971). For more on Leven's career, see Corliss and Clarens (1978: 48–51).

4. For more on this, see, for example, Pye and Myles (1979: 37–47).

5. Ironically the last film to be produced by Ned Tanen's programme at Universal, *American Graffiti* was made for $743 000 and grossed about $50 million, making it – in terms of return to outlay – the most profitable American film of the seventies.

6. Transamerica's seventies holdings included 'life insurance companies, a loan service, a capital fund, an investors' fund, a relocation service,

a microfilm company, a moving-and-storage company, a title insurance company, Budget Rent-A-Car, a computer service, and Trans-International Airlines' (Monaco 1984: 34).

United Artists had been sold to Transamerica in 1967 in a deal that enabled Arthur Krim and Robert Benjamin, who had run the studio since 1951, to retain control. In 1974, 'troubled' by Transamerica's 'involvement in studio management', Krim and Benjamin tried to buy United Artists back (Lewis 1995: 86). Not only did Transamerica refuse Krim and Benjamin's offer, but, 'in what in many in the industry saw as a kind of retaliation', appointed 'Transamerica executive James Harvey in charge of the studio's day-to-day operation' (*ibid*.).

7. For a discussion of some of the strategies by which the political is eclipsed by the nostalgic in *The Way We Were*, see Dyer (1976).

8. Note the opening of a review of *New York, New York* in *The Hollywood Reporter*: 'Martin Scorsese's tribute to the big band era, "New York, New York," should provide a great soundtrack album for United Artists Records. It is filled with excellent renditions of tunes from the period (supervised and conducted by Ralph Burns) and it also incorporates four wonderful new songs by John Kander and Fred Ebb that are brilliantly rendered by Liza Minnelli' (Pennington 1977: 4).

9. Scorsese and Cameron were divorced soon after *New York, New York*.

10. Lerner unexpectedly died of a heart attack on Christmas Day 1976. Lerner's place was taken by his assistant, David Ramirez, with Lucas joining the editing team to help Scorsese out. As *Taxi Driver* is dedicated to Bernard Herrmann, so *New York, New York* is dedicated to Irving Lerner.

11. It is this cut of *New York, New York* that will be discussed in this chapter.

12. Scorsese: 'It was a beautiful sequence... . But at the end, the movie was long and there was pressure to cut it. People said, "You are too close to it ... you are indulging yourself" ... I said, "Okay ... I'll show you that I'm not indulging myself. It *stays* out."' (Kelly 1992: 109).

13. With regard to Stander's past, the production notes for *New York, New York* only refer to his recent return 'to the United States after more than a decade in Rome' and to his having 'Years ago' having won an Oscar nomination. It would appear that, in 1977, HUAC was still an episode that Hollywood could/would not confront.

14. *The Godfather* presaged *Jaws* in having a blanket release, opening in 316 theatres. Taking $87.5 million at the box-office, it also presaged *Jaws* in becoming at the time the most successful film ever.

15. The integrated musical was so called because it sought 'to push the musical out of conventional patterns ... to link plot, song and dance together as an integrated whole' (Brown 1981: 259).

16. Rick Altman: 'Attacked from one side for commodifying activities which should be conceived as spontaneous expressions of pure joy or as disinterested artistic productions, attacked from the other side for the frivolousness of its commodities, Hollywood might well have looked to Madison Avenue to bolster its public image. But why bother with Madison Avenue when you have all Hollywood at your disposal? No doubt the world's most complex and expensive publicity scheme, the American film musical serves as Hollywood's own self-justification' (1989: 344).

17. Unless noted, all future references to *A Star Is Born* will be to the 1954 version.
18. 'Born in a Trunk' also 'reprises Garland's own career, with references to her roots in vaudeville' (Feuer 1993: 119–20).
19. In addition, both 'The Broadway Ballet' and 'Born in a Trunk' show their protagonists visiting three agents to obtain work and a segment in which the protagonist's rise is charted by performances in increasingly sophisticated settings.
20. See Altman (1989: 250–71).
21. That the female dancer is Minnelli in a blonde wig implicitly relates the incident and its connotations to the relationship between Jimmy and Francine. The male dancer is Gene Castle.
22. See Altman (1989: 62–80).
23. Michael Pye and Lynda Myles: 'Few cinemas can still project in the old ratio instead of the more usual widescreen, and it proved economically impossible to shoot in "Academy ratio". "But we could still frame within that ratio," Scorsese says, "and we did"' (1979: 216–17).
24. For more on the radical separation of elements, see Brecht (1930).
25. With regard to this, Altman somewhat intemperately commends the musical for being 'a *Gesamtkunstwerk*, an art form more total than even Wagner could imagine' (1981: 7). It is to combat the mystification of the *Gesamtkunstwerk* that Brecht calls for the radical separation of elements:

    so long as the arts are supposed to be 'fused' together, the various elements will all be equally degraded, and each will act as a mere 'feed' to the rest. The process of fusion extends to the spectator, who gets thrown into the melting pot too and becomes a passive (suffering) part of the total work of art. Witchcraft of this sort must of course be fought against. Whatever is intended to produce hypnosis, is likely to induce sordid intoxication, or creates fog, has got to be given up (1930: 37–8).

26. See Altman (1989: 246–60).
27. Jane Feuer draws a slightly different conclusion: 'Even after we are shown the tools of illusion at the beginning of the number, the camera arcs around and comes in for a tighter shot of the performing couple, thereby remasking the exposed technology and making the duet just another example of the type of number whose illusions it exposes' (1981: 165).
28. Martin Walsh offers a succinct rationalization: 'because the "means of expression" are ideologically determined it is no longer sufficient to place a new "content" within the old structures of expression. Instead, the signifying system itself must be attacked, in order to overthrow the basis upon which the dominant ideological message rests' (1974: 39).
29. Among Robert Altman's seventies films, *MASH* (1970) and *Brewster McCloud* (1970) parody the war and the cop film; *McCabe and Mrs Miller* (1971) and *Buffalo Bill and the Indians, or Sitting Bull's History Lesson* (1976) deconstruct the Western; *The Long Goodbye* (1973) and *California Split* (1974) rework *film noir* and the buddy movie; and *Nashville* (1975) explodes 'the very syntax on which the folk musical is based' (Altman 1989: 327).
30. Apart from the success of *MASH*, that took over $35 million at the box-office, up to 1977, and *Three Women*, only three of Robert Altman's films

had turned a profit: *McCabe and Mrs Miller, California Split* and *Nashville*. However, unlike *New York, New York*, most of his films had cost under $2 million. The exceptions were *McCabe and Mrs Miller*, that cost $3 million, and *Buffalo Bill and the Indians, or Sitting Bull's History Lesson*, that cost $6 million.

31. See Dyer (1976: 30–2).

32. The tilt also recalls that which reveals the 'Mohawked' Travis in *Taxi Driver*. Is this just an intertextual jokes, or does it seek to invite consideration of the relationship of the characters to each other and to the star?

33. Jimmy has registered at the hotel as Mr Powell, a nod to Michael Powell, the stylistic influence of whose films is again apparent in *New York, New York*. Of particular pertinence are three Powell and Pressburger 'musicals': *The Red Shoes, The Tales of Hoffmann* and *Oh Rosalinda* (1955). Apart from the factitious *mise-en-abyme* that is 'The Red Shoes' ballet, *The Tales of Hoffmann* and *Oh Rosalinda* are entirely studio-bound and consistently reflexive.

34. Shot before back projection of downtown New York, the 'taxi' recalls that of Hildy (Betty Garrett) in *On the Town*.

35. Minnelli's hair was styled by MGM/Garland's veteran stylist, Sydney Guilaroff, who – in a characteristically allusive/reflexive moment – appears diegetically preparing Francine's hair for 'Happy Endings'.

36. Incident here reflects that in *A Star Is Born* when Norman reveals his presence at the Downbeat Club after Esther sings 'The Man That Got Away'.

37. See Freud (1908).

38. Bruce makes similar points (1986: 90–2).

39. Jimmy and Frankie's touchy 'Oedipal' relationship was suggestively mirrored extra-diegetically by that between De Niro and Auld. To ensure that his fingering was correct, De Niro spent eight months learning how to play the tenor saxophone. Although De Niro became a competent player, Jimmy's solos were played by Auld who, in a long jazz career, had played with, among others, the Artie Shaw Orchestra and the Benny Goodman Sextet. While Auld was impressed by De Niro's commitment – 'it's incredible the way he learned' – he at times found it wearying: '[he] asked me ten million questions a day. It got to be a pain in the ass' (Cameron-Wilson 1986: 79). During the scene on the 'bus, Frankie admits that Jimmy 'blows a barrelful of tenor' but also insists that he is 'a top pain in the ass'.

40. In *A Star Is Born* Norman and Esther, fleeing the studio publicity machine, are similarly married, in a low-key ceremony, by a Justice of the Peace.

41. On the musical's correlation of the interpersonal and romantic with the creative and professional, Rick Altman writes: 'The formation of the couple is linked either causally or through parallelism to success in the ventures which constitute the plot... . Time and again, to solve the couple's problems becomes synonymous with, and thus a figure for, the solution of the plot's other enterprises' (1989: 108–9).

42. A further point of reference is *My Dream Is Yours* (Michael Curtiz, 1949), a film that Scorsese has claimed as 'a major influence' on *New York, New York* (Scorsese and Wilson 1997: 64), and in which crooner Gary Mitchell

(Lee Bowman) reacts with violent resentment when he is fired from his radio show for drunkenness. Exacerbating matters, he is replaced by his object of desire, Martha Gibson (Doris Day).

43. During the time of the studio system the front office was responsible for basic business and financial decisions.

    In the first version of *A Star Is Born* (William Wellman, 1937) Libby is played by Lionel Stander.

44. Cooke (1986: 103–4) discusses the Harlem Club sequence in detail. His analysis largely complements that presented here.

45. The scene led to De Niro, Minnelli and, somehow, Scorsese being treated for injuries: 'Liza almost broke her arm, Bobby hurt his knuckles, I hurt my knuckles. Of course, I wasn't in the car, it was from something else... . But we all got x-rayed' (Kaplan 1977: 43). Les Keyser writes: 'Some of [Scorsese's] crew found the scene too frightening to watch and left the set in disgust (1992: 91).

46. A similarly gendered divergence of failure and triumph informs the representation of Gary and Martha in *My Dream Is Yours*.

47. Richard Lippe hyperbolically states that the performance 'must be numbered among the finest moments in any musical' (1986: 100).

48. MacRauch's script has over the same period Jimmy unconvincingly becoming a successful writer and producer of early rock'n'roll and a vice-president of Columbia Records.

49. Kander and Ebb also wrote 'Happy Endings'. However, as an explicit parody, this presents a self-conscious contrast to their usual compositions.

50. Scorsese has claimed that the long-held close-up of Jimmy at the Harlem Club is balanced by the long-held close-up of Francine looking into the mirror, that cuts to a lengthy, masked close-up of her eyes. The shots, however, crucially lack Jimmy's close-up's intensive dramatic and thematic placement. That the shots were cut from the general release version of *New York, New York* would further appear to mark where Scorsese and the film's primary interest lies.

51. In MacRauch's script, Jimmy and Francine exit the narrative 'Arm in arm'.

Conclusion: 'That's the worst part. That's the whole thing, going on ... '

1. Scorsese commenting on the end of *Mean Streets* (Kelly 1980: 18).
2. Much of this money went to George Lucas's company, Lucasfilm. In setting up *Star Wars*. Lucas negotiated a contract that gave him merchandising rights, an 'error' that the majors have not since repeated.
3. See Britton (1986: 2).
4. Jameson describes nostalgia films as representing 'the pastiche of the stereotypical past' (1984: 68).
5. For a detailed account of the making of and fall-out from *Heaven's Gate*, see Bach (1985).
6. For an insider's account of MGM/UA's difficulties during the eighties, see Bart (1990).

7. For more on deregulation and the majors in the eighties, see Gomery (1989).
8. For accounts of developments in eighties and nineties Hollywood, see, among others, Schatz (1993), Balio (1998), Lewis (1998) and Maltby (1998). Wyatt (1994) provides the fullest account of the genealogy and contours of the high concept film.
9. Scorsese has stated that he was given Nikos Kazantzakis's novel *The Last Temptation* by Barbara Hershey after shooting *Boxcar Bertha*.
10. *The Color of Money* was completed for $13 million instead of $14.5 million and in 49 instead of 50 days. It took $24.4 million. The successful establishment of Touchstone in 1984 was instrumental in Disney achieving major status.
11. For more on CAA and agenting in contemporary Hollywood, see Kent (1991: 210–44). After resisting innumerable overtures, Ovitz finally trod the well-worn path from agent to executive by becoming President of Disney in the mid-nineties.
12. *GoodFellas* grossed $48.6 million.
13. Apart from his features, during the eighties and nineties Scorsese has directed an episode of the Steven Spielberg produced television series *Amazing Stories* ('Mirror, Mirror', 1985), pop videos for Michael Jackson ('Bad', 1987) and Robbie Robertson ('Somewhere Down the Crazy River', 1988), two commercials (1986 and 1988) and a promotional film (*Made in Milan*, 1990) for Giorgio Armani and a three-part documentary on American cinema (*A Personal Journey with Martin Scorsese Through American Movies*, 1995). To date, Scorsese has also co-produced four features – *The Grifters* (Stephen Frears, 1990), *Mad Dog and Glory* (John McNaughton, 1992), *Clockers* (Spike Lee, 1995) and *The Hi-Lo Country* (Frears, 1998) – and executive produced three others – *Naked in New York* (Dan Algrant, 1994), *Search and Destroy* (David Salle, 1995) and *Grace of My Heart* (Allison Anders, 1996).
14. For a discussion of the yuppie nightmare cycle, see Grist (1992: 276–81).
15. Note also *Seven Years in Tibet* (Jean-Jacques Annaud) and *Red Corner* (Jon Avnet).

Bibliography

Althusser, Louis (1964/1971) 'Freud and Lacan', pp. 177–202 in *Lenin and Philosophy and other essays*, translated by Ben Brewster, London: New Left Books.

Altman, Rick (1981) 'Introduction', pp. 1–7 in Altman, Rick (ed.), *Genre: The Musical: A Reader*, British Film Institute Readers in Film Studies, London, Boston and Henley: Routledge & Kegan Paul/BFI.

—— (1989) *The American Film Musical*, London: BFI.

Amata, Carmie (1976) 'Scorsese on *Taxi Driver* and Herrmann', *Focus on Film* 25: 5–8.

Andrew, Dudley (1993) 'The Unauthorized Auteur Today', pp. 77–85 in Collins, Jim, Radner, Hilary and Collins, Ava Preacher (eds), *Film Theory Goes to the Movies*, AFI Film Readers, New York and London: Routledge.

Andrew, Geoff (1994) 'Past Master', *Time Out* 1221: 18–22.

Arkush, Allan (1983) 'I Remember Film School', *Film Comment* 19 (6): 57–59.

Astruc, Alexandre (1948/1968) 'The birth of a new avant-garde: La caméra-stylo', translator not cited, pp. 17–23 in Graham, Peter (ed.), *The New Wave: Critical landmarks*, Cinema One 5, London: Secker & Warburg/BFI.

Bach, Steven (1985) *Final Cut: Dreams and Disaster in the Making of 'Heaven's Gate'*, London: Jonathan Cape.

Balio, Tino (1998) '"A major presence in all of the world's important markets": The globalization of Hollywood in the 1990s', pp. 58–73 in Neale, Steve and Smith, Murray (eds), *Contemporary Hollywood Cinema*, London and New York: Routledge.

Bart, Peter (1990) *Fade Out: The Calamitous Final Days of MGM*, London: Simon & Schuster.

Barthes, Roland (1957/1972) *Mythologies*, selected and translated by Annette Lavers, London: Jonathan Cape.

—— (1968/1977) 'The Death of the Author', pp. 142–8 in *Image–Music–Text*, essays selected and translated by Stephen Heath, London: Fontana.

—— (1970/1974) *S/Z*, translated by Richard Miller, New York: Hill and Wang.

Bazin, André (1957/1968) 'La politique des auteurs', translator not cited, pp. 137–55 in Graham, Peter (ed.), *The New Wave: Critical landmarks*, Cinema One 5, London: Secker & Warburg/BFI.

Belton, John (1994) *American Cinema/American Culture*, New York: McGraw-Hill.

Benveniste, Emile (1966/1971) *Problems of General Linguistics*, translated by Mary Elizabeth Meek, Coral Gables: University of Miami Press.

Biskind, Peter (1998) *Easy Riders, Raging Bulls: How the Sex-Drugs-and-Rock'n'Roll Generation Saved Hollywood*, New York: Simon & Schuster.

Bliss, Michael (1985) *Martin Scorsese and Michael Cimino*, Filmmakers 8, Metuchen and London: Scarecrow Press.

Bloom, Harold (1980) *A Map of Misreading*, Oxford and New York: Oxford University Press.

Booth, Wayne C. (1961) *The Rhetoric of Fiction*, Chicago and London: University of Chicago Press.

Bordwell, David (1979) 'The Art Cinema as a Mode of Film Practice', *Film Criticism* 4 (1): 56–64.

—— (1985a) 'Classical narration', pp. 24–41 in Bordwell, David, Staiger, Janet and Thompson, Kristin, *The Classical Hollywood Cinema: Film Style & Mode of Production to 1960*, London: Routledge & Kegan Paul.

—— (1985b) 'Time in the classical film', pp. 42–9 in Bordwell, David, Staiger, Janet and Thompson, Kristin, *The Classical Hollywood Cinema: Film Style and Mode of Production to 1960*, London, Routledge & Kegan Paul.

Bordwell, David and Staiger, Janet (1985) 'Since 1960: the persistence of a mode of film practice', pp. 367–77 in Bordwell, David, Staiger, Janet and Thompson, Kristin, *The Classical Hollywood Cinema: Film Style & Mode of Production to 1960*, London: Routledge & Kegan Paul.

Boyd, David (1976) 'Prisoner of the night', *Film Heritage* 12 (2): 24–30.

Brecht, Bertolt (1930/1964) 'The Modern Theatre is the Epic Theatre (Notes to the opera *Aufstieg und Fall der Stadt Mahagonny*)', pp. 33–42 in *Brecht on Theatre: The Development of an Aesthetic*, edited and translated by John Willett, London: Methuen.

Brewster, Ben (1971) 'Structuralism in Film Criticism', *Screen* 12 (1): 49–58.

Britton, Andrew (1986) 'Blissing Out: The Politics of Reaganite Entertainment', *Movie* 31/32: 1–42.

Brown, Geoff (1981) 'Musicals', pp. 252–61 in Pirie, David (ed.), *Anatomy of the Movies*, London: Windward.

Brown, Royal S. (1982) 'Herrmann, Hitchcock, and the Music of the Irrational', *Cinema Journal*, 21 (2): 14–49.

Bruce, Bryan (1986) 'Martin Scorsese: Five Films', *Movie* 31/32: 88–94.

Bygrave, Mike (1981) 'The New Moguls', pp. 62–79 in Pirie, David (ed.), *Anatomy of the Movies*, London: Windward.

Byron, Stuart (1979) '*The Searchers*: Cult Movie of the New Hollywood', *New York Magazine* 5 March: 45–8.

Cameron-Wilson, James (1986) *The Cinema of Robert De Niro*, London: Zomba.

Carducci, Mark (1975) 'Martin Scorsese: Now they're knocking at his door!', *Millimeter* 3 (5): 12–16.

Carney, Raymond (1985) *American Dreaming: The Films of John Cassavetes and the American Experience*, Berkeley, Los Angeles and London: University of California Press.

Caughie, John (ed.) (1981a) *Theories of Authorship: A Reader*, British Film Institute Readers in Film Studies, London: Routledge & Kegan Paul/BFI.

—— (1981b) 'Preface', pp. 1–6 in Caughie, John (ed.), *Theories of Authorship: A Reader*, British Film Institute Readers in Film Studies, London: Routledge & Kegan Paul/BFI.

—— (1981c) 'Auteurism: Introduction', pp. 9–16 in Caughie, John (ed.), *Theories of Authorship: A Reader*, British Film Institute Readers in Film Studies, London: Routledge & Kegan Paul/BFI.

—— (1981d) 'Notes on terms', pp. 292–301 in Caughie, John (ed.), *Theories of Authorship: A Reader*, British Film Institute Readers in Film Studies, London: Routledge & Kegan Paul/BFI.

Cawelti John G. (1971) *The Six-Gun Mystique*, Bowling Green: Bowling Green Popular University Press.

Chion, Michel (1982) *La Voix au cinéma*, Paris: *Cahiers du cinéma*/Editions de l'Etoile.

—— (1985) *Le Son au cinéma*, Paris: *Cahiers du cinéma*/Editions de l'Etoile.

—— (1988) *La Toile trouée: la parole au cinéma*, Paris: *Cahiers du cinéma*/Editions de l'Etoile.

—— (1994) *Audio-Vision: Sound on Screen*, edited and translated by Claudia Gorbman, New York and Chichester: Columbia University Press.

Ciment, Michel (1984) 'Les Enfants Terrible', *American Film* 10 (3): 36–42, 86, 91.

Ciment, Michel and Henry, Michael (1975) 'Entretien avec Martin Scorsese', *Positif* 170: 8–23.

Cohan, Steven and Hark, Ina Rae (1997) 'Introduction', pp. 1–14 in Cohan, Steven and Hark, Ina Rae (eds), *The Road Movie Book*, London and New York: Routledge.

Combs, Richard (1992) 'As time goes by', *Sight and Sound* 1 (12) NS: 24–6.

Comolli, Jean-Louis (1969/1980) 'Détour par le direct – Un corps en trop', translated by Diana Matias, pp. 225–43 in Williams, Christopher (ed.), *Realism and the Cinema: A Reader*, British Film Institute Readers in Film Studies, London: Routledge & Kegan Paul/BFI.

Cook, David A. (1996) *A History of Narrative Film*, third edition, New York and London: W.W. Norton.

Cook, Pam (1976) '"Exploitation" films and feminism', *Screen* 17 (2): 122–7.

—— (1985) 'The Art of Exploitation or How to Get into the Movies', *Monthly Film Bulletin* 52 (623): 367–9.

Cooke, Lez (1986) '*New York, New York*: Looking at De Niro', *Movie* 31/32: 101–7.

Corliss, Mary and Clarens, Carlos (1978) 'Designed for Film: The Hollywood Art Director', *Film Comment* 14 (3): 27–58.

Corliss, Richard (1978) 'The Hollywood Screenwriter: Take 2', *Film Comment* 14 (4): 33–47.

Corman, Roger (1974/1981) 'Encouraging the Young Director', pp. 22–5 in Hillier, Jim and Lipstadt, Aaron (eds), *Roger Corman's New World*, BFI Dossier 7, London: BFI.

Corman, Roger with Jerome, Jim (1990) *How I Made a Hundred Movies in Hollywood and Never Lost a Dime*, London: Muller.

Corrigan, Timothy (1991) *A Cinema Without Walls: Movies and Culture After Vietnam*, London: Routledge.

Crofts, Stephen (1998) 'Authorship and Hollywood', pp. 310–24 in Hill, John and Church Gibson, Pamela (eds), *The Oxford Guide to Film Studies*, Oxford: Oxford University Press.

DeCurtis, Anthony (1990) 'The *Rolling Stone* Interview: Martin Scorsese', *Rolling Stone* 590: 58–65, 106, 108.

—— (1993) 'What the Streets Mean: An Interview with Martin Scorsese', pp. 197–228 in McAuliffe, Jody (ed.), *Plays, Movies and Critics*, Durham and London: Duke University Press.

Delson, James (1973) '*Mean Streets*', *Take One* 3 (12): 28–9.

Dixon, Wheeler (1976) 'In Defense of Roger Corman', *The Velvet Light Trap* 16: 11–14.

Doane, Mary Ann (1987) *The Desire to Desire: The Woman's Film of the 1940s*, Language, Discourse, Society, London: Macmillan.

Dugas, David (1977) 'Why I wanted to make a forties musical', *Photoplay Film Monthly* 28 (11): 11, 58.

Dyer, Richard (1976) '*The Way We Were*', *Movie* 22: 30–3.

—— (1979) *Stars*, London: BFI

Editors of *Cahiers du cinéma* (1970/1972) 'John Ford's *Young Mr Lincoln*', translated by Helen Lackner and Diana Matias, *Screen* 13 (5): 5–44.

Ehrenstein, David (1992) *The Scorsese Picture: The Art and Life of Martin Scorsese*, New York: Birch Lane Press.

Elsaesser, Thomas (1975) 'The pathos of failure: American films in the 70s', *Monogram* 6: 13–19.

Feuer, Jane (1981) 'The Self-reflective Musical and the Myth of Entertainment', pp. 159–74 in Altman, Rick (ed.), *Genre: The Musical: A Reader*, British Film Institute Readers in Film Studies, London, Boston and Henley: Routledge & Kegan Paul/BFI.

—— (1993) *The Hollywood Musical*, second edition, British Film Institute Cinema Series, London: Macmillan.

Forbes, Jill (1998) 'The French Nouvelle Vague', pp. 461–65 in Hill, John and Church Gibson, Pamela (eds), *The Oxford Guide to Film Studies*, Oxford: Oxford University Press.

Foucault, Michel (1969/1977) 'What Is an Author?', pp. 113–38 in *Language, Counter-Memory, Practice: Selected Essays and Interviews*, edited by Donald F. Bouchard, translated by Donald F. Bouchard and Sherry Simon, Oxford: Blackwell.

Freud, Sigmund (1908/1990) 'Creative Writers and Day-Dreaming', translated by I.F. Grant Duff, pp. 129–41 in *Art and Literature*, edited by Albert Dickson, Penguin Freud Library 14, Harmondsworth: Penguin.

—— (1917/1991) *Introductory Lectures on Psychoanalysis*, edited by Angela Richards, translated by James Strachey, Penguin Freud Library 1, Harmondsworth: Penguin.

—— (1920/1991) 'Beyond the Pleasure Principle', translated by James Strachey, pp. 269–338 in *On Metapsychology: The Theory of Psychoanalysis*, edited by Angela Richards, Penguin Freud Library 11, Harmondsworth: Penguin.

—— (1927/1991) 'Fetishism', translated by James Strachey, pp. 345–57 in *On Sexuality* edited by Angela Richards, Penguin Freud Library 7, Harmondsworth: Penguin.

Friedman, Lawrence S. (1997) *The Cinema of Martin Scorsese*, Oxford: Roundhouse

Fuchs, Cynthia J. (1991) '"All The Animals Come Out at Night": Vietnam Meets Noir in *Taxi Driver*', pp. 33–55 in Anderegg, Michael (ed.), *Inventing Vietnam: The War in Film and Television*, Philadelphia: Temple University Press.

Gardner, Paul (1975) 'Martin Scorsese', *Action* 10 (3): 30–4.

Gaut, Berys (1997) 'Film Authorship and Collaboration', pp. 149–72 in Allen, Richard and Smith, Murray (eds), *Film Theory and Philosophy*, Oxford: Clarendon Press.

Gelmis, Joseph (1970) *The Film Director as Superstar*, London: Secker & Warburg.

Geraghty, Christine (1976) '*Alice Doesn't Live Here Anymore*', *Movie* 22: 39–42.

Goldstein, Richard and Jacobson, Mark (1976) 'Martin Scorsese Tells All: "Blood and Guts Turn Me On!"', *Village Voice* 9 April: 29–31.

Gomery, Douglas (1989) 'The Reagan Record', *Screen* 30 (1/2): 92–9.

Grimes, Teresa (1986) 'BBS: Auspicious beginnings, open endings', *Movie* 31/32: 54–66.

Grist, Leighton (1992) 'Moving Targets and Black Widows: Film Noir in Modern Hollywood', pp. 267–85 in Cameron, Ian (ed.), *The Movie Book of Film Noir*, London: Studio Vista.

Hark, Ina Rae (1997) 'Fear of Flying: Yuppie critique and the buddy–road movie in the 1980s', pp. 204–29 in Cohan, Steven and Hark, Ina Rae (eds), *The Road Movie Book*, London and New York: Routledge.

Haskell, Molly (1974) *From Reverence to Rape: The Treatment of Women in the Movies*, New York: Holt, Rinehart and Winston.

Heath, Stephen (1973) 'Comment on "The Idea of Authorship"', *Screen* 14 (3): 86–91.

—— (1975) 'Film and System: Terms of Analysis, Part I', *Screen* 16 (1): 7–77.

Heilman, Robert (1968) *Tragedy and Melodrama: Versions of Experience*, Seattle: University of Washington Press.

Henderson, Brian (1973) 'Critique of Cine-Structuralism (Part I)', *Film Quarterly* 27 (1): 25–34.

Hillier, Jim (1993) *The New Hollywood*, London: Studio Vista.

Hillier, Jim and Lipstadt, Aaron (1986) 'The Economics of Independence: Roger Corman and New World Pictures 1970–80', *Movie* 31/32: 43–53.

Hodenfield, Chris (1989) 'Martin Scorsese: The Art of Noncompromise', *American Film* 14 (5): 46–51.

Holmlund, Chris (1996) 'The eyes of Nelly Kaplan', *Screen* 37 (4): 351–67.

Hosney, Jim, Wollman, Jacquelyn and Engdahl, Jesse Ward (1993) 'The Passion of St. Charles: Martin Scorsese's *Mean Streets*', pp. 179–88 in McAuliffe, Jody (ed.), *Plays, Movies and Critics*, Durham and London: Duke University Press.

Howard, Steve (1975) 'The Making of *Alice Doesn't Live Here Anymore*: An Interview with Director Martin Scorsese', *Filmmakers Newsletter* 8 (5): 21–26.

Hugo, Chris (1980) 'The Economic Background', *Movie* 27/28: 43–9.

Jackson, Kevin (ed.) (1990) *Schrader on Schrader & Other Writings*, London: Faber and Faber.

Jameson, Fredric (1984) 'Postmodernism, or The Cultural Logic of Late Capitalism', *New Left Review* 146: 53–94.

Johnston, Claire (1973/1976) 'Women's Cinema as Counter-Cinema', pp. 208–17 in Nichols, Bill (ed.), *Movies and Methods, Volume I*, Berkeley, Los Angeles and London: University of California Press.

—— (1976/1985) 'Towards a Feminist Film Practice: Some Theses', pp. 315–27 in Nichols, Bill (ed.), *Movies and Methods, Volume II*, Berkeley, Los Angeles and London: University of California Press.

Kaplan, Jonathan (1977) 'Taxi Dancer: Martin Scorsese Interviewed', *Film Comment* 13 (4): 41–3.

Kay, Karyn and Peary, Gerald (1975) 'Waitressing for Warners', *Jump Cut* 7: 5–7.

Kelly, Mary Pat (1980) *Martin Scorsese: The First Decade*, Pleasantville: Redgrave.

—— (1992) *Martin Scorsese: A Journey*, London: Secker & Warburg.

Kent, Nicholas (1991) *Naked Hollywood: Money and Power in the Movies Today*, London: BBC.

Keyser, Les (1992) *Martin Scorsese*, Twayne's Filmmakers, New York: Twayne.

Kolker, Robert Phillip (1974) 'Night to Day', *Sight and Sound* 43 (4): 236–39.

—— (1988) *A Cinema of Loneliness: Penn, Kubrick, Scorsese, Spielberg, Altman,* second edition, New York: Oxford University Press.

Kouvaros, George (1998) 'Where does it happen? The place of performance in the work of John Cassavetes', *Screen* 39 (3): 244–58.

Kramer, Peter (1998) 'Post-classical Hollywood', pp. 289–309 in Hill, John and Church Gibson, Pamela (eds), *The Oxford Guide to Film Studies*, Oxford: Oxford University Press.

Krutnik, Frank (1991) *In a Lonely Street: 'Film noir', genre, masculinity*, London and New York: Routledge.

Lacan, Jacques (1948/1977) 'Aggressivity in psychoanalysis', pp. 8–29 in *Écrits: A Selection*, translated by Alan Sheridan, London: Tavistock.

—— (1949/1977) 'The mirror stage as formative of the function of the I as revealed in psychoanalytic experience', pp. 1–7 in *Écrits: A Selection*, translated by Alan Sheridan, London: Tavistock.

LaPlace, Maria (1987) 'Producing and Consuming the Woman's Film: Discursive Struggle in *Now, Voyager*', pp. 138–66 in Gledhill, Christine (ed.), *Home is Where the Heart Is: Studies in Melodrama and the Woman's Film*, London: BFI.

Lapsley, Robert and Westlake, Michael (1988) *Film Theory: An Introduction*, Manchester: Manchester University Press.

Laskos, Andrew (1981) 'The Hollywood Majors', pp. 10–39 in Pirie, David (ed.), *Anatomy of the Movies*, London: Windward.

Lévi-Strauss, Claude (1958/1968) *Structural Anthropology*, translated by Claire Jacobson and Brooke Grundfest Schoepf, London: Allen Lane.

Lewis, Jon (1995) *Whom God Wishes To Destroy ...: Francis Coppola and the New Hollywood*, Durham and London: Duke University Press.

—— (1998) 'Money Matters: Hollywood in the Corporate Era', pp. 87–121 in Lewis, Jon (ed.), *The New American Cinema*, Durham and London: Duke University Press.

Lippe, Richard (1986) '*New York, New York* and the Hollywood Musical', *Movie* 31/32: 95–100.

Lipstadt, Aaron (1981) 'Politics and Exploitation: New World Pictures', pp. 9–21 in Hillier, Jim and Lipstadt, Aaron (eds) *Roger Corman's New World*, BFI Dossier 7, London: BFI.

Livingston, Paisley (1997) 'Cinematic Authorship', pp. 132–48 in Allen, Richard and Smith, Murray (eds), *Film Theory and Philosophy*, Oxford: Clarendon Press.

Lloyd, Peter (1971) 'An outlook', *Monogram* 1: 11–13.

Lourdeaux, Lee (1990) *Italian and Irish Filmmakers in America: Ford, Capra, Coppola, and Scorsese*, Philadelphia: Temple University Press.

MacCabe, Colin (1974) 'Realism and the Cinema: Notes on some Brechtian theses', *Screen* 15 (2): 7–27.

—— (1976) 'Days of Hope – a Response to Colin McArthur', *Screen* 17 (1): 98–101.

—— (1980) *Godard: Images, Sounds, Politics*, British Film Institute Cinema Series, London: Macmillan.

Macklin, F. Anthony (1975) '"It's a personal thing for me:" an Interview with Marty Scorsese', *Film Heritage* 10 (3): 13–28, 36.

Maher, Kevin (1998) 'Twenty years ago, these men were the toast of Hollywood. How the mighty are fallen ...', *Guardian* G2 section 3 July: 8–9.

Maltby, Richard (1998) '"Nobody knows everything": Post-classical historiographies and consolidated entertainment', pp. 21–44 in Neale, Steve and

Smith, Murray (eds), *Contemporary Hollywood Cinema*, London and New York: Routledge.

Maltby, Richard and Craven, Ian (1995) *Hollywood Cinema*, Oxford: Blackwell.

Margulies, Ivone (1998) 'John Cassavetes: Amateur Director', pp. 275–306 in Lewis, Jon (ed.), *The New American Cinema*, Durham and London: Duke University Press.

McClintick, David (1982) *Indecent Exposure: A True Story of Hollywood and Wall Street*, New York: William Morrow.

McGreal, Jill (1993) '*Mean Streets*', *Sight and Sound* 3 (4) NS: 64.

Medhurst, Andy (1991) 'That special thrill: *Brief Encounter*, homosexuality and authorship', *Screen* 32 (2): 197–208.

Metz, Christian (1975/1981) 'History/Discourse: a note on two voyeurisms', translated by Susan Bennett, pp. 225–31 in Caughie, John (ed.), *Theories of Authorship: A Reader*, British Film Institute Readers in Film Studies, London: Routledge & Kegan Paul/BFI.

Monaco, James (1976) *The New Wave: Truffaut, Godard, Chabrol, Rohmer, Rivette*, New York: Oxford University Press.

—— (1984) *American Film Now: the People, the Power, the Money, the Movies*, revised edition, New York: Zoetrope.

Morris, Gary (1975) 'Interview with Roger Corman', *Bright Lights* 1 (2): 21–5.

Morrison, Susan (1986a) 'An Interview with Martin Scorsese', *CineAction* 6: 3–11.

—— (1986b) 'Sirk, Scorsese, and Hysteria: A Double(d) Reading', *CineAction* 6: 17–25.

Muller, John P. and Richardson, William J. (1982) *Lacan and Language: A Reader's Guide to Écrits*, New York: International Universities Press.

Mulvey, Laura (1975) 'Visual Pleasure and Narrative Cinema', *Screen* 16 (3): 6–18.

Naha, Ed (1982) *The Films of Roger Corman: Brilliance on a Budget*, New York: Arco.

Naremore, James (1988) *Acting in the Cinema*, Berkeley, Los Angeles and London: University of California Press.

—— (1990) 'Authorship and the Cultural Politics of Film Criticism', *Film Quarterly* 44 (1): 14–22.

Neale, Steve (1976) 'New Hollywood Cinema', *Screen* 17 (2): 117–22.

—— (1980) *Genre*, London: BFI.

—— (1981) 'Art Cinema as Institution', *Screen* 22 (1): 11–39.

—— (1990) 'Questions of genre', *Screen* 31 (1): 45–66.

Newman, Kim (1985a) 'The Roger Corman Alumni Association', *Monthly Film Bulletin*, 52 (622): 360.

—— (1985b) 'The Roger Corman Alumni Association II', *Monthly Film Bulletin* 52 (623): 392.

—— (1992) '*The Big Shave*', *Sight and Sound* 2 (2) NS: 56.

Nowell-Smith, Geoffrey (1967) *Visconti*, Cinema One 3, London: Secker & Warburg/BFI.

—— (1976) 'Six Authors in Pursuit of *The Searchers*', *Screen* 17 (1): 26–33.

Pennington, Ron (1977) '*New York, New York*', *The Hollywood Reporter* 247 (3): 4.

Perkins, V.F. (1972) *Film as Film: Understanding and Judging Movies*, Harmondsworth: Penguin.

―――― (1990) 'Film Authorship: The Premature Burial', *CineAction* 21/22: 57–64.
Phillips, Julia (1991) *You'll Never Eat Lunch in this Town Again*, London, Heinemann.
Pirie, David (1981) 'The Deal', pp. 40–61 in Pirie, David (ed.), *Anatomy of the Movies*, London: Windward.
Powell, Anna (1994) 'Blood on the borders – *Near Dark* and *Blue Steel*', *Screen* 35 (2): 136–56.
Pye, Michael and Myles, Linda (1979) *The Movie Brats: How the Film Generation Took Over Hollywood*, London: Faber and Faber.
Quart, Leonard and Auster, Albert (1984) *American Film and Society Since 1945, The Contemporary United States*, London: Macmillan.
Ray, Robert B. (1985) *A Certain Tendency of the Hollywood Cinema, 1930–1980*, Princeton: Princeton University Press.
Rice, Julian C. (1976) 'Transcendental Pornography and *Taxi Driver*', *Journal of Popular Film* 5 (2): 109–23.
Rosen, Marjorie (1975) 'New Hollywood: Martin Scorsese Interview', *Film Comment* 11 (2): 42–46.
Sarris, Andrew (1962) 'Notes on the Auteur Theory in 1962', *Film Culture* 27: 1–8.
Schatz, Thomas (1981) *Hollywood Genres: Formulas, Filmmaking and the Studio System*, New York: Random House.
―――― (1983) *Old Hollywood/New Hollywood: Ritual, Art, and Industry*, Studies in Cinema 15, Ann Arbor: UMI Research Press.
―――― (1993) 'The New Hollywood', pp. 8–36 in Collins, Jim, Radner, Hilary and Collins, Ava Preacher (eds), *Film Theory Goes to the Movies*, AFI Film Readers, New York and London: Routledge.
Schrader, Paul (1972a) 'Notes on Film Noir', *Film Comment* 8 (1): 8–13.
―――― (1972b) *Transcendental Style in Film: Ozu, Bresson, Dreyer*, Berkeley and Los Angeles: University of California Press.
―――― (1990) 'Introduction: Interview with Martin Scorsese by Paul Schrader', pp. ix–xxii in *Taxi Driver*, London: Faber and Faber.
Sconce, Jeffrey (1995) '"Trashing" the academy: taste, excess, and an emerging politics of cinematic style', *Screen* 36 (4): 371–93.
Scorsese, Martin (1975) 'Martin Scorsese Seminar', *Dialogue in Film* 4 (7): 2–24.
―――― (1978) 'Martin Scorsese's Guilty Pleasures', *Film Comment*, 14 (5), 63–6.
―――― (1981) 'Confessions of a Movie Brat', pp. 132–9 in Pirie, David (ed.), *Anatomy of the Movies*, London: Windward.
―――― (1995) 'Preface', p. 1 in Romney, Jonathan and Wootton, Adrian (eds), *Celluloid Jukebox: Popular Music and the Cinema Since the 50s*, London: BFI.
―――― (1997a), 'An Authentic Passion', pp. 3–4 in Boorman, John and Donohue, Walter (eds), *Projections 7*, London: Faber and Faber.
―――― (1997b) 'De Niro and Me', pp. 36–59 in Boorman, John and Donohue, Walter (eds), *Projections 7*, London: Faber and Faber.
―――― (1997c) 'A Passion for Film', pp. 93–102 in Boorman, John and Donohue, Walter (eds), *Projections 7*, London: Faber and Faber.
Scorsese, Martin and Wilson, Michael Henry (1997) *A Personal Journey with Martin Scorsese Through American Movies*, London: Faber and Faber.
Sharrett, Christopher (1993) 'The American Apocalypse: Scorsese's *Taxi Driver*', pp. 220–35 in Sharrett, Christopher (ed.), *Crisis Cinema: The Apocalyptic Idea*

in Postmodern Narrative Film, Postmodern Positions 6, Washington, DC: Maisonneuve Press.

Shklovsky, Victor (1917/1965) 'Art as Technique', pp. 3–24 in Lemon, Lee T. and Reis, Marion J. (eds), *Russian Formalist Criticism: Four Essays*, Regents Critics, translated by Lee T. Lemon and Marion J. Reis, Lincoln: University of Nebraska Press.

Siclier, Jacques (1961) 'New Wave and French Cinema', *Sight and Sound* 30 (3): 116–20.

Slotkin, Richard (1973) *Regeneration through Violence: The Mythology of the American Frontier, 1600–1860*, Middletown: Wesleyan University Press.

Sontag, Susan (1964/1967) 'Spiritual style in the films of Robert Bresson', pp. 177–95 in *Against Interpretation and other essays*, London: Eyre & Spottiswoode.

Stam, Robert, Burgoyne, Robert and Flitterman-Lewis, Sandy (1992) *New Vocabularies in Film Semiotics: Structuralism, Post-structuralism and beyond*, Sightlines, London and New York: Routledge.

Stern, Lesley, (1995) *The Scorsese Connection*, Perspectives, London: BFI.

Stoddart, Helen (1995) 'Auteurism and film authorship theory', pp. 37–57 in Hollows, Joanne and Jancovich, Mark (eds), *Approaches to Popular Film*, Manchester: Manchester University Press.

Taubin, Amy (1999) 'God's lonely man', *Sight and Sound* 9 (4) NS: 16–19.

Taylor, Bella (1981) 'Martin Scorsese', pp. 293–368 in Tuska, Jon (ed.), *Close-up: The Contemporary Director*, Metuchen and London: Scarecrow Press.

Thompson, David and Christie, Ian (eds) (1996) *Scorsese on Scorsese*, updated edition, London: Faber and Faber.

Thompson, Richard (1976a) 'Screenwriter: *Taxi Driver*'s Paul Schrader', *Film Comment* 12 (2): 6–19.

—— (1976b) 'In the American Grain: an interview with Robert Getchell', *Sight and Sound* 45 (3): 140–4.

Truffaut, François (1954/1976) 'A Certain Tendency of the French Cinema', translator not cited, pp. 224–37 in Nichols, Bill (ed.), *Movies and Methods, Volume I*, Berkeley, Los Angeles and London: University of California Press.

—— (1978) *Hitchcock*, updated edition, London: Paladin.

Walker, Michael (1982) 'Melodrama and the American Cinema', *Movie* 29/30: 2–38.

—— (1992) 'Film Noir: Introduction', pp. 8–38 in Cameron, Ian (ed.), *The Movie Book of Film Noir*, London: Studio Vista.

Walsh, Martin (1974/1981) 'Political Formations in the Cinema of Jean-Marie Straub', pp. 37–59 in *The Brechtian Aspect of Radical Cinema*, edited by Keith M. Griffith, London: BFI.

Weaver, David (1986) 'The Narrative of Alienation: Martin Scorsese's *Taxi Driver*', *CineAction* 6: 12–16.

Webb, Teena and Martens, Betsy (1975) 'A Hollywood Liberation', *Jump Cut* 7: 4–5.

Weiss, Marion (1987) *Martin Scorsese: a guide to references and resources*, A Reference Publication in Film, Boston: G.K. Hall.

Will, David and Willemen, Paul (eds) (1970) *Roger Corman*, Edinburgh: Edinburgh Film Festival.

Williams, Raymond (1966) *Modern Tragedy*, London: Chatto & Windus.

Wilson, George M. (1986) *Narration in Light: Studies in Cinematic Point of View*, Baltimore: Johns Hopkins University Press.

Wollen, Peter (1972) *Signs and Meaning in the Cinema*, Cinema One 9, revised and enlarged edition, London: Secker & Warburg/BFI.

—— (1972) 'Counter-Cinema: *Vent d'Est*', *Afterimage* 4: 6–16.

Wood, Robin (1975) 'Smart-ass & Cutie-pie: Notes Towards an Evaluation of Altman', *Movie* 21: 1–17.

—— (1980) 'The Incoherent Text: Narrative in the 70s', *Movie* 27/28: 24–42.

—— (1986) *Hollywood from Vietnam to Reagan*, New York and Guildford: Columbia University Press.

—— (1989) *Hitchcock's Films Revisited*, New York and Oxford: Columbia University Press.

Wright, Will (1975) *Sixguns and Society: A Structural Study of the Western*, Berkeley, Los Angeles and London: University of California Press.

Wyatt, Justin (1994) *High Concept: Movies and Marketing in Hollywood*, Texas Film Studies, Austin: University of Texas Press.

Filmography

A bout de souffle/Breathless (Jean-Luc Godard, 1960)
After Hours (Martin Scorsese, 1985)
The Age of Innocence (Martin Scorsese, 1993)
Airport (George Seaton, 1970)
Alice Doesn't Live Here Anymore (Martin Scorsese, 1974)
American Boy: A Profile of Steven Prince (Martin Scorsese, 1978)
American Gigolo (Paul Schrader, 1980)
American Graffiti (George Lucas, 1973)
An American in Paris (Vincente Minnelli, 1951)
The Andromeda Strain (Robert Wise, 1971)
Angels Die Hard! (Richard Compton, 1970)
Angels Hard as They Come (Joe Viola, 1971)
Angels with Dirty Faces (Michael Curtiz, 1938)
The Arena (Steve Carver, 1973)
At Long Last Love (Peter Bogdanovich, 1975)

Badlands (Terrence Malick, 1973)
The Band Wagon (Vincente Minnelli, 1953)
Barefoot in the Park (Gene Saks, 1967)
The Barkleys of Broadway (Charles Walters, 1949)
Le Beau Serge/Bitter Reunion (Claude Chabrol, 1958)
Believe in Me (Stuart Hagmann, 1971)
The Big Bird Cage (Jack Hill, 1972)
The Big Doll House (Jack Hill, 1971)
The Big Heat (Fritz Lang, 1953)
The Big Shave (Martin Scorsese, 1967)
The Birds (Alfred Hitchcock, 1963)
Black Narcissus (Michael Powell and Emeric Pressburger, 1946)
Bloody Mama (Roger Corman, 1970)
Bonnie and Clyde (Arthur Penn, 1967)
Boxcar Bertha (Martin Scorsese, 1972)
Breakout (Tom Gries, 1975)
Brewster McCloud (Robert Altman, 1970)
A Bucket of Blood (Roger Corman, 1959)
Buffalo Bill and the Indians, or Sitting Bull's History Lesson (Robert Altman, 1976)
Il buono, il brutto, il cattivo/The Good, the Bad and the Ugly (Sergio Leone, 1966)
Bury Me an Angel (Barbara Peeters, 1971)
Busting (Peter Hyams, 1974)
Butch Cassidy and the Sundance Kid (George Roy Hill, 1969)

Cabaret (Bob Fosse, 1972)
Caged Heat (Jonathan Demme, 1974)
California Split (Robert Altman, 1974)

Candy Stripe Nurses (Allan Holleb, 1974)
Cape Fear (J. Lee Thompson, 1962)
Cape Fear (Martin Scorsese, 1991)
Casino (Martin Scorsese, 1995)
Charlotte et son Jules (Jean-Luc Godard, 1958)
The China Syndrome (James Bridges, 1979)
Chinatown (Roman Polanski, 1974)
Citizen Kane (Orson Welles, 1941)
Clockers (Spike Lee, 1995)
Close Encounters of the Third Kind (Steven Spielberg, 1977)
The Color of Money (Martin Scorsese, 1986)
Come Back Africa (Lionel Rogosin, 1959)
Un Condamné à mort s'est échappé/A Man Escaped (Robert Bresson, 1956)
Coney Island (Walter Lang, 1943)
The Connection (Shirley Clarke, 1961)
Coogan's Bluff (Don Siegel, 1968)
Cool Breeze (Barry Pollack, 1972)
The Cool World (Shirley Clarke, 1963)
The Critic (Ernest Pintoff, 1963)

Death Wish (Michael Winner, 1974)
2 ou 3 choses que je sais d'elle/Two or Three Things I Know About Her (Jean-Luc Godard, 1966)
Dial M for Murder (Alfred Hitchcock, 1954)
Diary of a Mad Housewife (Frank Perry, 1970)
Dillinger (John Milius, 1973)
Dirty Harry (Don Siegel, 1971)
Donovan's Reef (John Ford, 1963)
Double Indemnity (Billy Wilder, 1944)
Double Trouble (Norman Taurog, 1967)
Drive, He Said (Jack Nicholson, 1972)
Duel in the Sun (King Vidor, 1946)

East of Eden (Elia Kazan, 1955)
Easy Rider (Dennis Hopper, 1969)
Edge of the City (Martin Ritt, 1957)
El Dorado (Howard Hawks, 1967)
Elvis on Tour (Pierre Adidge and Robert Abel, 1972)
The Exorcist (William Friedkin, 1973)

The Fast and the Furious (Edwards Sampson and John Ireland, 1954)
Une Femme est une femme/A Woman is a Woman (Jean-Luc Godard, 1961)
Five Easy Pieces (Bob Rafelson, 1970)
Force of Evil (Abraham Polonsky, 1948)
For Me and My Gal (Busby Berkeley, 1942)
Frenzy (Afred Hitchcock, 1972)

The Gambler (Karel Reisz, 1974)
The Gang That Couldn't Shoot Straight (James Goldstone, 1971)

Gas-s-s-s (Roger Corman, 1970)
Giant (George Stevens, 1956)
Glen or Glenda (Edward D. Wood, 1953)
The Godfather (Francis Ford Coppola, 1972)
The Godfather, Part II (Francis Ford Coppola, 1974)
Gone With the Wind (Victor Fleming, 1939)
GoodFellas (Martin Scorsese, 1990)
Grace of My Heart (Allison Anders, 1996)
The Graduate (Mike Nichols, 1967)
The Grapes of Wrath (John Ford, 1940)
The Grifters (Stephen Frears, 1990)
Gun Crazy (Joseph H. Lewis, 1950)

Hardcore (Paul Schrader, 1979)
Hearts and Minds (Peter Davis, 1974)
Heaven's Gate (Michael Cimino, 1980)
Hello, Dolly! (Gene Kelly, 1969)
Hello Frisco, Hello (H. Bruce Humberstone, 1943)
The Hi-Lo Country (Stephen Frears, 1998)
The Hired Hand (Peter Fonda, 1971)
Hiroshima mon amour (Alain Resnais, 1959)
The Honeymoon Killers (Leonard Kastle, 1970)
The Hot Box (Joe Viola, 1972)
The Hustler (Robert Rossen, 1961)

I Escaped from Devil's Island (William Witney, 1973)
Invaders from Mars (William Cameron Menzies, 1953)
Italianamerican (Martin Scorsese, 1974)
It Happened One Night (Frank Capra, 1934)
It's Not Just You, Murray! (Martin Scorsese, 1964)

Jackson County Jail (Michael Miller, 1976)
Jaws (Steven Spielberg, 1975)
Johnny Guitar (Nicholas Ray, 1954)
Journal d'un curé de campagne/Diary of a Country Priest (Robert Bresson, 1950)
Jules et Jim/Jules and Jim (François Truffaut, 1961)

The King of Comedy (Martin Scorsese, 1983)
The King of Marvin Gardens (Bob Rafelson, 1972)
Kundun (Martin Scorsese, 1997)

Ladri di biciclette/Bicycle Thieves (Vittorio De Sica, 1948)
The Last Movie (Dennis Hopper, 1971)
The Last Picture Show (Peter Bogdanovich, 1971)
The Last Temptation of Christ (Martin Scorsese, 1988)
The Last Waltz (Martin Scorsese, 1978)
Leo the Last (John Boorman, 1970)
Light Sleeper (Paul Schrader, 1992)
Little Big Man (Arthur Penn, 1970)

The Little Shop of Horrors (Roger Corman, 1960)
The Long Goodbye (Robert Altman, 1973)
Love on the Run (W.S. Van Dyke, 1936)
Love Story (Arthur Hiller, 1970)
Lovers and Lollipops (Morris Engel, 1955)
Lucky Lady (Stanley Donen, 1975)

Machine Gun Kelly (Roger Corman, 1958)
Mad Dog and Glory (John McNaughton, 1992)
The Man I Love (Raoul Walsh, 1946)
The Man Who Knew Too Much (Alfred Hitchcock, 1956)
The Man Who Shot Liberty Valance (John Ford, 1962)
La Mariée était en noir/The Bride Wore Black (François Truffaut, 1967)
Marnie (Alfred Hitchcock, 1964)
MASH (Robert Altman, 1970)
A Matter of Time (Vincente Minnelli, 1976)
McCabe and Mrs Miller (Robert Altman, 1971)
Mean Streets (Martin Scorsese, 1973)
The Mechanic (Michael Winner, 1972)
Medicine Ball Caravan (François Reichenbach, 1971)
Minnie and Moskowitz (John Cassavetes, 1971)
Mishima: A Life in Four Chapters (Paul Schrader, 1985)
Murder by Contract (Irving Lerner, 1958)
My Dream Is Yours (Michael Curtiz, 1949)

Naked in New York (Dan Algrant, 1994)
Nashville (Robert Altman, 1975)
The New Centurions (Richard Fleischer, 1972)
New York, New York (Martin Scorsese, 1977)
New York Stories (Martin Scorsese, Francis Coppola and Woody Allen, 1989)
Nickelodeon (Peter Bogdanovich, 1976)
Night Call Nurses (Jonathan Kaplan, 1972)
North by Northwest (Alfred Hitchcock, 1959)
Notorious (Alfred Hitchcock, 1946)
Novecento/1900 (Bernardo Bertolucci, 1976)
The Nutty Professor (Jerry Lewis, 1963)

Obsession (Brian De Palma, 1976)
Oh Rosalinda (Michael Powell and Emeric Pressburger, 1955)
The Oklahoma Woman (Roger Corman, 1955)
On Dangerous Ground (Nicholas Ray, 1951)
On the Bowery (Lionel Rogosin, 1956)
On the Town (Gene Kelly and Stanley Donen, 1949)
On the Waterfront (Elia Kazan, 1954)
Otto e mezzo/8$\frac{1}{2}$ (Frederico Fellini, 1963)

Paper Moon (Peter Bogdanovich, 1973)
Papillon (Franklin J. Schaffner, 1973)
Peeping Tom (Michael Powell, 1960)

Per qualche dollaro in più/For a Few Dollars More (Sergio Leone, 1965)
A Personal Journey with Martin Scorsese Through American Movies (Martin Scorsese, 1995)
Per un pugno di dollari/A Fistful of Dollars (Sergio Leone, 1964)
Pickpocket (Robert Bresson, 1959)
Pierrot le fou (Jean-Luc Godard, 1965)
The Pirate (Vincente Minnelli, 1948)
Play It As It Lays (Frank Perry, 1972)
Point Blank (John Boorman, 1967)
The Postman Always Rings Twice (Tay Garnett, 1946)
Prima della rivoluzione/Before the Revolution (Bernardo Bertolucci, 1964)
Private Duty Nurses (George Armitage, 1972)
Le Procès de Jeanne d'Arc/The Trial of Joan of Arc (Robert Bresson, 1962)
Psycho (Alfred Hitchcock, 1960)

Les Quatre Cents Coups/The 400 Blows (François Truffaut, 1959)

Raging Bull (Martin Scorsese, 1980)
The Raven (Roger Corman, 1963)
Rear Window (Alfred Hitchcock, 1954)
Rebecca (Alfred Hitchcock, 1940)
Red Corner (Jon Avnet, 1997)
The Red Shoes (Michael Powell and Emeric Pressburger, 1948)
Rio Bravo (Howard Hawks, 1959)
The Roaring Twenties (Raoul Walsh, 1939)
Rocky (John G. Avildsen, 1976)
Roger Corman's Frankenstein Unbound (Roger Corman, 1990)
Rolling Thunder (John Flynn, 1977)

A Safe Place (Henry Jaglom, 1971)
Scarface (Howard Hawks, 1932)
Scorpio Rising (Kenneth Anger, 1962)
Search and Destroy (David Salle, 1995)
The Searchers (John Ford, 1956)
Seven Years in Tibet (Jean-Jacques Annaud, 1997)
Shadows (John Cassavetes, 1959)
Shane (George Stevens, 1953)
The Shanghai Gesture (Josef von Sternberg, 1941)
Shockproof (Douglas Sirk, 1949)
Silent Runing (Douglas Trumbull, 1971)
The Silver Chalice (Victor Saville, 1954)
Singin' in the Rain (Gene Kelly and Stanley Donen, 1952)
Sisters (Brian De Palma, 1973)
Sorcerer (William Friedkin, 1977)
The Sound of Music (Robert Wise, 1965)
The Split (Gordon Flemyng, 1968)
SPYS (Irvin Kershner, 1974)
A Star Is Born (William Wellman, 1937)
A Star Is Born (George Cukor, 1954)

Star Wars (George Lucas, 1977)
Steelyard Blues (Alan Myerson, 1973)
The Sting (George Roy Hill, 1973)
The Strawberry Statement (Stuart Hagmann, 1970)
Street Scenes 1970 (New York Cinetracts Collective, 1970)
The Student Nurses (Stephanie Rothman, 1970)
The Sugarland Express (Steven Spielberg, 1973)
Sullivan's Travels (Preston Sturges, 1941)
Summer of '42 (Robert Mulligan, 1971)
Summer Stock (Charles Walters, 1950)

Taking Off (Milos Forman, 1971)
The Tales of Hoffmann (Michael Powell and Emeric Pressburger, 1951)
Taxi Driver (Martin Scorsese, 1976)
Teenage Caveman (Roger Corman, 1958)
The Terror (Roger Corman, 1963)
The Texas Chainsaw Massacre (Tobe Hooper, 1974)
That's Entertainment! (Jack Haley Jr, 1974)
They Live by Night (Nicholas Ray, 1948)
They Shoot Horses, Don't They? (Sydney Pollack, 1969)
Thieves Like Us (Robert Altman, 1974)
This Gun for Hire (Frank Tuttle, 1942)
Three Women (Robert Altman, 1977)
THX-1138 (George Lucas, 1971)
Tirez sur le pianiste/Shoot the Piano Player (François Truffaut, 1960)
Tobacco Road (John Ford, 1941)
The Tomb of Ligeia (Roger Corman, 1965)
Tous les garçons s'appellent Patrick/All Boys Are Called Patrick (Jean-Luc Godard, 1957)
Tout va bien (Jean-Luc Godard and Jean-Pierre Gorin, 1972)
The Trip (Roger Corman, 1967)
The Trouble With Harry (Alfred Hitchcock, 1955)
True Grit (Henry Hathaway, 1969)
Two-Lane Blacktop (Monte Hellman, 1971)

Ulzana's Raid (Robert Aldrich, 1972)
Unholy Rollers (Vernon Zimmerman, 1972)
Up the Sandbox (Irvin Kershner, 1972)

Vanishing Point (Richard C. Sarafian, 1971)
Vertigo (Alfred Hitchcock, 1958)
Vivre sa vie/My Life to Live (Jean-Luc Godard, 1962)
Von Richthofen and Brown (Roger Corman, 1971)

Walking Tall (Phil Karlson, 1973)
The Way We Were (Sydney Pollack, 1973)
West Side Story (Robert Wise, 1961)
What's a Nice Girl Like You Doing in a Place Like This? (Martin Scorsese, 1963)
Where Danger Lives (John Farrow, 1950)

Who's That Knocking at My Door? (Martin Scorsese, 1969)
The Wild Angels (Roger Corman, 1966)
The Wild Seed (Brian G. Hutton, 1965)
The Wind and the Lion (John Milius, 1975)
The Wizard of Oz (Victor Fleming, 1939)
Woodstock (Michael Wadleigh, 1970)
The Wrong Man (Alfred Hitchcock, 1956)

X – The Man with the X-Ray Eyes (Roger Corman, 1963)

The Yakuza (Sydney Pollack, 1975)
Young Mr Lincoln (John Ford, 1939)
The Young Nurses (Clinton Kimbrough, 1973)
You Only Live Once (Fritz Lang, 1937)

Index